ADVANCE ACCLAIM FOR
SECRETS OF SLOANE HOUSE

"Shelley Gray writes a well-paced story full of historical detail that will invite you into the romance, the glamour . . . and the mystery surrounding the Chicago World's Fair."

—COLLEEN COBLE, *USA TODAY*
BEST-SELLING AUTHOR OF *ROSEMARY*
COTTAGE AND THE HOPE BEACH SERIES

"*Downton Abbey* comes to Chicago in Shelley Gray's delightful romantic suspense, *Secrets of Sloane House*. Gray's novel is rich in description and historical detail while asking thought-provoking questions about faith and one's place in society."

—ELIZABETH MUSSER, NOVELIST,
THE SWAN HOUSE, *THE SWEETEST THING*,
THE SECRETS OF THE CROSS TRILOGY

Secrets of
SLOANE HOUSE

Secrets of

SLOANE
HOUSE

SHELLEY GRAY

ZONDERVAN®

ZONDERVAN

Secrets of Sloane House

Copyright © 2014 by Shelley Gray

This title is also available as a Zondervan ebook. Visit www.zondervan.com.

This title is also available as a Zondervan audiobook. Visit www.zondervan.com.

Requests for information should be addressed to:
Zondervan, *Grand Rapids, Michigan 49546*

Library of Congress Cataloging-in-Publication Data

Gray, Shelley Shepard.
  Secrets of Sloane House / Shelly Gray.
    Pages cm
  ISBN 978-0-310-33852-9 (trade paper)
  1.   Family secrets—Fiction. I. Title.
  PS3607.R3966S45 2014
  813'.6—dc23
                              2014015970

Cover design: Gearbox

Cover photography: Trevillion and Library of Congress

Interior design: Mallory Perkins

Printed in the United States of America

14 15 16 17 18 19 20 / RRD / 20 19 18 17 16 15 14 13 12 11 10 9 8 7 6 5 4 3 2 1

Sometimes the journey to publication is as much a story as the novel itself! This is one of those books for me. I am indebted to two very special people who never gave up on either me or Secrets of Sloane House.

Thank you to my agent, Mary Sue Seymour, who tirelessly talked to everyone and anyone about this novel. For years. Agents like you are what writers dream about, MSS!

Thank you, also, to Sue Brower, who made me feel like both me and this novel were worth fighting for. Bless you, Sue! It's my dream that you will find this book well worth your efforts!

"Though your sins are like scarlet, I will make them as white as snow. Though they are red like crimson, I will make them as white as wool."

—Isaiah 1:18 NLT

There is the muffled beating of tom-toms, the shuffling of many feet, the popcorn and lemonade, and thousands of dull, dusty, frowzy folks who stare and gape and imbibe ox-like impressions.

—Frederic Remington, as quoted in *Harper's*

CHAPTER 1

Chicago, August 1893

As circumspectly as she could, Rosalind Perry smoothed her dark gray skirts before meeting the wide, assessing gaze of Douglass Sloane, the twenty-four-year-old son and heir of the Sloane estate.

"And who might you be?" he asked.

"Rosalind, sir."

"I haven't seen you here before, have I?" His dark eyes scanned her form, her face.

"No, sir. I'm new." A prickling ran up the length of her spine. Why was he watching her so closely? Had she done something wrong that she wasn't aware of?

Below them, down the stairs, the steady ticking of a mahogany grandfather clock floated upward, echoing the quick beating of her heart. The surrounding walls, with the rose trellis wallpaper and great array of samplers and portraits, seemed to close around her.

As if he had nowhere else to go, Douglass leaned a shoulder

against the wall. The movement nudged the corner of a frame displaying the likeness of one of his dead relatives, showing a patch of dark wallpaper underneath. Rosalind did her best to stand still, though her hands longed to fidget. These questions were out of the ordinary. Never had the other members of his family conversed with her. Never had she expected it.

Cook had warned her that all four Sloanes were particular about the servants remembering their station in the formidable home. Hired help who spoke too much, didn't follow directives, or proved slovenly were soon replaced. Rosalind didn't doubt that to be true.

As she stood as still as a statue, Douglass Sloane continued to examine her as if she were one of the World Fair's new inventions.

"So . . . Rosalind." A dimple appeared. "Shakespeare, yes?"

She nodded. The name was from the play *As You Like It.* Her mother was a great fan of all things literary. Her children's names had been a reflection of that. And perhaps to show the world that she was more than merely a farmer's wife.

Clarifying her mother's reasons for naming her Rosalind, however, seemed unnecessary. Too personal.

Not asked.

His arms crossed. The white linen of his shirt shone against the dark woodwork behind him. "And where might you be from?"

"Wisconsin, sir." A small dairy farm near Milwaukee, to be specific.

"Ah, Wisconsin. That veritable utopia to our west." Skimming her features again, he almost smiled. "And now here you are. In Chicago. Dusting."

"Yes." Her shoulders began to relax. Obviously, this member of the household meant her no harm. He was just curious about the newest housemaid on staff.

Perhaps that made sense. During the three weeks she'd worked in the home, the master's son had been on a buying trip with his father to New York City. She heard they'd returned just two days ago—and the downstairs talk was filled with gossip about his escapades.

Rumor had it that Douglass had spent every waking hour in city pubs and gaming halls. Anywhere he liked, actually. With a name like Sloane, a man could do what he liked whenever he chose.

"Really, Douglass," Veronica Sloane called out as she entered the hall on the arm of an extremely handsome man. "Leave the girl alone. If you cause her to tarry, she won't get all her work done." Somewhat mockingly, she raised a finely curved eyebrow. "And then what will we do?"

"I'm doing nothing out of the ordinary." He dared to wink, and his gaze gripped Rosalind again. "Merely getting acquainted. As I've done many times before," he added, almost as an afterthought.

With those words, alarms sounded in Rosalind's head again. Perhaps it was only her imagination, but she was certain his statement was laced with another meaning.

"There's little to get acquainted with," his sister said as she and her companion joined Douglass, their bodies effectively circling Rosalind. Her voice was sharp. "She's a servant, Douglass. Not a debutante."

Rosalind clutched her dust rag more tightly. Yes, in their world she was only a servant. But in her heart, she knew she was more than that. She was a child of God. In his eyes, she counted as much as anyone.

As much as her sister, Miranda, had . . . before she'd gone missing.

Douglass stepped forward, bringing with him the faint scent of scotch. "Tell me, Rosalind, are you liking our home?"

His voice had turned silky. Rosalind's mouth turned dry. The question felt loaded, but she wasn't sure what the expected answer was. Her heartbeat quickened.

Oh, why had she been dusting in this spot at this moment?

Staring at her intently, Veronica once again raised a brow. "Do you? Are you happy?" Her voice lowered. "Content?"

Content? "I . . . I—"

"Rosalind, Miss Sloane is right, you'd best get your chores done," the handsome stranger interrupted. "Why don't you run along now?"

His voice was so commanding, so direct, that she took a step back. Then stopped just as abruptly. She wasn't supposed to leave until she'd been dismissed.

Douglass turned to the man and frowned. "Armstrong, are you now giving orders to the servants in my home?"

"Not at all. I'm merely repeating what Veronica said. She is right. This maid surely has a great many things to do other than stand here with us."

Rosalind noticed a slight softening around the corners of Veronica's lips. "Reid, you actually listened to me."

Mr. Armstrong smiled at Veronica, and his voice became warmer. "Of course I listened. I always listen." There was no such warmth in his eyes when he turned back to Rosalind, however. His gaze was cool and almost piercing. "Miss, you had best go about your business. Now."

Staring at him, Rosalind stepped back. Her body was trembling so much that she feared it would be commented upon, giving them yet another opportunity to taunt her.

But when neither Douglass nor Veronica protested, only chuckled softly, she pivoted on her heel and scurried down the hall.

Brittle feminine laughter followed her steps. "Oh, Reid, I do think I'll keep you close to me all day. You're beyond amusing. Besides, it's nice having someone nearby who heeds what I say."

"Some might have a problem with your heavy-handed ways, though," Douglass added, his voice carrying a thread of malice. "The way you shooed away our new girl was a bit of a surprise. It almost seemed as if you were worried about her welfare."

"Perhaps I am concerned about her. You do have quite the reputation, you know, Sloane," their guest retorted. "If we're not careful, you'll charm the girl, break her heart, and next thing you know? Why, she'll be leaving. Then who would dust your furniture?"

The laughter continued as Rosalind turned a corner. But just as she was hurrying down a half flight of stairs, she faintly heard Veronica's reply. "Don't be silly, Reid. Servants can be replaced. Always."

A jolt of fear shot up Rosalind's spine. Was that what had happened to her sister? Had she been dismissed for neglecting her chores and then promptly forgotten?

Or had she been snatched up from the city's busy streets and simply vanished?

Quickly, Rosalind turned right, then left. She struggled to recall where she was. The house was so vast, such a jumbled maze of curious rooms and narrow, winding halls, that she was continually getting lost. One wrong turn could lead to her flying down a corridor where she had no business being.

Which, of course, could lead to her coming into contact with members of the family.

As she stopped and rested a palm on a wall covered in rich scarlet and burnished gold paisley wallpaper, she let her mind drift, remembering how Miranda had written that she, too, had gotten lost in the mansion more than a time or two. Of course, she'd also confided that some of the people in the house frightened her.

Remembering that the letters had stopped coming before she'd revealed who had frightened her—and how—Rosalind closed her eyes and tried to fend off a new wash of pain.

Oh, Miranda! Where are you?

Her sister, older by only eleven months, was the twenty-one-year-old beauty of the family. Blessed with thick, curly auburn hair, set off by bright blue eyes, she was striking. Rosalind's mahogany hair and faded blue eyes had always paled in comparison.

As did her personality. Miranda was the more headstrong, the one who was the most self-reliant. Rosalind? Ever the follower.

Over the years, Miranda's strong personality had always gotten her what she wanted. So much so that Rosalind had often wished she had even a small portion of her sister's determination.

When things had gone from bad to worse at their farm, Miranda had up and left, leaving behind a note saying that she'd gone to Chicago to find work and she'd send money home as soon as she could.

But Rosalind knew financial concerns weren't the only reason Miranda had ventured east. No, she'd always been plagued by the need to push limits and boundaries. Even the wide open fields of their farm had seemed far too confining for a woman of her light and exuberance.

Soon after she left, Miranda wrote that she'd gotten a position as a maid in a grand house. More letters arrived over the next two months, each one with a bit of money.

But then they heard nothing.

With a heavy heart, Rosalind was beginning to fear that her earnest prayers for her sister had not only been unanswered, but had also been in vain.

Either Miranda had decided to move on and forget about them all . . . or something dire had happened to her.

Sometimes, in the dark of night, Rosalind admitted that she wasn't sure which scenario would be easier to bear.

CHAPTER 2

"Mrs. Sloane just changed the numbers for dinner. Now we're going to have twenty people instead of ten," Cook announced grumpily when Rosalind arrived in the perpetually steamy kitchens for a bite of lunch. "That means not a one of you is going to be taking a break anytime soon. I need you, Rosalind, to run to the market and pick up another batch of squash for the soup."

Still feeling off-kilter after her run-in with Douglass and Veronica, Rosalind blinked. "Do you mean the farmer's market?"

Mrs. Martha Russell—"Cook" to everyone in the house—folded her arms over an ample bosom and glared. "None other."

Rosalind's heart dipped. She barely knew her way around the two blocks surrounding the mansion. Chicago streets were crowded and winding, difficult to traverse in the best of circumstances.

Now, with the World's Fair in full swing and thousands of visitors swarming along the sidewalks, it was near impossible to navigate the streets with any expediency. She feared that there was a very good chance she'd become lost and ruin Cook's schedule.

But that was the least of her worries. Never a moment passed when she wasn't completely aware of the dangers that lurked in the city and that, somehow, her sister had vanished in them.

"I'm sorry, ma'am. But I'm not sure if I'm the right—"

Cook cut her off with a stern expression brewing in her toffee-colored eyes. "I can't be sparin' no one else. I need that squash." Pulling away the bowl Rosalind had just picked up, she snapped, "You've got no time to eat! Go now."

Only Cook's reputation of being all bark and no bite prevented Rosalind from shaking in her shoes. "Yes, ma'am. Um, where is the market?"

With exaggerated patience, Cook said, "Take a grip car and be quick about it. When you get there, look for Tom. He's the head grocer, and Sloane House has an account with him."

"Tom," she repeated.

"He's youngish. Has a red beard, and he knows all about Mrs. Sloane's wants and particulars. He'll help you find what you need."

It sounded as if finding Tom might not be too much of a problem, but she dreaded taking the grip car. The only time she'd been on it alone she'd worried she'd miss her stop, get off too early—or worse, too late—far from the neighborhood she was just starting to become accustomed to.

Traveling in the large city was excruciatingly nerve-racking and scary. Especially after Miranda had mentioned time and time again in her letters how dangerous the streets were. Just the descriptions alone made Rosalind wish for eyes in the back of her head. Yes, there were multiple dangers on the streets of Chicago, and a woman alone was always at risk.

But perhaps there were dangers most anywhere? Once again, she found her mind drifting back to Douglass and his piercing gaze . . .

A pair of saucepans clanged together. "Rosalind, what more do you need for me to say? Go on with ya, now."

"Yes, ma'am. I mean, yes, I'm off to the market right now."

Now that she was getting her way, Cook's voice gentled. "Take some coins from housekeeping just in case you don't be seein' Tom. Go on, now. There's a good girl."

Nanci, her one good friend in the house, smiled sweetly at Rosalind as their paths crossed in the doorway. "You can do it. It'll be just like the time we took the trolley to the park. Just take it again, but head south, toward the market. If you get lost, ask for help. Most people in Chicago are honest folk. Most will help you."

Most. That one word made all the difference between comfort and wariness. Not everyone was honest. Or helpful. Some, it seemed, were much worse.

Once again, Rosalind recalled Miranda's letters. She'd written stories of women coming to the fair and getting pulled into brothels, never to be heard from again.

Like a newsboy calling out the day's headlines, Cook's voice rang down the hall. "Don't you be comin' back without my squash, Rosalind. You do, and I'll have you be the one to tell the missus herself why her dinner party will be ruined, and you know what will be happenin' then!"

She'd be let go, that was what would be happening.

Rosalind didn't doubt Cook's threat in the slightest. From her first day, she realized the whole staff lived in fear of the mercurial moods of the family. Mrs. Sloane could be at once exceptionally benevolent and malicious. Stories abounded of servants being fired for the slightest offense while others were paid while recuperating from the influenza.

Removing her apron and hanging it in the servants' closet, Rosalind grabbed four coins from the cook's top desk drawer, then, at last, darted out the back door.

"Lord, please help me find my courage," she whispered. "Please help me become strong and not such a ninny. I need to keep my wits about me to find my sister. Please help me become more confident and more hopeful too. Help me be more like the girl I was back home."

Back home, she'd hardly ever worried about her safety. Back home, she'd known everyone and had felt secure, not only in her surroundings, but in the knowledge that she mattered. To the townspeople nearest to their farm. To her family. To the Lord.

Stepping out onto the broad cavalcade of Michigan Avenue, Rosalind was immediately swept into the crowd of people hurrying among the drays, carriages, and curricles. She was sure her starched gray blouse and skirts were about to be hopelessly stained.

Then she knocked into the side of a lad no more than twelve.

"Watch it," he muttered with a fierce scowl. He was a messenger boy, distinguishable as such by his hat, sturdy satchel, and single-minded expression.

"Sorry." Suddenly, with a burst of steam, the trolley squealed to a halt in front of her. Though she'd only traveled on the crowded conveyance twice before, she knew she had to push her way on and hold on tightly. Within seconds, the trolley car moved forward, pushing its way through the cacophony of carriages and people filling the street.

Noise filtered by the congestion rang in her ears. Rosalind gripped the leather strap more tightly. Looking around, she sought a friendly face. Directly across from her stood a woman, most likely a typist, given her black skirt and crisp white shirtwaist. "Pardon me, have you ever gone to the market? I mean, to the farmer's market," she clarified. "You know, for vegetables?"

"I have," the woman said with a regal nod. Long black feathers circling the brim of her hat fluttered with the motion.

"Am I going in the right direction?"

If the lady heard, she didn't deign to give a reply. Flummoxed, Rosalind resigned herself that she'd have to wait and see.

"Exit the next stop, miss," an older man in multiple layers of brown tweed and tan muttered from her other side. "Exit and walk toward the west. Can't miss it."

A young woman dressed in a plain dress flashed a reassuring smile. "He's right, lamb. You'll see the stalls before you've walked too far. You'll smell them too. Nothing smells better than the market in the afternoon."

Rosalind took their advice with a grateful smile. "Thank you."

"Have a care, now," the working girl warned. "The streets can be a challenge for one who's not familiar with them."

Rosalind nodded but said nothing more. The girl's warning told her nothing she didn't already know. And nothing her sister hadn't already found out.

───

Rosalind made it back in two hours. She had no idea if she'd made good time or had taken twice as long as necessary. All she cared about was that she'd accomplished her mission, by herself, with little problem. That, she felt, was something to celebrate.

"This is what Tom had today," she said as she handed over a cloth sack filled to the brim with squash. "I hope it will do."

The cook's fleshy face brightened as she looked into the parcel. After pulling out one of the yellow vegetables, she held it to her nose, breathed deeply, then nodded. "It will."

Rosalind breathed a hearty sigh of relief.

Her gaze warmer, Cook clucked a bit. "Now you'd best sit down before you fall down and have something to eat. You're so thin, sometimes I fear a sharp wind is going to take you away from us," she teased. "Not a one of us will be getting any rest 'fore midnight, I expect. Master Douglass is entertaining this evening too. He's hosting a rowdy crowd of gentlemen in the billiard room."

Rosalind took a thick stoneware bowl, filled it with mutton stew, and sat down at the far end of the kitchen table. No meal had ever looked so good.

With a brief prayer of thanks, she dived in. She was hungrier than she realized. Each bite brought her warmth and felt cozy and filling. It was a welcome oasis amid the hustle and bustle of the busy kitchens.

"And who might you be?" a man asked as he pulled up a chair and sat next to her. It was the same question Douglass had asked her upstairs.

Off-kilter by the nerve-racking events of the day, Rosalind looked at the short, mustached man with more than a slight degree of suspicion. "I'm sorry . . . Have we met?"

"I should say not," Cook said, her voice merry. "This here's Jim Quinn. He's doing a bit of repair work in the wine cellar today." After a moment, she added kindly, "And no need to worry about him. Jim's a mite too forward, that's true enough. But he's harmless enough."

"Pleased to meet you." He tipped his cap. "I'm a carpenter, miss. I do odd jobs, doing my best to make a dime, you know."

"I'm Rosalind."

"I know that. I do." He winked. "As soon as I saw there was a looker new on staff, I asked about you."

"Out with ya, Jim," Cook exclaimed. More confidentially, she leaned closer to Rosalind. "His mouth is going to get him in trouble yet, you mark my words. But if you learn to ignore most of his silly flirting, you'll see that Jim's as good a man as they come. I'd trust him with my soul, I would."

Before Rosalind could think of a reply to that, Jim started speaking. "Have you been to the fair yet?" When she shook her head, he grinned. "Didn't think so. If you had, you'd be smiling."

Still too rattled to even think about attending the World's Fair, she murmured, "I doubt I will go."

"You should. I mean, you should if you can get the time off." Jim rested his elbows on the table as he continued. "It's something to see, make no mistake. If you had seen Jackson Park before we got to work, you'd be right amazed at all the changes that have come about. Us carpenters have been right busy, making one building after another into a thing of beauty."

"Beauty where there was none," Cook interjected.

"I worked on several of the buildings, I tell you that. The Agricultural Building, Fisheries, even the Gov'ment one too."

"They got carrier pigeons and a redwood in that one," Cook interjected importantly. "I saw them meself."

"I even helped with fourteen of the state buildings," Jim continued, his voice sounding prouder than punch. "Maybe I even worked on yours. Where are you from, Rosalind?"

"Wisconsin."

Jim frowned. "Sorry, can't say's I worked on that one."

"Oh." She was starting to realize Wisconsin sounded as foreign to these Chicagoans as Japan or Russia sounded to her.

"But I'm sure it's there. Somewhere. You'll have to see it, all the same."

"The fair does sound special," Rosalind murmured. "It's hard to believe such a big event is taking place right here in Chicago."

"We live in a wondrous age, for sure. And our city is plumb in the middle of it! You be sure you go and see the sights, if you dare," Jim said as he stood up.

Rosalind was about to smile when he lowered his voice dramatically. "But if you do go, don't forget to be careful, now. The city can be a dangerous place. For a young woman likes yerself, there's trouble around almost every corner."

In a flash, the cozy atmosphere of the kitchen darkened.

Cook scowled as she used a paring knife to cut the squash into long yellow ribbons. "Jim, there ain't no reason for you to be bringing things like that up."

For the first time, Jim looked embarrassed. "Martha always tells me to watch my tongue. Guess I should start listening. I'm sorry. I didn't mean to be scaring you."

Feeling apprehensive, but for the first time slightly hopeful, Rosalind struggled to keep her voice tempered. "No, no, I want to hear what you mean."

"I was only thinking of another pretty maid, that's all."

"Jim's speaking of Miranda," Tilly, the scullery maid, whispered.

Rosalind's heart slammed into her chest. "Miranda?"

She had to be careful. Because she went by Rosalind Pettit instead of Perry, which was her real last name, no one at Sloane House knew she was Miranda's sister. And so far she'd been afraid to start asking questions. Now that the subject of Miranda had unexpectedly come up, she had to make the most of it.

Cook left her position and ponderously approached the table. After a second's pause, she said with obvious reluctance, "Miranda was a maid who worked here."

"But she didn't last long, though," Tilly said with a troubled expression. "Barely a couple of months."

"Why such a short time?"

"She was real pretty," Jim continued, ignoring her question. "She was about your age, now that I think of it." He snapped his fingers. "And from Wisconsin just like you." Eyeing her a bit more closely, he murmured, "Did you know her?"

"I . . . I . . ."

"Go on with you, Jim," Cook scoffed before Rosalind could utter a lie. "Even though Wisconsin is no Illinois, there's still a fair number of folks living there!"

While another of the maids snickered, Rosalind stared at Jim. "Wh–what about Miranda? What happened to her?"

"No one really knows." Looking at her a bit more closely, he added, "She was here one day, gone the next."

"Left without so much as a by-your-leave, she did," Cook added. "I was good to that girl too."

But Rosalind noticed that Cook's voice wasn't bitter. No, it sounded worried.

"Where do you think Miranda went in such a hurry?" Remembering some of the dark things Miranda had written, about being frightened by someone in the house, she swallowed hard. "Do you think she got hurt or something?"

Cook shrugged. "Don't know."

Feeling slightly sick, Rosalind attempted to sound more hopeful. "Maybe she fell in love and ran away to get hitched or something?"

"Not a chance. She left without her clothes and paycheck," Tilly said.

Cook glared. "Tilly!"

"Well, I'm sorry, but love can only get a girl so far, you know," Tilly said with a lift of her chin. "Takes money to eat."

After sending a dark look to the cheeky girl, Cook answered.

"Miranda's leaving was a sudden thing. Too sudden, if you ask me." After a furtive glance at the door to the hallway, she lowered her voice. "I, for one, don't believe she left the house on her own will. By all accounts, she seemed happy enough here—at least until the last few days or so."

"Always had a smile for us all, she did," Stanley, valet to Mr. Sloane and Douglass, said.

Cook continued. She shivered dramatically. "No one leaves a good job like this without giving notice first. I fear somethin' terrible happened to her."

"Like what?" Rosalind asked, fearing the answer. She could feel tears wanting to fill her eyes. With effort, she blinked them away. No one could know how affected she was by this news.

"You could choose any number of things," Jim said. "She could have been abducted, murdered. Maybe even fallen onto the train tracks."

"Or maybe even something worse," Tilly whispered. "Maybe someone she *knew* did her in."

"What do you mean by that?" Rosalind asked. Vivid pictures of her sister in terrible situations came to mind. Each one ended with her being beaten and bleeding. Broken and alone. Maybe even dead.

After glancing at Cook, Tilly flushed. "Nothing."

What was Tilly not saying? Why didn't Cook want Tilly to tell what she knew? And why did Cook sound like Miranda wasn't happy just before she left?

"Her going missing has been a real mystery, for sure. It's affected us all, and that is the truth," Cook stated after the briefest of pauses. "We read about girls getting snatched all over Chicago all the time in the *Tribune*. But bad things feel different when they happen to you. Know what I mean?"

Rosalind nodded. She knew exactly what Cook meant. It was one thing to hear about a nameless woman getting injured or killed. But if it were a sister? Well, there were no words.

"Mrs. Sloane was in a state about it too." A line formed in between Cook's brows. "She still kind of is, if you want to know the truth." Wagging her finger, she said, "If you know what's good for you, don't ever bring up Miranda's name. It sets Mrs. Sloane off something awful."

"Rosalind?" Tilly called out. "You're looking as white as a sheet."

Cook narrowed her eyes. "Are you all right?"

No. No, she was not. But that hardly mattered.

Lifting her chin, Rosalind tried to think of her mission and not her worst fears. "I'm surprised, that's all. I never would have imagined something horrible happening to a girl working in a grand house like this. And, uh, I would have thought she would have been more protected."

"Protected? Well now. No one can promise you that you'll always be safe." Cook wagged a finger again. "But I can promise that our lady makes sure she knows just about everything that happens. And what she doesn't know Mrs. Abrams does," she said, speaking of the housekeeper who hired Rosalind.

Rosalind didn't know if that made her feel better or worse. Struggling to keep her expression neutral, she murmured, "I'll be sure to remember that. And keep my eyes open."

"Good. But remember, child, whatever you do . . . Rosalind, don't you get it in your head to start asking about poor Miranda. As far as you are concerned, young Miranda never existed."

The lump that had formed in her throat was threatening to choke her. She bent down to her stew, attempting to concentrate on it instead of her broken heart.

"Like I said, I hope I didn't scare you none. Just wanted you to be aware of things, you know." Jim tipped his hat again. "A fetching girl like you can't be too careful, by my way of thinking. Now I best be gettin' back to work or I won't get paid."

She stared at him, almost woodenly. What had happened to Miranda? What did people know that they weren't saying? Her mind awhirl, she barely heard Stanley approach. "If I were you, I'd forget this whole conversation, Rosalind," he murmured. "We get paid to mind our own business, not to speculate on others' affairs. It's best for us all if you remember that."

"Yes, of course."

Rosalind tried to concentrate on her stew again, but her mind was churning. Could that be what had happened? Her sister had gone walking in the streets one day and simply never returned? Had disappeared against her will?

Or was it intentional? But if that had been the case, where had she taken off to? Why had she never written home?

Her plan to get hired on at Sloane House and discover what had really happened during Miranda's stay had seemed so logical back on the farm. She'd assumed a new name, made up a story about always wanting to work for a prestigious family like the Sloanes, and somehow convinced the clerk at the employment agency to send her for an interview. When she'd gotten the job after a brief meeting with Mrs. Abrams, Rosalind had been sure that the Lord had wanted her to find out what, exactly, had happened to her sister.

Now she realized that wasn't the case. She'd been woefully ignorant of the things she was expected to do. Of the hard, hidden life of a servant in a big, prominent house. Of the gap that divided the Sloane family and the people who served them.

Most of all, she realized that she'd never imagined that so many people could live together and still keep so many secrets. Furthermore, it was becoming obvious that there were things no one in the house wanted to talk about. The more Rosalind learned about the people who lived inside Sloane House, the more she was sure Miranda's fear had been real. If only she could determine what, exactly, her sister had been so afraid of.

After finishing her meal, Rosalind walked quietly out of the kitchen. Never had she felt so alone.

CHAPTER 3

"I do love it when you make time to talk with me when you're home," his mother announced when Reid entered the drawing room shortly after six. "It's a bit lonely with your sister away. But the opportunity to travel in Europe with her schoolmate's family was too special to keep her here, even with your father being ill."

After lunching with the Sloane siblings, Reid had taken his leave and gone to his father's offices, where he continued work on the incoming reports and updates from the family's silver mining holdings in Colorado.

After that, he completed correspondence for his own company, the fledgling Armstrong Construction. Since he'd always had an interest in building things, he'd begun a small company with a band of twenty workers. Each of his men had worked on the construction of the Exposition buildings. Now he was actively bidding on work in other parts of the city.

No, they weren't making much money as of yet, but he had dreams. One day, he wanted the Armstrong name to mean something. He hoped his children and grandchildren would be able to take pride in the Armstrong name the way Douglass and Veronica did being Sloanes.

Currently, the Armstrong name meant very little to most of Chicago's upper crust. If it was noticed at all, it was probably only coupled with luck, which meant little to the pillars of their society.

Many of Chicago's great men, such as Field and Pullman, cemented their reputations through ingenuity, hard work, and esteemed bloodlines. A fortune gained from a windfall at the silver mine was not impressive.

But Reid knew the truth. His father was a great man too. He was burly and strong and full of good humor. However, math and education had never been his strong points, which was why he'd sent Reid to fancy boarding schools and to Harvard for his education.

Now that his father's health was failing, it was Reid's responsibility to make sure the fortune his father had uncovered stayed solvent and to do everything he possibly could to make the Armstrong name one to respect.

However, at the moment it was his mother whose interests he focused on. "I miss Beth too, but I'm very glad she is having such a good time in London and Paris. Did you have many callers today, Mama?"

Her slim shoulders slumped. "Only a few, and those were my lady friends from church." Gesturing to her most recent acquisition, the black walnut Louis XV desk, she added, "No matter how hard I try, I'm afraid our neighbors will never see me as someone with whom they should associate. Only the Sloanes have welcomed me among the best circles, and that is, I think, merely because of your association with Douglass and Veronica."

In many ways, Reid deemed it no great loss. So far, the society ladies his mother had tried to impress seemed a particularly rigid and unforgiving lot. They spoke of their temperance and high moral standards with pride, yet preferred to ignore the mass of citizens who toiled at the slaughterhouses and other factories for barely enough to feed their families.

He'd watched them practically shun women for wearing outmoded dresses or socializing at the wrong homes. And the men weren't much better. However, it was from this very group his father ached for acceptance for their family. And since his mother constantly ached for her husband's praise and approval, she continually strived to win the society matrons' regard.

He gently squeezed her shoulders, thinking that though elegantly encased in copper taffeta, they looked a little frail. "Who did stop by?"

"Eloisa Carstairs, briefly. It's lovely that she visits, though her mother seems reluctant to do so."

"Eloisa has told me that her mother is determined she make a good match. We might not be quite high enough in the instep for Mrs. Carstairs."

His mother smiled softly. "You may be right about that." Smoothing a wrinkle from her sleeve, she added, "However, Millicent Arnold and her daughter, Louise, came calling. Millicent is a member of the women's temperance society, you know."

"I do know." She'd also been one of the few who'd made an effort to befriend his mother.

"Louise mentioned that she is very glad that you joined the choir."

Reid felt his cheeks heat. "I see." He liked to sing. Unfortunately, his baritone had been discovered during one especially rousing church service. Soon after, he'd been pressed into the choir.

Though it definitely was not the most masculine of pursuits, it did have its benefits. The bulk of the choir members were available young ladies—some of them in the upper classes, like Louise Arnold—each one eager and amiable to his regard. His parents had made no secret that they hoped he would form an alliance with a woman who was both of his social stature and a Christian.

Smiling sweetly, his mother leaned forward. "Have you made Louise's acquaintance?"

He had. He also had not been impressed with the young lady's mousy demeanor or gossipy nature. "I've noticed a great many women there."

She leaned forward. "Yes?"

"But no one in particular yet."

"Oh."

Reid hid a smile as Penny, his mother's parlor maid, brought in a heavily laden silver tray with fresh tea and buttered scones. Before his mother could offer, he helped himself to the bounty.

Oh, he did love to tease his mother about the many available ladies she pushed his way, especially from their church. But the fact was, so far no one had interested him—not even the lovely Eloisa Carstairs—even though he'd been doing his best to keep an open mind.

His mother casually pulled out a bit of embroidery while he ate two scones. When he'd set aside his napkin, she picked up her needle and spoke again. "So you visited the Sloane home today?"

"Yes. I saw both Veronica and Douglass."

"And did you have an enjoyable time?"

"Enjoyable enough, I suppose." His relationship with Douglass Sloane was complicated. Reid knew he owed him a great deal. Douglass had stuck his neck out for him when Reid had been blamed for vandalism during his first term at Lawrenceville.

Reid had been innocent, of course. But he'd been new and a

relative nobody. The headmaster and the other boys had been more than happy to let him take the blame and get expelled. Seeing that he was an easy mark, they began to pull pranks on him. Some rather harmless. Others? They'd been far more painful and difficult to ignore.

Each day had become a trial and a difficult journey to get through. He'd become miserable and withdrawn and had considered dropping out of the school. It would have been a serious blow to his father, but Reid had begun to think that it was either quit or descend into an even greater hell.

When a few of the boys had made up the story about him destroying property, Reid had had enough. He'd been formulating a letter to his father to explain his reasons for departure when Douglass had stepped in and given him an alibi.

Douglass had told a heap of lies, of course. In actuality, Reid had not been with Douglass during the time the vandals had broken into the groundskeeper's cottage. But no one ever would dare cross a Sloane, and one would definitely never call Douglass a liar. Not when the library and the dining hall were named after his revered ancestors.

As Douglass had assured him would happen, the alibi had been accepted without question. The dean of students had apologized profusely.

And from that point on, his life had become better. All the hazing stopped. Boys sought him out at mealtime. Invited him to parties and their older sisters' coming outs.

The difference in his social standing had been remarkable, and it was all due to Douglass Sloane. His family's reputation was that influential.

To his credit, his friend never once brought up that incident. But Reid knew it was always between them, as bright as a blazing red cloth, binding Reid to Douglass.

But today, even for all that, Reid had been eager to leave Douglass's presence that morning. Perhaps it had something to do with the pretty maid they'd practically run into. Unaccountably, his pulse had beat a little faster when she'd looked his way. Her eyes had been wide and innocent. Her manner as scared as a hare near a den of wolves.

He'd felt the need to make her day a little easier, since she was so obviously hard at work.

And since both Douglass and Veronica had seemed to enjoy their power over her.

The interaction had left Reid feeling vaguely disturbed. He was from proud, working stock. His grandparents had been little more than skilled laborers. In many ways, it was those people with whom he felt an affinity. He understood the working man's mind. There was something to be said for caring about God, country, and an honest day's wage.

Now that his status had risen and his parents were hoping he'd help to guide their way into high society, he was doing his best to concentrate only on the other people in his social circle. But it was a difficult undertaking. Much of the time he found himself following his parents' steps and treating the servants in their home as friends.

As he sipped his tea, he said, "Douglass invited me to accompany him to the fair next week."

"And?"

"And . . . I imagine I'll go," he said with a smile.

"I've visited the Women's Pavilion but only a few other buildings. Your father has refused to let me visit the fair without him. He says it's a dangerous place for a woman on her own."

"He's right, Mother. Ladies of good reputation don't frequent the fair unaccompanied."

"I know. But with your father doing poorly at the moment . . ." She wrinkled her nose. "And I do believe he's exaggerating things.

Not that I would know. He's refused to let me read the majority of the newspaper too."

Reid knew why. The papers were filled with stories of debauchery and ribald accounts of the many tourists who had descended on the city. More than once, he'd read stories detailing the rise in crime. Pickpockets were having a fine business at the fair, as were rapists and robbers in the dark alleyways of the city. "I've heard more than a few . . . rumors circulating about women going missing. One can never be too careful, Mama."

Instead of looking shocked, she merely nodded. "I realize single women are at risk in our city. But those are women of the lower class, don't you think?"

Reid wasn't so sure. Just the other day he'd heard a story about a well-to-do father combing the streets, asking questions of anyone and everyone about his missing daughter. But he certainly didn't want to alarm his mother with that bit of information. He sufficed with merely saying, "No good will come of you worrying about things you can't control. That's what the police are for."

"I suppose." She sighed as she sipped from her teacup. "Before we know it, the Exposition will be a thing of the past. It's hard to believe."

Yes, it was. Though danger surrounded the amusement, the world's most entertaining destination was already in its fourth month and becoming more popular each week. But like a tulip blooming in spring, the fair would only last a short time, closing at the end of October. All that would remain of the beautiful White City would be the stories told and the memories made.

Reid hoped there would be as many good ones as bad.

Now that they'd discussed his mother's callers and the fair, Reid knew he couldn't delay his most important reason for wanting to talk with her. "So . . . how is Papa doing today?"

His mother's hand shook a little as she hastily set her cup back on its saucer. "Not so well, I'm afraid. The tuberculosis doesn't care for this city's harsh climate. The doctor came today, but he doesn't hold out much hope for improvement."

As always, the knowledge that his father's health was declining rapidly hit him hard. "Perhaps we should think about taking Papa to Arkansas? I heard the spring there does wonders."

"You know your father would never leave Chicago. He'd see leaving as a sign of weakness. This great city is our home now. For better or worse."

For better or worse indeed. One day in the near future, his father would meet his Maker. Reid hoped he'd be man enough to cope with the loss the way he was expected to. "I . . . I think I'll go visit Papa for a few moments. We've been reading the book of Luke together, you know."

"Don't tire him out, son."

"Of course not."

He knew everything she was not saying. He'd better not tell his father any news that might prove distressing.

She didn't have to worry. Years ago, Reid had promised himself he would be everything his father wanted him to be . . . even if, sometimes, it was never what he had wanted at all.

CHAPTER 4

Two days had passed since that terrible conversation in the kitchen. For Rosalind, however, it felt as if it had taken place only hours before. Trying not to think about Miranda's last days at Sloane House was that difficult.

Her only recourse was to keep busy. Whenever she had a moment's peace, Jim's words and Cook's warnings reverberated in her head, making every person seem suspicious and every corner filled with danger.

In spite of her worries and fears, she was becoming accustomed to the rhythm of working at Sloane House. She had learned to get up with the dawn, quickly eat breakfast, then help with the breakfast service. Each day, she laid out the breakfast silver in neat, orderly rows, making sure each fork, spoon, and knife gleamed in the early morning light.

Working with a dozen strangers, some who had never really

known a life other than serving the Sloanes, was feeling easier too. Rosalind was slowly but surely getting to know everyone, making them less like strangers every day. She was learning which servants she could talk to and which ones were best to avoid. She'd become close to Nanci and had begun to form friendships with some of the other girls as well, especially Emma and Emily.

Mrs. Abrams and Cook—and even the butler, Mr. Hodgeson—began to trust her more too. Soon, little by little, she was allowed to be around the family more often. This was good for Rosalind and her sleuthing, but so far she'd been too intimidated by them and her job to do anything but concentrate on the duties she was assigned.

None of the previous tasks had brought anything close to the fear she was facing at the moment.

Her mouth went dry as she stared at the large tray holding a silver coffeepot, a delicate china teacup and saucer, a basket of toast, and a plate filled with eggs. "Are you sure you would like me to take this up to Miss Veronica, Cook?"

Cook looked her over in that way she always did, as if she was still attempting to understand how someone so ill equipped had come to work in her kitchen. "There ain't no one else. Emma is off this morning and Nanci is attending to Mrs. Sloane as she always is."

"I see."

Jerome, one of the footmen, crossed his arms over his chest as he glared at her. "Surely even you can handle carrying a tray?"

"Of course I can." She could handle it. She was just afraid of tripping on the stairs, dropping everything on the way to Veronica's bedroom, and, of course, saying the wrong thing to the woman. So far, it seemed as if she was often saying the wrong thing.

Cook clucked. "Good. Now, I've checked and double checked, and you should have everything Miss Veronica needs. Don't forget that she likes her coffee to be mixed with a fair bit of cream and sugar in the cup."

Thinking of pouring Veronica's coffee in front of her brought forth a whole new host of terrible worries. Already Rosalind had visions of splashing the hot liquid on the young lady.

"All right then, off you go," Cook said with a reassuring smile. "Remember, knock twice, count to five, then let yourself in, easy like. Miss Veronica will be in a frightful mood, but don't take it personal. She's not a morning person."

Rosalind had never known Veronica to be anything but waspish. "Anything else?"

"Yes, indeed." Cook pointed to the stairs. "You'll be needin' to go up right this minute or I'm going to have to make Miss Veronica a fresh breakfast. She won't be pleased if the coffee and eggs are cold," she said sharply. "Go on now, and be quick about it."

After whispering a quick prayer for strength, Rosalind gripped the silver tray with both hands, took a deep breath, then ascended the stairs.

By the eighth step, the muscles in her arms began to protest. She was a strong girl—anyone brought up on a dairy farm would be—but the effort of carrying a heavy silver tray loaded with china, coffee, toast, and eggs was not to be disputed. By the tenth step, she was already longing for a place to rest for a few seconds.

It was half past ten in the morning. She'd already been up for five hours, and truthfully, the time felt decidedly mid-morning. For most of her life, she'd had to rise at dawn to help feed and tend to the animals. Now, here she was, tending one of the most popular girls in Chicago society.

Not for the first time, she reflected on what it must feel like to simply expect to be looked after. To assume that others would make her breakfast, bring it to her, and pour her coffee.

Rosalind was slowly realizing that she was the only person who seemed to think it odd. But perhaps that was because most of the other servants in the house had always worked for the rich and powerful. Even Nanci had reminded Rosalind that they each had their role to play in the house. They were to complete tasks as perfectly as possible and strive to be invisible.

Veronica's role was to marry well; Douglass's responsibility was to continue the family fortune.

Nanci said she'd heard from Jerome that Douglass and Veronica's last guests hadn't left the house until after three in the morning, after all of them had been drinking gin, no less! Rosalind had never drunk spirits, but she had a feeling that she would want to stay abed late in the morning, too, if she'd had that kind of evening.

Slowly and with care, she walked up the narrow servants' stairs, the tray growing heavier by the second. Each of her steps seemed to fall heavier too, each landing with a dull thud. When she arrived at the second floor, she caught her breath. Thankful that the hallway was empty, she straightened and walked to Veronica's closed door.

She stood staring at it, yearning for a third hand to knock and turn the door handle. She was just considering putting down the tray in order to knock when she heard footsteps on the main staircase.

Finding an extra amount of strength she hadn't known she possessed, she gripped the tray with one hand, braced it against her body, and smartly knocked once, then twice.

Then she counted to five and opened the door just as Mrs. Sloane herself approached.

After giving the lady a hasty curtsy, she walked into Veronica's room and faced the daughter of the manor, who was peering out at her from under an intricately embroidered coverlet.

"Good morning, Miss Veronica. I have your breakfast."

Veronica said nothing as Rosalind approached the large bed dressed in pale pink silk sheets, cream-colored lace, and a plethora of down pillows. She noticed that the delicate table next to the bed was littered with a long strand of pearls, two rings, and two tortoiseshell combs inlaid with silver.

"Where would you like me to set the tray?"

Veronica glanced at the table, seemed surprised that no one had already cleared it, then sighed. "I suppose you may set it over there," she said, pointing to the finely crafted desk by the window.

"Yes, miss." By now Rosalind's arms were shaking from the weight of the tray. She used her last bit of strength to gently rest it on the center of the desk. "Coffee?"

"Of course."

Rosalind carefully set the cup and saucer to rights, then poured in a small amount of cream and a spoonful of sugar. Finally, she poured in the coffee, stirred it once, and carried it to Veronica.

By now, thankfully, Veronica had sat up in bed. Her nightgown was a frothy mixture of gray satin and ecru lace. Her auburn-colored hair was still neatly bound in a thick braid and rested over one slim shoulder.

It was almost the same exact shade of Miranda's hair. Unbidden, a memory spilled forth, one of her sister laughing as Rosalind tried to tame her hair into perfect curls, just like they'd seen in a magazine at the mercantile. Miranda's hair had been shiny and full of body, but much like the woman herself, the curls had a mind of their own. They no sooner would have agreed to be tamed than Miranda would have taken Rosalind's advice.

For a brief second, Rosalind stared at it, remembering her sister, feeling her loss as acutely as if she had only recently vanished.

Realizing what she'd been doing, Rosalind felt her embarrassment rise. "Your coffee, miss."

Veronica took the coffee without a word and sipped.

Anxious to leave, Rosalind stepped backward. "Will you be needing anything else, Miss Veronica?"

Veronica lifted her head as her mouth twisted into a sardonic smile. "Do you ever think how odd it is for you to call me 'miss'? After all, we're almost the same age. I might even be older. How old are you?"

"I'm twenty, ma'am."

Veronica laughed. "Now I'm a ma'am, am I? Though you haven't asked, I'll reveal that I'm all of twenty-three. Practically ancient. Almost a spinster. And almost a disappointment to my mother." She paused, then murmured, almost to herself, "Almost. But not yet."

If they'd known each other better, or if Veronica had been a nicer person, Rosalind's heart might have gone out to her. At this moment in time, however, all that counted was their position in society, and especially their position in the house.

"You don't have anything to say to me about that, Rosalind?" she murmured, sarcasm lacing each word. "No quaint comment, no maudlin, sanctimonious saying about how I'm worth more than my name? That I'm more than a myriad of social graces learned from a mother's knee?"

"W–would there be anything else, Miss Veronica?"

Her eyes narrowed. "No."

Rosalind turned and quickly left the room. Only when she had closed the door behind her and leaned against the wall did she exhale. She'd been holding her breath and hadn't even realized it. Veronica's bitter diatribe had unnerved her—and had made her feel as if her quest was forever unobtainable. How was she ever going to discover what happened to Miranda when she could hardly even serve coffee to Veronica?

"Rosalind, why are you loitering in the hall?"

She sprang to attention. "I'm sorry, Mrs. Abrams. I'm on my way downstairs now."

The formidable housekeeper's gray gaze narrowed. "See that you leave the floor immediately."

"Yes, ma'am." Hastily, she turned to her right and rushed down the hallway, anxious to make it to the servants' stairs and the dimly lit emptiness of the stairwell.

She'd almost made it when yet another door opened and Douglass appeared.

"Ah, Rosalind," he murmured, forcing her to stop. "Look at you." As he scanned her form, his lips curved slightly upward. "You're up early. And so bright-eyed too."

"Y–yes, sir. I mean, Mr. Sloane."

"Only my father is Mr. Sloane. I'm Douglass. I think the very least you could do is call me by my Christian name, don't you think?" he asked, his voice turning low and silky. "I mean, here we are, living together."

Well aware of Mrs. Abrams still standing at the other end of the hallway, watching her, she felt her cheeks heat again. She opened her mouth—to say what, she wasn't sure.

But then she felt his gaze settle on her lips.

Anxiety coursed through her, whether from his heated stare or her nerves or her fear, she didn't know. Too afraid to guess, she turned and practically ran to the stairs.

Behind her she heard Douglass chuckle.

Finally alone in the servants' passage, she pressed her shoulder blades against the cool plaster and closed her eyes.

Never before had she felt so much like one of the ivory balls on the billiard table, rolling to and fro. Always at everyone else's mercy. She forced herself to breathe in more slowly and gather her thoughts.

Perhaps she *was* at everyone else's mercy, but if she was, then Miranda had been too. And that meant she needed to do whatever it took to discover what had happened to Miranda.

Only now was she beginning to realize what "anything" might be. And though she was afraid, she was more determined than ever. For Miranda, she had to be.

CHAPTER 5

When Rosalind came down for breakfast the next morning, a far different scene greeted her. Mrs. Abrams' dress was wrinkled, her hair hastily pinned. Cook's apron was stained and tied crookedly about her waist. Both women looked weary.

The other servants were wandering around somewhat aimlessly. A strange, strained silence permeated the room.

Jerome was standing against the back door. His usually polished appearance looked a bit on the shabby side. His eyes fastened on hers when she entered the room.

"What is going on?" Rosalind asked. "What happened?"

After glancing in Mrs. Abrams' direction and seeing her slight nod, Cook spoke. "It's Tilly."

"What about her? Is she sick?"

"No. Um. I'm afraid . . . I'm afraid she's gone missing."

Rosalind felt as if someone had suddenly taken a hammer to her senses. Remembering that offhand remark Tilly had made in the kitchen about what could have happened to Miranda, and how Cook had pushed it aside with a meaningful look, she began to feel dizzy. Did this have anything to do with secrets about her sister?

Nanci rushed to her side and unceremoniously pushed her to a chair. "Pull yourself together."

She'd hardly known Tilly. Certainly not as much as the rest of the staff. With sheer force of will, she told herself to pull herself together as Nanci had commanded. "What happened? You don't think she simply decided to leave?"

Cook shrugged. "I can't imagine that she would. Tilly is a good girl. She doesn't run off or leave when she's not supposed to."

"Besides, where would she go?" Nanci asked.

"Her day off was yesterday. She was going to go to the fair with two other girls from other houses," Cook murmured. "But they said she never showed up. And she never came home."

"Oh my goodness. What do Mr. and Mrs. Sloane say?"

"They don't know as of yet." Mrs. Abrams sighed. "When Mr. Hodgeson discovered that some of her things were still here, he called for a police officer to stop by, but that man was no help. Said no scullery maid was 'missing' unless she was gone for a full week."

Rosalind was shocked. "But by then, anything could have happened to her!"

Cook nodded. "That would be true. If something did happen."

"We'll all just have to keep a lookout for anything unusual," Jerome murmured.

"And you, Rosalind, will need to help us out a bit in here until we decide what to do next," Cook stated. "Don't bother trying to get out of going to the market for me, neither. You ain't got no choice."

Rosalind got a cup of coffee, then sat down to her breakfast. For some reason, things seemed to get harder at Sloane House instead of easier.

≡

Two days later, Tilly was still missing.

Mrs. Sloane had been informed, but as of yet the lady had not given Cook permission to replace her. Mrs. Abrams said she was holding out hope that Tilly would return to the house one day soon.

Did Mrs. Sloane give Miranda the same consideration? Rosalind wondered. Was that why there was an opening when she applied for a job at Sloane House? Cook had said Miranda's disappearance was still upsetting to Mrs. Sloane all these weeks later. That fit with the stories she'd heard about how kind Mrs. Sloane sometimes was toward her servants.

Would she ever know?

Rosalind had spent much of the previous day in the kitchen, carefully chopping vegetables and dressing chickens. Today, on the other hand, she'd been mostly in the company of Mrs. Abrams, cleaning the east wing guest rooms in preparation for yet another group of guests. The last group, a party of six from Philadelphia, had left only minutes before.

The Sloanes' next guests, friends from New York City, were expected within three hours. Frantically polishing and cleaning silver and crystal, dusting and ironing sheets and pillowcases, they worked as quickly as they dared to set things to rights.

Indeed, the spacious home had become a hotel of sorts for some of the fair's most esteemed visitors. At least, much of the staff was starting to feel that way. Because of the fair's popularity, rooms at hotels such as the Fairmont had become not only exorbitantly expensive but scarce. That left even wealthy out-of-town guests relying on the hospitality of Chicago society.

Rosalind had always imagined that no one worked harder than farmers, whose lives were dependent on caring for livestock and growing crops. But she was slowly coming to realize that until her arrival in Chicago, she had led a very sheltered life.

Now her hours were spent cleaning and arranging rooms to perfection, unpacking and then packing a dizzying array of gowns, and doing her best to stay invisible.

That was what was so difficult, she realized. A good job was an unnoticed one. Where no one realized she'd even been in the room.

At the moment, she was by Mrs. Abrams' side in the blue bedroom. One of the Philadelphia ladies had been especially messy, and it was taking even the housekeeper's diligent efforts to clean and prepare the room for the next round of visitors.

"I don't understand how one woman can make such a mess," Rosalind said as she eyed the crumpled stationery on the floor and the boxes and tissues from the shopping trips. And the faint stains of powder and kohl that stained the dressing table cushion.

Her hand in an old sock, Mrs. Abrams was carefully swiping the stains with a baking soda paste. Little by little, the streaks of kohl were being removed. "Ours is not to wonder why. Only to clean it."

"Yes, ma'am." She looked up gratefully when Emma brought in the new set of freshly ironed sheets. "Thank you."

"I'll stay and help you get the bed made up," Emma said. "Mrs. Abrams, Cook was lookin' for ya."

After giving the cushion one last thoughtful swipe, she nodded. "I imagine she's in a dither about tonight's menu. Girls, when this room is done, don't forget to check in with the laundry. They might need your assistance pressing dresses or even napkins."

"This work, it's enough to make one dizzy, it is," Emma said when they were alone.

"I've been so exhausted when I fall into bed, I hardly move." Remembering her sister's chatty letters, the first ones so filled with excitement and wonder, Rosalind wondered how Miranda had handled it all.

Or had she not? Had her early letters about how wonderful her new life was really been full of lies? Had she opted to write about a world that never was, choosing to share her wishful dreams of her life instead of the stark, vacant reality?

"How long have you worked here, Emma?"

"Three years, I have."

Emma couldn't be more than eighteen. "That long?"

"Started here when I was fifteen, in the laundry," she said proudly. "Now, here I am, a parlor maid. One day I aim to be what Nanci is."

"A lady's maid?"

Emma nodded. "I figure one day Nanci will leave to get married or something. When that happens, I aim to take her place."

"You think that's possible?"

"I'm praying it is. I can sew better than Nanci, and I'm almost as good with hair as she is."

"Who taught you how to do hair?"

"Miranda." She smiled softly. "She was talented."

"Did you know her well?" Rosalind let her voice drop softly, hoping that she added just enough of a touch of openness to encourage more sharing.

Emma tilted her head to one side. "As well as anyone did. She was beautiful. Almost too beautiful, you know? I heard Mrs. Abrams caution her to watch herself."

"Why would she do that?"

"It wouldn't do to be so pretty around Miss Veronica, you know. Plus, looks like hers would have gotten her into trouble. Men start to notice things they shouldn't, you know. Or the ladies begin to feel threatened."

"I wish I could have met Miranda."

"Oh, you would have liked her, I bet. Almost everyone did."

"Almost?"

Emma's cheeks turned red. "I didn't mean anything. That was just an expression."

Desperate to learn something, anything of use, Rosalind reached out to Emma. Grabbed her sleeve. "Who didn't like her?"

Emma's eyes widened. With a jerk, she pulled her arm out of Rosalind's grasp. "What's wrong with you? You almost tore my sleeve."

"I'm sorry. It's simply that I'm curious about what you said."

"Why?"

"Miranda sounds like a really nice girl," she improvised. "And competent, too. So if she wasn't well liked, it seems like I wouldn't have a chance." Hesitantly, she smiled at her little joke. "So who didn't like her? Was it someone on staff? Or a member of the family?"

"I was just talking, that was all," Emma replied in a rush. She turned, picked up two of the delicately embroidered pillows, and set them neatly on the center of the bed. "What do you think?"

Realizing that the conversation was through, Rosalind picked up the two dust cloths Mrs. Abrams left, then scanned the room with a critical eye. Light streamed in from the sheer curtains, sending rays of sunshine across the polished cherry writing desk and freshly cleaned yellow chair cushion.

The bed was made, the pillows were arranged perfectly, the blue-and-ivory-striped coverlet was pressed. The fireplace was cleaned and logs set in. Fingerprints had been removed from silver trinkets. The crystal decanter was filled with fresh water. The carpet was brushed clean.

"I think it looks beautiful in here. Perfect." Still feeling a bit cautious, she murmured, "Is that what you think?"

"It's not what I think that matters. We both know that to be true, don't we?" Before Rosalind could think of anything to say to that, Emma clasped her hands together. "As far as I can tell, we're done. We'd best go on to the next room. We've got a lot to do and no time to do it."

Reluctantly, Rosalind nodded. She'd heard Emma's warning loud and clear.

Now all she had to do was wonder if she should heed it.

—

Rosalind was still stewing about Miranda being liked by "almost" everyone and Emma's steadfast refusal to explain herself, when she entered the small attic room she shared with Nanci.

Nestled in the attic's eaves, it boasted a sloping ceiling, a small window, two twin beds, two nightstands, and one very plain and rickety dresser standing tall and regal in between the two beds.

When Rosalind had first come to work at Sloane House, she'd felt like these attic rooms were scary and full of ghosts. The bedroom next to them was empty, and the window was stuck shut so they couldn't get a breeze on hot July nights. Rosalind had been sure a person could be forgotten up in the eaves, practically never seen or heard from again.

But Nanci, being Nanci, had soon dispelled her of that notion. Together with her matter-of-fact manner and a bounty of discarded fabrics, she'd made their bedroom a happy place. What it lacked in elegance, Nanci had more than made up for in comfort and coziness. She'd covered her bed with a marvelous wedding ring quilt her grandmother had long ago stitched. On her bedside table were an ornate filigree frame and a small silver snuff box, a favor from a gentleman friend whom she'd so far refused to name.

In comparison, Rosalind's side was as bare and functional as

Nanci's was inviting. It made her homesick for the comforts of her cozy bedroom at home.

Just last week, Nanci had even wheedled Jim's services, asking him to see to the window. She'd asked Jim so sweetly and explained the need for repairs so easily to Mrs. Abrams that they got the window fixed with hardly a word of complaint.

Their room was a popular spot with the other girls in the house, despite the sometimes stifling hot summer temperatures. More often than not, Rosalind would come upstairs to find two or three other maids sitting in the room with Nanci, chatting or looking at magazines or newspapers pilfered from the trash. And, as was always the case with Nanci, the conversation would be lively.

Luckily, this evening Nanci seemed as tired as Rosalind, just as happy to slip out of her starched uniform and retire early.

"What a time we had of it today. And for that matter, all week!" Nanci said as they hastily prepared for bed. "I'm exhausted."

Watching Nanci carefully unpin her hair and begin brushing it with her nightly hundred strokes, Rosalind said, "You seem to be handling it better than me. I almost fell asleep during the dinner service."

"You've had a time of it, for sure. You're doing both Tilly's job and yours now."

"Do you ever worry about Tilly?"

Nanci's hand slowed. "From time to time, I do. But it's best not to think about her too much."

"That sounds kind of harsh."

"Maybe so, but there's nothing we can do. Not really."

"Do you think she'll return?"

Nanci shook her head. "If she returned, she'd probably be fired. We all know that. Whatever the reason, she's most likely gone for good."

Rosalind shivered as she unpinned her waist-length brown hair.

Though it was the fashion to cut hair at least to shoulder-blade length, Rosalind had never felt the urge to do so. The problem with that, however, was that it weighed heavily against the dozen pins she used to keep it in place. It was always a blessed relief to release it at the end of each day.

"Just you be glad you weren't standing behind hot irons all day today," Nanci said. "Every time I turned around, another woman was needing her dress pressed."

"I've never seen anything like it," Rosalind said, thinking about the ladies who had been in the house. "There were more women here than I could shake a stick at."

Nanci chuckled at her country phrase. "Like I said, it's bound to continue, fair or no fair. Mrs. Sloane is determined to marry off Veronica as soon as possible. Add that to all the ladies who want their daughters to have Douglass? We're certain to always have a house full of guests now."

"I'm already even more exhausted just thinking about it," Rosalind teased. But still, this evening's party had been exciting, even from her vantage point, which was firmly in the background.

The Sloanes' dinner for forty-eight had kept all of them on their toes—and their tongues wagging too. Each young lady looked beautiful, and their mothers were just as handsome and well turned out. One by one they had alighted from their carriages and strolled into the home's brightly lit entryway in an array of exquisitely styled taffeta and satin gowns, each jewel-colored dress seeming to have more yards of fabric than the last.

The men by their sides wore black tuxedos and top hats, white gloves, and bored expressions.

Together, the group looked like something out of a picture postcard or one of the society magazines Miranda used to spend too much money on and examine in awe.

Thinking of how much Miranda must have enjoyed seeing the gowns at parties when she worked there, she mused, "The ladies looked bright and beautiful. Truly lovely."

"That they did."

"Did you notice Mrs. Anderson's bustle?" Rosalind mused, thinking back to the petite woman dressed in unrelieved black. "It was very stylish for a lady in mourning."

Nanci wrinkled her nose as she continued to pull the horsehair brush through her caramel-colored tresses. "From the way her cheeks were blooming, I wouldn't put it past her to already be looking for a new man."

The thought was appalling. Turning to Nanci, Rosalind shook her head. "Surely not. I mean, ladies in mourning are the same everywhere, don't you think? No amount of money could ever bring back a cherished husband."

"You've got to learn about life here at Sloane House. The people who live here aren't like anyone you've ever met, and some of their friends are even more outlandish." Lowering her voice, she cast a concerned eye at the door, just as if she imagined someone was listening at the keyhole. "You should prepare yourself to be shocked."

"By what?"

Looking as if she'd said something she shouldn't, Nanci shook her head. "Never you mind that."

"You're not going to even give me a hint? Perhaps I should consider looking through some of those keyholes."

"Don't you ever do that," Nanci said, her voice hard. "Some things go on here that you don't want to know about. Ever. And I shudder to imagine what would happen to you if one of the family discovered you were spying on them."

"I was only joking." It was all Rosalind could do not to shake off the words with a bit of a nervous giggle. Never before had she received a warning like that. Had Miranda been warned like this? Was that what had frightened her so?

Looking a bit chagrined, Nanci spoke more lightly. "I hope I didn't scare you none. I don't mean to frighten you. It's just that a home like this is a big change from your life in Wisconsin. The people here do things a bit different too. And if you don't get used to it, well, it can cause a lot of problems in the long run."

Nanci's change of tone gave Rosalind confidence to ask questions.

"Is that what happened to Miranda? Did she never get used to things here?"

"Miranda refused to listen to reason. That's what happened with her. If she would have listened in the first place, it would have saved her a lot of trouble."

"I'll keep my eyes and ears open, though. Just like you suggested."

"Good. You're the best roommate I've ever had. I don't want to lose you anytime soon!"

"Thank you for that."

Now dressed in her nightgown, Nanci crawled into her narrow bed. "We should get some sleep, since tomorrow is sure to be wonderful."

"I'd almost forgotten."

"I don't know how! Can you believe our luck? We both get tomorrow afternoon and evening off. And Mr. Sloane has given us tickets for admission to the fair and tokens for the midway!"

Just a few hours before, Mr. and Mrs. Sloane had lined up all the staff and presented each member with tokens and tickets for both the fair admission and the Ferris wheel in the midway. Even the most senior members of the staff had trouble containing their excitement.

Mr. Hodgeson and Mrs. Abrams had then, in turn, made up a schedule that allowed a few of them at a time to visit the fair, in addition to their usual half day off once a week. Nanci and Rosalind were paired together.

The idea of going to the fair was tremendously exciting . . . and terribly hard for Rosalind to accept. She didn't feel she should do anything other than hunt for Miranda or work. Taking part in even the most harmless of amusements felt wrong.

But perhaps she could show her sister's daguerreotype to a few of the workers while she was there. It was a long shot, to be sure, but at least it was an attempt to find some answers. As Nanci continued to prattle on, Rosalind tried to look excited too. But as she washed her face and then got under her sheet, her mind drifted to other things. About how she used to share her bed at home with Miranda.

And how at the moment, the cold cotton settling against her skin felt like ice despite the warmth of the room. Whether it was the coolness of the sheet or the direction of her thoughts, Rosalind felt her skin break out in chill bumps. A tremor coursed through her as her body attempted to warm itself. Thinking about how cold their attic room would be when winter came . . . Oh, what she'd give then for just one of the down comforters that were in the guest rooms, not to mention how wonderful it would be to have a fireplace in a bedroom like Veronica did.

Yet she should know better than to not count her blessings. She was lucky, and that was the truth. Back home, the work was just as hard, only there was little gaiety or anything to break up the days. Early morning brought milking, then the hard labor of sterilizing the buckets and milking areas. Afterward, a long line of chores blended each day into the next, and all the while she was pestered by her younger brothers. Only gardening gave her much pleasure.

But the worst part was sitting at her parents' table and feeling their despair and exhaustion cloud the room. Her mother, though not even forty, looked twenty years older. Her father's perpetually grim expression was weighted down with the burdens of the nation's recession and the responsibility of caring for the four children still at home.

And then, of course, there was the ever-present worry about Miranda. From the time her dear sister's letters had stopped arriving, Rosalind had tossed and turned at night and worried and fretted. She had to find her. She had to. Or she had to discover what had become of her. There was no choice.

After the kerosene lamp was dimmed and their attic room was wrapped in darkness, Rosalind finally remembered to tell Nanci her news. "Guess what? I talked to Douglass the other day."

"Oh? Where did you see him?"

"In the east hallway. I turned around, and there he was. He remembered my name."

"Did he?"

Rosalind noticed that Nanci wasn't responding the way she'd imagined she would. Instead of teasing Rosalind, she almost sounded . . . jealous?

"We didn't say much to each other."

"What did you talk about?"

"Nothing." Now Rosalind wished she'd never even brought it up, and she was glad she'd never told Nanci about her first encounter with Douglass. "I had just delivered Miss Veronica's tray. He wished me good morning."

"Ah. Well, he would. He's special that way," Nanci replied in a much warmer tone. "I bet he was just curious about the new maid in the house."

She certainly hoped that was still the case, though something about him had made her feel a little uncomfortable again. "What's he like?"

"What do you mean?"

"You seem to know him well. What's special about him?"

Nanci laughed softly. "Douglass is the master's son. *That's* why he is special, silly. That's all that matters, anyway."

"No, I mean, is he kind? Mean? Have you ever talked with him?"

"Talked with him?"

"Yes. I mean, you've worked here for two years. Surely you've had occasion to speak to him once or twice. What do you know about him?" Rosalind bit her tongue so she wouldn't ask any more questions.

"I know he likes his shoes polished every Thursday until they shine. He likes his eggs poached and his fireplace swept clean daily. At least, he did back when I was just a house maid."

"Come now, you have to know something more."

"Actually . . . I do," Nanci said after a moment's pause. "Mr. Douglass has been seein' someone special, but I hear he don't care for her hoity-toity ways all that much." She cleared her throat. "I've even been told that he doesn't always find all those ladies to his taste."

"Truly?"

"Truly." Lowering her voice, Nanci added, "I've never told anyone this, but once I noticed him smiling my way."

Eager for more, Rosalind pounced on that bit of information. "Oh? And what did you do?"

"Why, I smiled just as sweet as you please right back, that's what I did."

Rosalind was disappointed by the answer, but promptly pushed her reaction aside. "I would have been too surprised to do anything but stand there with a smile. I was practically shaking in my boots and all I was trying to do was stay out of his way."

"Don't worry, Rosalind. Before you know it, you'll understand how everything works in this house. You'll know when to smile and know when to stay in the shadows." Before Rosalind could comment on that,

Nanci said, "Well, we'd best stop talking and get to sleep. It'd be a pity if we was too worn out to enjoy our afternoon and evening off."

Dutifully, Rosalind closed her eyes. But all she could think about were Nanci's words about knowing how to get along in the house. She wondered if Miranda had ever learned all the rules to working in the household.

And what might have happened if she hadn't.

"Lord, please be with Miranda," Rosalind whispered into the darkness. "Please keep her safe, free from harm." As disturbing images swirled in her head, and as she recalled how Miranda had written about the Sloanes' power and the way they did things, she added one more plea. "Or at least free from pain."

CHAPTER 6

The World's Columbian Exposition was far bigger than Rosalind had ever imagined. From the majestic fountains greeting visitors at the entrance to the vast array of animals and foreigners, there was plenty for all to see. Each stately columned building was filled with remarkable machinery and exotic inventions from faraway locales. The papers proclaimed that a person could spend two weeks at the fair and still not see everything.

Rosalind imagined that to be true.

Each stately building glowed in ethereal white, encouraging even the most hardened of gentlemen and women to speak in soft, respectful tones. The giant buildings, each glimmering in the twilight, promised magical wonders within. Together, their arrangement produced a unique serenity that soothed one's soul.

Yet what kept Rosalind mesmerized was the great number of people. Ladies and maids, gentlemen and dockworkers, children and soldiers all filled the area. But instead of being worried about the crowds, for the first time since her arrival in Chicago, Rosalind felt her spirits lift. She wished she could live in the White City.

Nanci felt the same way. "It's a shame we can't come back again tomorrow," Nanci said with a pout. "We've walked so far and have only visited a few of the states' buildings. I've a mind to visit Pennsylvania's display next. We need to see the Liberty Bell, don't you think?"

Nanci had been that way all afternoon, holding her Columbian Exposition newspaper tightly in one hand while pointing out sights and sounds with the other.

"Perhaps one day we'll get to come again. You never know," Rosalind ventured, though in truth, she had no idea how she would ever get to visit again. She'd neither the funds nor the opportunity to visit twice.

"Perhaps." With a sigh, Nanci reached for her hand, and together they traipsed over gravel walkways and picturesque bridges. "Since the newspaper says the lines are long for the Liberty Bell, let's make our way to the midway. I hear Blarney Castle is right magical."

Their journey to the other end of the park took quite some time. It was impossible not to stop often to investigate different sights and sounds.

It was also impossible for Rosalind not to scan every face that passed, on the off chance that she'd find her sister. She carried the small photo she had of Miranda in her reticule, though fearing she was on a fool's errand. The one time she dared show it to a vendor while Nanci was looking elsewhere, he laughed heartily at her question, saying thousands of people passed him each day.

The situation felt overwhelming. Rosalind wasn't very brave. She wasn't very good at subterfuge. Every time she left the confines of the grand mansion, she became more and more aware that she had a very limited view of the world.

In Wisconsin, she'd spent the majority of her time with either animals or her family. Here in Chicago, it seemed very few people ever spent time with their own kin. Instead, they chose to flit here and there, to accept jobs in a city that was dangerous and exciting. They'd made the choice to try something new, to be in strange surroundings.

She, on the other hand, was there only because her family was that desperate. After her father made a short trip to Chicago and could not convince either Mr. or Mrs. Sloane or the police to help him find Miranda, she'd been the only person in her family who could leave the farm and look for her. So she'd gone, not because she was the best choice, but because she was the only choice.

And now, as each day passed, she worried that perhaps she was merely making things worse. In many ways, she feared she was going to let her parents down, her whole family down. And most of all, Miranda herself.

As the sights and the sounds of the fair surrounded her, Rosalind's earlier fascination disappeared. She felt almost claustrophobic. There were too many people, too close together.

Nanci, however, seemed to glow from her excitement. "Do you hear them folks behind us?" she asked when they were standing in a line of at least twenty deep for cider. "I think they're speaking Chinese!"

"How do you know what Chinese sounds like?"

"I don't, but I've got a good imagination!"

Despite her fears, Rosalind laughed. "That you do, Nanci. You have a very good imagination."

"You need to relax and learn to look around you a bit, you know," Nanci warned. "Here you are at the one place in the world where everyone is coming together, and you're looking as if you're about to jump out of your skin!"

Rosalind was in awe of the many foreigners who wandered

through the buildings. But instead of looking at them like prospective friends as Nanci did, she looked at them as possible kidnappers. She couldn't help it. Her sister's disappearance made her fear and distrust almost everyone.

"I can't wait to see the belly dancers," Nanci whispered. "I heard the women wear veils too."

After they each got a cold glass of cider, they sipped their drinks near one of the many parks and viewing areas. "We need to see as much as we possibly can, Rosalind." Without stopping for air, Nanci continued. "And, of course, I'm eager to see all the curious people and animals. Do we dare visit the Egyptian temple?"

At last, Rosalind felt herself getting more excited about their adventure as well. "I'll go wherever you would like."

"There's a girl. I knew you'd get the hang of things sooner or later."

"I guess it's finally happened then." Picking up a handout a previous visitor had tossed to the ground, Rosalind's eyes grew wide. "But perhaps we could take in one of the many shows today? I see there's an opera here."

Nanci wrinkled her nose. "I've never been much for opera." Pointing to another flyer that littered the ground, she said, "But I would like to see the funhouse."

"And the wax museum."

Nanci moaned. "There's so much to see. Do you think Mrs. Sloane will notice if we don't come home tonight?"

"Only if her dress isn't pressed for tomorrow," Rosalind joked. Truly, she couldn't imagine what her employers would do if she and Nanci stayed very late at the fair. They might wonder if they were missing, like Miranda and Tilly.

As they approached the entrance to the midway, they both looked at the giant Ferris wheel looming over them. It was a massive structure.

Each enclosed car held sixty people. As it revolved in its lit splendor, Rosalind blanched. "Should we go on the wheel now?"

Nanci shuddered. "I don't care that we got tokens. The thought of being so high up scares me to death."

They'd just passed the signs for Wild Bill Cody's Wild West Show when Rosalind felt her heart jump . . . but this time because of something far different than a fear of heights.

Approaching them were Douglass Sloane and his gentleman friend, Reid Armstrong. Gripping her friend's hand, she whispered, "Nanci, that's Douglass Sloane coming this way."

Nanci's cheeks bloomed pink. "Truly?" She craned her neck. "Oh, look at him now, Rosalind! Isn't he something? Douglass is so handsome. Do you think they've seen us yet?"

"I sincerely hope not. Hurry, let's go visit the wax museum."

"The what?"

"The wax museum. That building, there." Her tone had become urgent. Though they had been given the time off, she still felt uneasy about being seen by one of their employers. More than that was the slow, worrisome sensation she always ended up feeling whenever Douglass was nearby. He made her uneasy. She wasn't sure if it was because he was a man about town, wealthy and sophisticated, and she was merely a farmer's daughter pretending to be a sleuth, or because she had a terrible feeling that he was somehow connected to her sister's disappearance.

No matter the reason, she certainly didn't want his company to ruin their day of freedom.

Gripping her friend's arm, she gave it a little yank. "Hurry, Nanci. We don't want to run into them."

But instead of heeding Rosalind's wishes, Nanci smiled gamely at the two approaching men. Both nodded in return, then Douglass's eyes widened in recognition.

"Well, what do you know? Two of my housemaids. Rosalind and . . ."

"Nanci, sir." She gave a little curtsy.

"Ah, yes. Are you two having a good time?"

"Oh yes, indeed, sir. I mean, Mr. Sloane, sir. I mean, we were given the afternoon and evening off by your father."

He leaned close. "My father is Mr. Sloane. Call me Douglass, yes?"

"I couldn't." But all the same, Nanci leaned a little closer.

His dimple appeared. "Sure you could. Especially here. After all, no one back home will ever know what we do."

Rosalind felt her nerves tighten as his words floated over them. To her way of thinking, they sounded vaguely threatening. But it seemed she was the only one who thought that. Nanci was smiling flirtatiously, and Douglass looked pleased.

And Mr. Armstrong? He simply looked bored.

Feeling slightly silly, Rosalind forced herself to relax. Her problem was that she saw danger at every turn. Because her sister's welfare and disappearance rested at the top of her concerns, she most likely saw problems where there were none.

Worried about things that she shouldn't concern herself about.

Standing beside Nanci, even Rosalind had to admit that Douglass Sloane was charming. Furthermore, it truly was a blessing that he was so friendly. She'd served enough men and women in the dining rooms to realize that most of the guests barely deigned to even notice the servants, let alone bother to learn their names. Still fewer took the time to ever have a conversation with them.

She should have known better than to assume anything about Douglass. After all, she'd been raised with her mother's constant gentle reminder that they were all God's children, and therefore equal in his eyes.

With all that in mind, Rosalind tried her best to be a bit more lighthearted. "Perhaps I will call you Douglass too."

Dramatically, Douglass patted his chest. "Be still, my heart. My name sounds so sweet on your lips."

Unable to stop herself, Rosalind giggled. Yes, Douglass Sloane flirted too much. And surely a respectful woman would never give any of his words credence. She did not. But she would be lying to herself if she didn't admit that having a sophisticated man like Douglass Sloane take notice of a country girl like her made her slightly breathless.

You have been a foolish girl, she scolded herself. *Imagining problems where there are none and blackguards where only friends appear.*

Douglass Sloane really was terribly charming. And he seemed nice too. Surely all of that wasn't pretense. She didn't know society's ways, but she liked to think that she did know people. Surely she'd be able to know immediately if a person was dangerous. Really dangerous.

Yes, she liked to think so. And she needed an ally in the house if she was ever going to truly uncover all the mysteries surrounding Miranda's disappearance. Instinctively, she knew she couldn't rely only on information passed to her by servants. She needed the perspective and knowledge that only one of the family—someone in society—could know.

The first spark of real hope lit inside of her. Maybe her working in the house, maybe all this subterfuge, wasn't for naught after all.

Reid cleared his throat, bringing her thoughts back to the present. "I believe it's time we let you, uh, ladies go on your way. You no doubt have other things to do, as do we." Though unspoken, the meaning under his words was unashamedly evident. He'd had enough of two maids' company.

"Oh yes, sir," Nanci said. Almost imperceptibly, her shoulders straightened and her expression turned a bit more wooden.

Rosalind found she wasn't able to revert to her supposed place so easily. Instead blood began to pound in her temples as embarrassment flowed over her. It seemed that while Douglass might be inclined to let some of the walls between their stations crumble, Reid Armstrong had no intention of forgetting everyone's place in society.

"Whatever are you speaking of, Armstrong?" Douglass retorted. "I don't recall a single place I'd rather be than right here."

Pointedly, Reid pulled out a silver timepiece from a vest pocket. "Did you forget the meeting we have scheduled? We told those *ladies* we'd meet them at one of the restaurants facing the Court of Honor ten minutes ago."

Rosalind inwardly flinched. Even the way he said *ladies* this time left no doubt about the perceived differences. This time there was no awkward pause.

Douglass blinked, then a new warmth entered his eyes. "Oh. Oh yes. Quite so." With a slight bow, he said, "Beg pardon, girls. Perhaps we'll tour the fair together one day in the future."

Reid nodded as well before abruptly turning his back on them. But Rosalind had noticed that his gaze had turned harder. Less languid.

In the barest of seconds, their elegant forms had blended into the crowds, mixing with the confetti of people. Effectively disappearing from their view.

Rosalind and Nanci stood motionless, staring after them in confusion.

"What just happened?" Nanci whispered.

"I'm not sure," Rosalind said. "I think we were almost escorted around the fair by two of the richest gentlemen of the city."

The corners of Nanci's lips curved up. "Is it a good thing or bad that they walked away?"

"I couldn't tell you that."

The truth was, for a moment, she'd been as affected as her sister must have been at first. For a split second, all that mattered was money and looks and power and elegance. For a brief time, she'd been able to imagine what it would be like to have her hand resting on an elegant man's arm.

She could feel other women's envious glances as they wondered what made her so special. And she'd been drawn to that feeling like a moth to a flame. In the span of just minutes, she'd pushed aside everything she'd vowed to remember just so she could feel good about herself. It was shocking.

In a burst of clarity, she wondered if, perhaps, that was what had happened to Miranda. Perhaps she had let herself yearn for something that was as fake and as treacherous as a relationship with the wrong kind of man.

Had she let herself believe that a man like Douglass Sloane or Reid Armstrong would ever actually care about a lowly maid who worked in his house?

"We should start walking," Nanci said with a nervous laugh. "Folks are going to think we're one of those Roman statues if we stand here like this much longer."

"Indeed," Rosalind murmured.

And so finally they, too, joined the throng of tourists and Chicagoans. The throng of everyone. Blending into anonymity.

So much so, they might as well have never been there. They might as well have been completely gone. And she realized that if they did disappear, few would care, and certainly even fewer would have any idea how to locate them.

Rosalind felt the stark, tremulous feeling of worry. And, ironically, relief.

For the moment, at least, they had nothing to fear.

CHAPTER 7

The following day proved to be a test of Rosalind's will and patience. By ten that morning, she realized she'd failed on both counts. By the half-pitying, half-annoyed looks cast her way by the rest of the staff, she knew everyone else noticed her mishaps as well.

Nanci had woken up with a light fever and an upset stomach. After Mrs. Abrams visited her, she confined Nanci to bed for the day and transferred most of Nanci's duties onto Rosalind's shoulders.

That would have been hard enough, but there was the added stress of having to rush through more than a few unfamiliar chores. First, she'd been called to help iron Veronica's gowns before dawn. The process of heating irons and carefully pressing each voluminous layer was a stressful, painstaking one. A girl with an indelicate hand could scorch a gown within seconds. That, of course, would cause the fabric irreparable damage, as well as the loss of a job with no reference.

It also meant a thorough scolding from Mrs. Abrams.

With all that in mind, it took double the time for Rosalind to press a gown than it did for anyone else. Which, of course, caused her to fall behind on her other chores.

When she finished the ironing at last, she tripped on the rug while helping to set the table for a luncheon. Only the quick hand of Jerome prevented her from dropping the stack of plates she was carrying.

While the family had their luncheon, she was sent to help Emma prepare a guest room in the west wing.

While she was rushing to help Emma, she managed to spill ash on the carpet. Which necessitated Emma preparing the room by herself while Rosalind cleaned the stain.

"I really am sorry," she said to Emma. "I don't know what happened. I am usually not so clumsy."

Emma sniffed. "Are you certain about that?"

After the briefest of breaks, Rosalind responded with a good dose of apprehension when she was summoned to help tidy the conservatory.

"Will you be able to handle this on your own, Rosalind?" Mrs. Abrams asked, a healthy bit of impatience and doubt lacing her tone. "Miss Veronica is expecting a dozen women to attend, some of whom are very important."

The conservatory was only named so because of a lumbering, somewhat garishly painted harp in the corner. Otherwise, its purpose seemed to be to display Mrs. Sloane's collection of gilt clocks and porcelain figurines. Every tabletop and shelf held either a ticking clock or a pair of shepherdesses. All seemed to attract dust like honey attracted bees. "Yes, ma'am."

If the formidable woman heard the doubt in Rosalind's voice, she gave no sign of it. "Good," she said. However, on her way out the door, the housekeeper threw one more warning over her shoulder.

"And do try to be quick about this. The party will begin at the top of the hour."

"Yes, ma'am," Rosalind repeated, hastily brushing the harp with her feather duster just before Mrs. Abrams turned back.

"By the way, I'm still confused by Nanci's illness. When did she fall ill? Was she sick last night? This morning?"

Rosalind shrugged. "I'm not sure, ma'am. She seemed fine last night. At least, she did when I went to sleep."

Mrs. Abrams narrowed her eyes. "You two didn't eat anything strange at the fair, did you?"

"I don't believe so, ma'am. Though we didn't eat exactly the same things . . ."

"I suppose it doesn't really matter who ate what when, does it?" Mrs. Abrams muttered. "Not when we're all working as best we can to keep this house running efficiently."

"Yes, ma'am."

"Well, tut, tut. Finish the dusting as quickly as you can. I'll return shortly with the tea service."

Frustrated with herself, Rosalind glanced at one of the clocks decorating the gold-and-ivory-wallpapered room. She had twenty minutes.

She pulled out a clean rag and prayed that her fingers wouldn't suddenly slip each time she painstakingly picked up a delicately carved clock, china vase, or scantily clad porcelain woman.

Ten minutes later, Lolly, the tweeny, ran in with an armful of linen napkins. "Sorry it took me so long to bring these to you," she said. "Things are a bit backed up in the laundry."

"That's all right," Rosalind said as she rested them in the center of the coffee table, where she assumed the tea service would sit.

"I'm supposed to stay and help you," Lolly said nervously. "What do you want me to do?"

Rosalind bit her lip. Unfortunately, Lolly had even more to do than she did. "Just make sure everything's in perfect order as quickly as possible. Oh! And don't forget to start the fire in the grate."

Lolly groaned. "Ooh, but I hate starting the fires. I can never get the flame to catch."

"I'll do it then," Rosalind soothed. She'd built many a fire at home. At least here she didn't have to worry about fuel to feed it. At Sloane House, there was as much wood and coal as anyone could ever dream about.

While she removed the grate and began filling the coal bucket, Lolly scurried around the room like she was on fire herself.

While Rosalind continued to prepare the fireplace, Lolly picked up one of the three ornate clocks that were grouped on an occasional table. "Have you ever seen the like?" she asked as she fingered the dove carved at the top.

"You'd best put that down. And I already dusted that clock."

Lolly set it down with a hasty thump, rattling the china, almost toppling the stack to the floor.

"Please be careful," Rosalind warned.

"Oh, I am. It's just . . . are you almost done? We need to finish, and quickly."

Rosalind turned and stared at the tiny young housemaid. She didn't look like her usual self at all. She looked pale and agitated. "Lolly, you are shaking like a leaf! What is wrong?"

"Since Nanci's sick, I'm supposed to go up to help Mrs. Sloane dress. And she likes her hair real particular, you know. If Emma doesn't get to her room on time, Mrs. Abrams said I'm supposed to try to help her!" A line formed between her brows. "Oh, I could wring that Nanci's neck, I could! Why in heaven's name did she have to pick today to be sick?"

That seemed to be the question of the day. Since she had no answer, Rosalind merely shooed her on her way. "Go on now. I've got things under control."

"You sure?"

"Of course. As soon as I get the fire started, I'll double check that everything's set up perfectly, and then will be right behind you."

Lolly sent her a grateful smile, then trotted out of the room.

Alone again, Rosalind breathed a sigh of relief. For a moment there, she'd been sure Lolly was going to upset the stack of china or knock over a lamp. She'd been very unlike herself—not only clumsy, but extremely nervous too.

After striking the match, Rosalind watched the flame take hold with a feeling of satisfaction. The heat emanating from it felt so comforting that she let herself relax some and watch the flames dance across the coals.

Kind of like how the staff all jumped and darted through the house, she mused.

It was amazing how everyone who raced to do the Sloane family's bidding was in a constant state of panic. The slightest frown or admonition from a member of the family could set some maids to vapors.

Rosalind supposed the obligation to see to the family's every whim came from a lifetime of being in service. Working all day at pleasing other people was still new to her since her father had always said there was only one being—the Lord—whom he needed to please.

Now that the fire was blazing, she efficiently replaced the grate and took one last turn around the room. It all looked to be in order. The china was neatly stacked; linen napkins were carefully folded. Trays were laid out for the tea sandwiches and cakes Cook would deliver shortly. Yes, it was all as perfect as it could be. So much so that even Mrs. Abrams would surely find no fault with her efforts.

"You are still here? This room should have been readied ten minutes ago!"

Startled to hear Veronica's voice, Rosalind whirled and jostled three sets of cups and saucers close to the server's edge. With a crash, they fell and broke at her feet. Letting out a cry, Rosalind quickly crouched down and scooped up two pieces. However, the clumsy movement only served to create more chaos. She gasped as a shard pierced her skin.

"What have you done?" Veronica yelled.

With a feeling of doom, Rosalind met her gaze. "I'm so sorry! I don't know . . ."

Veronica's stormy gray gaze eclipsed her beautiful sky-blue gown with its exquisitely designed leg-of-mutton sleeves—sleeves that Rosalind herself had pressed to perfection just that morning!

Pointing at the broken china littering the floor, Veronica glared. "Girl, don't just sit there! My guests will be here any moment."

Dutifully, Rosalind bent and grasped more of the broken shards. Another piece sliced her palm. As a thin trail of blood oozed from the cut, she clumsily curved her hand upward. What would she do if blood stained the expensive Persian carpet?

"Where is everyone? Abrams?" Veronica shouted. "Mother? Mother!"

Mrs. Abrams came running, followed by Mrs. Sloane herself, who had obviously not gotten her hair restyled by either Emma or Lolly. When they surveyed the scene, they stopped abruptly.

"Oh, Rosalind," Mrs. Abrams murmured.

Mrs. Sloane's usually lovely expression turned pinched. Her eyes narrowed as they focused on her daughter. "Veronica, what is the meaning of all this commotion?"

"This 'commotion' is the product of our newest housemaid."

Still crouched, Rosalind wished she could dig herself a hole through the floor. "I'm so sorry," she said again, her voice quavering. "I turned quickly and must have jostled—"

"You have just managed to break three Haviland teacups and saucers. I promise, you will pay for this," Veronica said.

"Yes, ma'am." After all, what else could she say?

However, Veronica continued on, her voice gaining speed and volume with each word. "You obviously have no care for anything of worth. You, with your direct looks and coarse accent. With your clumsy hands and inability to do even the simplest of tasks."

Each word felt like a slap in the face.

As the harsh words continued, Rosalind carefully got to her feet, the broken pieces of china in her hands. Obviously, she was about to be fired. Then she would be let go without a reference, without pay, and with no way to get home. And even worse? There would be no way to continue the search for her sister.

As Veronica drew breath, apparently preparing to deliver yet another vindictive diatribe, Mrs. Sloane stepped forward. "That is more than enough, Veronica." Turning to Rosalind, the lady softened her expression. "Oh my dear. Look at you, you're bleeding." After handing the broken shards to Mrs. Abrams, she gripped Rosalind's elbow and walked her toward the doorway. "Come now, let's let someone help you before you get hurt worse. Abrams—"

"Mother, she broke three cups and saucers," Veronica interrupted in a shrill voice. "Of the Haviland."

"It is only china, darling."

Veronica's cheeks burned red. "But—"

"And you've broken more in fits of rage than any of us can count," Douglass interjected as he joined them, a sardonic smile playing on his lips. "Really, Veronica. You'd think she broke your heart."

Still holding Rosalind's elbow, Mrs. Sloane sighed in relief.

"Douglass, thank goodness you're here. Please help your sister greet her guests while I help . . ." Her voice faltered.

"I'm Rosalind, ma'am."

"Yes. While I help Rosalind."

Veronica's look was pure venom. "Mother, she doesn't need your help. She needs to be fired."

"For a couple of broken teacups?" Douglass drawled. "Surely even you can't be that heartless, sister."

Jerome arrived and helped Mrs. Abrams efficiently pick up the remaining shards of china and set everything to rights. Still standing next to Mrs. Sloane, Rosalind knew she was on the verge of tears. "I'm so sorry, madam," she murmured. "I'm not sure what happened."

Mrs. Sloane clucked. "Don't distress yourself any further. As I said, it's only china. Now, go on to the kitchen and have Cook tend to you."

"Yes, ma'am. Thank you. I really am so sorry." Before she turned to exit the room, she looked at the crowd in the once pristine conservatory. Veronica was standing in the center of the room, glowering. Mrs. Sloane looked pensive. Mrs. Abrams eyed her with disapproval. Jerome looked mildly amused.

And Douglass . . . Douglass's gaze was unwavering as he walked out of the room by her side. "Don't fret, pet," he said almost kindly. "All that really matters is that you weren't hurt any worse."

"Yes, sir," she murmured.

"And don't let my sister scare you too much. I'll take care of her."

"Thank you, Mr. Sloane."

When she met his gaze, he winked.

"It's Douglass. Remember, you said you were going to call me that when we were alone."

As she parted ways with him just a few feet from the servants' hall, Rosalind knew something important had just happened. Douglass had come to her defense against the wishes of his sister. Unequivocally. She now was in his debt.

Rosalind was certain that they both knew it.

CHAPTER 8

Mrs. Russell frowned when she studied the cuts on the palm of Rosalind's hand. They were bleeding, and some shards were no doubt embedded deep inside at least one of the cuts. "This looks as bad as if you'd gotten on the losing end of a knife fight! You're going to need some stitches, I think."

Rosalind looked at her smarting hand. "Cook, are you sure?"

"Oh, I am certain." Glancing at Dora, the assistant cook, Mrs. Russell snapped her fingers. "Fetch the doctor, wouldja?"

Right after the shy woman flew from the kitchen, Cook clucked a bit. "Everything'll be as right as rain before you know it. Dora don't look like much, but she's fast on her feet, she is. And the Sloane name gets results. That doctor will be here in a jiffy."

But even the thought of getting patched up quickly didn't make Rosalind feel any better. "I don't see why Mrs. Sloane would pay for the expense of having the doctor here." Especially since she'd just broken several pieces of expensive china.

Cook waved off her worries. "Don't you worry about that none. Here at Sloane House, appearance is everything. The last thing anyone—most especially Mrs. Sloane—will want to get out is that the family pinched pennies on their servants." Peering at her a bit more closely, she frowned, her usually merry golden eyes looking worried. "Now sit down before you fall down. You're looking peaked."

Because she did feel rather light-headed, Rosalind gladly sank down on the kitchen chair, trying not to focus on the pain throbbing in her hand or the way it continued to bleed.

As if Cook was thinking the same thing, she placed a neat stack of old dishcloths under Rosalind's hand, no doubt to save the oak table from permanent stains. There was already some blood on Rosalind's uniform.

Less than ten minutes later, Dora reappeared.

Cook looked up. "You must have run like the wind."

Dora rolled her eyes. "Jerome told me to tell you that Mrs. Sloane had already sent him for Dr. Nolan. Jerome said the doctor should be here presently."

"See there, Rosalind? Things will be just fine in no time." Cook smiled kindly, but even through her pain, Rosalind could tell that things were very far from fine.

"Do you think I'll be dismissed?"

"Over a few broken teacups? I shouldn't think so."

But Rosalind noticed that Cook didn't look her in the eye when she spoke and that Dora looked worried.

Turning to Stanley, who had just wandered in, she said, "Miss Veronica said those dishes were Haviland. That means they were expensive, right?"

He nodded. "Everything's expensive here."

Well, that certainly didn't make her feel any better.

"You know what?" Cook blurted. "I think we could all use a nice cup of tea." Turning to Dora, who had just gotten out her rolling pin, she said, "Dora, be a love and make us a cuppa, would you? Bring one for Dr. Nolan too. He's always a mite parched when he arrives."

"Coming right up."

Dora had just handed Cook, Stanley, and Rosalind each a steaming cup when the door opened. In walked Mrs. Abrams, followed by a man in a charcoal suit. "Here is Dr. Nolan, Rosalind. He'll be seeing to your hand."

Dr. Nolan looked to be in his early forties, was bald, had a mustache, and wore wire-rimmed glasses. Somehow his unusual looks made him more handsome than the opposite. He also had a calm, competent way about him that eased Rosalind's fears for the first time all day.

Tears pricked her eyes. Even if she was about to be fired, she was grateful to have a real doctor stitch her up. "Thank you, Mrs. Abrams. I hope it wasn't too much trouble."

Mrs. Abrams' cool expression looked a bit incredulous, reminding Rosalind that of course all the events over the course of the last two hours had been too much trouble.

Instead of answering Rosalind, she merely turned to Cook. "Please inform Jerome when the doctor is ready to depart. I'll make sure he is paid."

"Will do."

While the women had been talking, Dr. Nolan had removed his coat, rolled up his sleeves, and washed his hands with some of the strong kitchen soap. Now he opened his bag and pulled out a pair of tweezers, bandages, a needle, and what appeared to be thread.

Once settled, he sat next to Rosalind and looked at her through his lenses in a kind way. "What is your name, miss?"

"Rosalind."

"Let's see how things look, shall we?" After a moment, he picked up her hand, gently cradling her knuckles and wrist as he peered into the wound. "You've got yourself a sizable injury. It's a blessing that the china didn't cut you an inch higher. If it had, your wrist could have been scored."

Imagining the blood that would have come from that injury, she felt dizziness wash over her.

Cook whistled low. "Chin up, dear. We can't take your vapors right now."

Kind Dora sat down on her other side and grabbed Rosalind's other hand. "Squeeze my hand if you start to feel woozy."

With a shaky smile, Rosalind nodded.

"Rosalind, this is going to hurt, but there's no getting around it, I'm afraid. You have shards embedded." With Cook's able assistance, the doctor carefully used his tweezers and pulled out the shards that were visible. Then, with a regretful wince, he said, "I'm sorry," and dug a bit more.

Through barely opened eyes, she saw him pull out a thin splinter of china. "Success!" he said, looking genuinely pleased. Next he cleansed her hand, poured a little powder into the wound, threaded his needle, and began to stitch.

Feeling more light-headed by the second, Rosalind closed her eyes, desperately trying not to sway and succumb to weakness.

As if she knew just how much Rosalind was on the verge of breaking down, or at least fainting into a slump, Dora started talking. "You know what? This reminds me of the last time you were here in the kitchens, Dr. Nolan."

"I remember that well." The doctor chuckled. "I was here to stitch up another housemaid," he explained to Rosalind. "For the second time in as many weeks."

"That Miranda," Cook said with a laugh. "She was always raising havoc."

Dora nodded. "Pretty girl, terrible maid—except for doing hair."

"Did you say Miranda?" Rosalind asked. After their first conversation about her, she was surprised Cook was willing to discuss Miranda again.

"Yes. Remember, she's the housemaid who went missing," Cook replied, a new, uneasy tone edging into her voice.

"The one before Tilly, that is," Dora said helpfully.

Cook scowled. "Did you hear? The grocer told me that our Tilly ran off with a soldier she'd met at the market."

"No wonder she never minded going to the market for you!" Dora teased.

"Wish she woulda been honest with me. I would've been understanding." After spying Dora's incredulous look, she chuckled. "Well, maybe not. But still, her taking off without a word to anyone gave me a fright, it did."

"I'm glad Tilly is all right," Rosalind said as the doctor poked and prodded some more. "I was worried about her," she squeaked out as he poked around an especially tender spot.

"You would have liked Miranda very much, Rosalind," Cook went on. "In some ways, you actually remind me of her."

"How so?"

"She was pretty, like you are. Though her coloring was a bit more vivid," Cook explained.

"Red hair. Striking, it was," Dr. Nolan murmured, just as his needle pinched her palm again.

"Oh, but she was a flighty thing," Dora added. "Always had her head in the clouds, she did."

"And always late," Cook murmured.

"Why . . . why did she need Dr. Nolan's services?"

Dr. Nolan paused, no longer smiling. "The first time I saw her? She'd walked into the corner of a mantel and cut her eye."

"She never did look where she was going," Cook murmured.

"But that second time, it was for a far more serious reason," Dr. Nolan said. "She had cuts. Lot of them."

Miranda had never mentioned this in her letters, Rosalind thought.

"It was the queerest thing," Dora mused. "She was in the billiard room and dropped a whole tray of glasses right to the floor. A whole tray!"

"It made quite a racket," Cook said. "The whole house practically went running to the room to see what had happened."

Rosalind's heart was pounding, this time nothing to do with her injury and everything to do with the story she was hearing unfold. "And what had happened?"

"As a matter of fact, no one really knows. Miranda wouldn't say a word about it. Always swore that she was alone, but I, for one, never thought that was true," Dora said.

Cook sniffed. "Anyways, she got cut trying to pick up all that glass."

"She needed stitches in three different places and would hardly sit still for any of it," Dr. Nolan reflected. "It was like it pained her to remain in a chair."

"Why was that? Had she fallen or something?"

"She wouldn't say. Actually, she refused to discuss it at all."

Pausing, he met Rosalind's eye. "You're a much better patient, my dear."

She was so stunned to hear the story, she felt as if her whole body had gone numb. "So you never found out what really happened?"

"Nope, but it weren't like we had much of a chance." Cook's voice dropped. "She left us soon after."

"Without a word of good-bye to any of us," Dora added. "Just like Tilly."

With a snip of his scissors, Dr. Nolan said, "The important thing is that I am sure Miranda healed up just fine, as I am sure you will, Rosalind. However, I must caution you not to use your hand for at least two days. The wound was deep. You needed twelve stitches."

Twelve! Almost as bad as the wound was the thought that she wouldn't be able to do her job. If she couldn't do her job, she could get fired. Then she would have no way of learning more about her sister. "Are you sure?"

"I counted them myself." His voice was firm, allowing no argument. "If you don't allow the sutures to heal, infection could set in and that could be very dangerous."

"Listen to him, Rosalind," Cook warned as the doctor wiped down his instruments, then set them all back in his bag before walking to the sink and washing his hands again.

"But Mrs. Sloane—"

"I doubt she'll even wonder where you are," Dora said. "She hardly ever lets her temper get the best of her."

"I can't imagine Mrs. Sloane ever losing her temper."

Dora laughed. "Only Master Douglass and Miss Veronica can make her truly upset. Or someone who threatens them," she said with a laugh.

Cook stepped closer. "Ignore Dora, Rosalind. Don't you worry about Mrs. Sloane. All that matters is that the house continues to run smoothly. We'll all help you as best as we can."

"Oh. Yes. Yes, of course. Thank you."

"My advice is to go lie down for a while," Dr. Nolan said. "Your hand will hurt like the devil, but that's to be expected. Change the dressing once a day. If you start to develop a fever or it begins to bleed, or if the skin around your stitches seems more tender or red and swollen, have someone fetch me." With a kind look, he added, "We don't want anything to happen to you too."

"No. I mean, of course not. I mean, thank you, Doctor."

After the doctor took a few sips of his cooling tea, he stood up and Emma led him to Jerome.

When they were sitting alone at the table, Cook stared at Rosalind hard. "If you don't mind me saying so, I'm thinking that there's more going on with you besides a hurt hand. Is there anything you'd like to discuss?"

Rosalind met the older woman's eyes. Noticed how sharp and perceptive she looked. This was a woman who knew more than she let on.

Was there anything more she wanted to discuss? Absolutely.

Could she? Definitely not.

If today's story about her sister was correct, it was becoming very apparent that not only had some disturbing things happened to Miranda, but also she hadn't trusted anyone in the household with secrets.

Rosalind figured she should take that as advice. She was completely alone. There wasn't a single person she could trust with her own secrets.

Not a single solitary one.

"No, Mrs. Russell. There's nothing at all."

CHAPTER 9

Reid Armstrong might have been heir to one of the wealthiest fortunes in Chicago, but for the most part, he still felt a bit like a fish out of water along Michigan Avenue.

Perhaps it was because his parents hadn't come from money. Instead, his father had gotten lucky in the silver market and had been shrewd in his investments right after the War of Southern Aggression.

Those investments tripled, then tripled again, propelling their somewhat comfortable existence into a whole new direction. And because his parents had always dreamed of creating a better life for their only son, they'd pushed Reid forward into a series of prestigious boarding schools, followed by a finishing year at Harvard.

So now he was firmly embedded in high society, yet always most comfortable around folks who were far less pretentious. He liked going to church. He liked spending an evening listening to music or playing cards. There, he felt at ease. At rest.

But those days had become few and far between. His parents

wanted him to marry well, to do justice to their plans. So he'd learned to curb his tongue and look a bit bored. He'd learned to dance well and play poker and billiards even better. He'd learned to be quick-witted— or to at least appreciate that gift in others.

And he did well.

But even so, he sometimes found himself at a loss for words in certain situations. Which was what was happening at that moment.

He'd gone to see Douglass to seek his opinion on a certain investment he was considering, when Veronica spied him in the Sloane House entryway and came running to his side.

"Reid, I'm so glad to see you," she said, her voice wavering and her eyes looking to be on the verge of tears. "Everything here is falling apart. Help me escape!"

He was taken aback. Though they'd certainly spent time together, their relationship had definitely not progressed to him providing her comfort.

In an effort to lighten her mood, he teased, "And where shall we escape to? Would you care to take a stroll down Michigan Avenue? Go to the fair again?"

"Neither of those things. I want to stay away from the crowds. Be alone." Her voice lowered. "Let's do something more private, Reid. At the moment, I don't want to be around anyone but you."

Stunned by her comment, he curved his hand around hers. "What is wrong, Veronica? Are you hurt?"

"I'm not hurt. Simply exhausted. It has been a terrible day."

"What on earth happened?"

"The new housemaid broke several pieces of china just minutes before my guests were to arrive." She shuddered dramatically. "It was simply awful. All the ladies had to wait in my mother's private receiving room for a full ten minutes while everyone set things to right."

He blew out the breath he'd been holding. "You're crying over a broken teacup? Come now, Veronica. I can never imagine you getting so worked up about something so insignificant."

"You're only thinking that way because you weren't there to witness it all. Our new maid is ghastly."

"Oh?"

"I wanted to fire Rosalind, but my mother said we were already short one servant. Then she declared I was getting too emotional. And then Douglass got in the middle of things."

"The maid's name is Rosalind, you say?"

She stilled as a new, sharp awareness filled her eyes. "Why are you looking at me like that?"

"It's just that I, uh . . . met her the other day in the hall, remember?" Not wanting to create a problem where there wasn't one, he said, "Tell me, where are your guests now?"

"Oh, they left." Her gaze warmed as she reached out and pressed her palm against his lapel. "So, where should we go?"

"I'm afraid I don't have the time to take you anywhere today. I only dropped by to get some stock advice from Douglass."

She leaned in a little closer. "Are you sure you can't change your plans?"

"I'm afraid not." He tried his best to look regretful.

"You're as bad as everyone else." With a flounce of her lovely pale pink gown, she strode down the hall, leaving him to wonder where Douglass was. Seeing one of the footmen, he asked.

"Mr. Sloane is in his rooms, sir," the footman replied. "He asked not to be disturbed."

"Oh." He paused, half waiting for the man to give some explanation. When the servant merely stared back at him, his gaze revealing nothing, Reid stepped away. "Well, thank you. I'll be on my way then."

When he was back on the street, he felt at a bit of a loss. He wished he'd brought his carriage instead of choosing to walk to the Sloane mansion. Now he had little choice but to walk back home to get it.

He'd just turned the corner when he spied a riot of brown curls. He picked up his pace, wondering if he'd guessed right. Just as he got close enough to realize that he had, Rosalind crossed the street to the park.

Though he feared it wasn't proper, he followed. He was curious about her, about her side of Veronica's story, and, he had to admit, drawn to this little slip of a girl.

The park was several acres, a wide expanse that many had seen as wasted space when it had first been planned. Only the grove of maple, birch, and oak trees prevented it from becoming mowed over for someone's home. Eventually, however, it became a popular spot for many of the well-to-do families in the area and for many middle-class families seeking a respite from the bustling city.

When Rosalind slowed, he closed the distance between them. When he did so, he noticed the thick bandage on her hand. That, combined with the careful way she was holding her arm, told him much about Veronica's complaints.

Obviously, her version of the events wasn't the whole story.

He debated briefly before approaching her. But when Rosalind looked up at him, and the startled look in her eyes faded into suspicion, he knew he had no choice but to speak to her.

"Hello, Rosalind. I thought that might be you."

Her expression turned wary. "Yes, sir? I mean, beg pardon, Mr. Armstrong?"

Feeling vaguely foolish, he murmured, "Deciding to take a respite outside?"

"Yes. Mrs. Abrams, the housekeeper, said I might have a short break."

"I'm not checking up on you," he assured. "I was out walking and happened to notice your hand. I didn't want to walk by without ascertaining if you needed any help." He waved a hand at the nearby bench. "Please, sit down. That is, if you'd care to."

She sat. Moving her bandaged hand to her lap, either to shelter it from his gaze or to ease its pain, he didn't know. "I don't need any help. But thank you for asking. Sir."

He felt a little foolish, looming over her like he was. "May I join you on the bench?" When she stiffened slightly, he added, "I promise, I only want to talk to you. To pass the time." He waved a hand and tried to look as innocent and unassuming as he wished he felt. "We are out in the open too."

"Of course, sir. Please do sit down, if you'd like." Looking away, she murmured, "I'm sure you've never seen a woman as skittish as me."

"It's a big city. And we don't know each other well . . ."

Hugging her bandaged hand a little tighter to her stomach, she added, "Being around so many people can be overwhelming, you see. I grew up on a farm in Wisconsin."

"It is natural for a girl like you to be apprehensive. Even a young lady raised in the city would be." He paused. "Some would say that is even a smart decision, though I will say that you have nothing to fear from me. I assure you of that."

She rolled her eyes. "If it is a smart one, it is surely the only smart thing I've done today."

"It's been that bad?"

"The worst."

"How did you hurt your hand?"

"I accidentally broke some china and sliced my palm when I was picking up the pieces."

He winced. "That sounds painful. Do you need to go to the doctor?"

"I've already seen one. Mrs. Sloane called for him." She shook her head with a bit of wonder. "Their personal physician came to the kitchens and took care of my hand. Can you even imagine? A doctor being called to care for a maid's hand?"

"I'm glad she sent for the doctor. By the looks of that bandage, his assistance was needed." When she smiled, he ventured, "What did he say?"

"That I needed twelve stitches," she quipped. "But he also said that after a day or two of rest I'll be right as rain."

"Twelve!" Irritation flooded him as he recalled Veronica's callous version of the incident. "Rosalind, that was no mere scratch, was it?"

"No, it wasn't, sir." A line formed between her brows as she fingered the fabric of her dress. "This is my Sunday dress. We're soaking my uniform, hoping to get the bloodstains out of it. I hope we can."

It seemed a trifling thing to worry about, what with her injury and all. "I'm sure the Sloanes will procure you a new uniform if one is needed."

"I've cost them quite enough with the doctor's visit. I don't dare imagine that they'll be too eager to spend another cent on my behalf."

He ached to tell her that a single pair of Veronica's gloves were most likely double the price of one of her uniform dresses, but he was afraid that would only make her feel worse about her situation. "Please don't worry," he said. "Accidents happen. And china cups practically beg to get broken."

She smiled for the first time. "Thank you for saying that, Mr. Armstrong."

Glancing at her again, he noticed how the smattering of freckles on her nose made her seem adorably innocent. "Tell me about your farm and your family. Do you have any siblings?"

To his surprise, a dark shadow appeared in her eyes. "I have a large family. My parents, three brothers, and . . . a sister."

"You hesitated." Seeking to tease a smile from her, he raised his brows. "Are you not sure if you have a sister?"

If anything, her expression became more stricken. "There were five of us growing up. Miranda, me, then Henry, Stephen, and Ethan. But a few months ago, my sister moved to Chicago."

"And?"

"And after the first couple of months, we didn't hear from her again. She's disappeared."

"She's missing? Are you certain?"

"To be honest, I don't know what has happened to her." She paused, eyed him more closely, then blurted, "That's the real reason I've come here to Chicago. I promised my family that I'd try to discover what has happened to her."

"I'm surprised your parents allowed such a thing." Reid was shocked. He couldn't deny that.

"I'm afraid they didn't have much choice. We are all desperate, you see. And very worried. Plus, when my father came to Chicago, he didn't get much help. The police said she'd probably run off with a man."

The police response shocked him as well. But he was also curiously drawn into her story. "Where was she when she left? Was she with a man? Did she have a job?"

Rosalind opened her mouth, then closed it just as quickly as she scrambled to her feet. "I must go."

Reid got to his feet, too, and attempted to stop her. "Why must you leave this very minute? I could help you. I mean, I'd like to try."

"I don't know how you could help." Nibbling her bottom lip, she blurted, "I probably shouldn't have even told you this much."

"What about the Sloanes? What do they say?"

Looking even more distressed, she stared hard at him. Then, as if she'd suddenly made a momentous decision, she whispered, "My sister was working for the Sloanes, sir. I fear that someone in the house had something to do with her disappearance."

▬

Without a word, they both sat down again.

"You can't be serious," Reid finally scoffed.

And she knew at once that telling Mr. Armstrong had been the absolute worst thing to do. As his statement rang in her ears, Rosalind could practically feel her sister's exasperation. From the time she'd been old enough to be embroiled in any sort of conflict, Rosalind had been miserable at keeping secrets. Time and again, Miranda would glare at her, whisper that if she could ever be trusted, it wouldn't be too soon. Rosalind would promise to do better in the future.

But yet, here she was again, sharing the most important secret she'd ever kept in her life . . . to one of the people she should be treating as a suspect, not a confidant.

She kept her eyes trained on her injured hand, but couldn't resist taking a peek at him through the corner of her eye.

As one might have expected, he looked flummoxed.

After taking a long moment—she assumed to gather his thoughts—he turned slightly so that he was more or less facing her on the cool iron bench.

"Who accompanied you? Who has been sharing your burden here?"

The question couldn't have been more surprising. "My family knows, of course. But I am here by myself."

"Have you talked to the Sloanes? Asked them for their help?"

"No, sir. When my father came here to find answers, he went to the Sloanes first. They wouldn't give him the time of day. So if none of the servants are to blame . . . I fear that someone in the Sloane family might have had something to do with her disappearance."

"Nonsense. They're one of the oldest families in the area. Very respected."

"I fail to see how that means anything at the moment." She made a move to rise and leave him. This had been a mistake, a terrible one, and one that she sincerely hoped wouldn't cause further difficulties in her investigation. "I had best go back now, sir," she said stiffly.

He whipped out a hand and held her in place. "Not yet."

"Sir?"

"Why would you think the Sloanes would be suspects?"

She debated saying any more, but she realized that only the truth, not further evasiveness, was going to bring her sister's fate to light. And she had a feeling that the search wasn't meant to be easy. Not the things she learned and not the pain and worry she was going to subject herself to.

Slowly, she said, "My sister wrote the family letters. In them, she talked about everyone she came in contact with. At first, it was only because her experiences were so exciting and so different from anything we'd ever known."

"That makes sense."

"Later, though, she told us things that made us worry for her. She said some of the Sloane family seemed . . . ruthless. And secretive." She gazed at him, not trusting him entirely, but needing for someone to know the truth of what she was saying. "Mr. Armstrong, she began to fear the family, that she would lose her job. I think she may have discovered some of their secrets. But she needed the job, needed the recommendation that only staying—no matter what—could bring her. But she was not terribly happy."

"Chicago is a dangerous city, Rosalind. Especially now, with so many foreigners and tourists here. The police are overwhelmed and underpaid. Anything could have happened to a young woman on her own."

"Yes, sir. I am aware of that." Feeling more frustrated and confused than ever before, she made to stand up again. "I must go. If you wouldn't mind, I'd be very grateful if you kept this between the two of us."

He closed his eyes, obviously striving for patience. "Rosalind, I want to talk to you about this some more. I want to help you."

"There is nothing you can do."

"I disagree. By the very nature of your job, you have limited access." Lifting his chin a little, as if he were daring her to disagree, he said, "I can speak to people you cannot. I can speak to the men and women of my society, see if they have heard of any tales about a missing housemaid."

"Don't you imagine that they'd find your sudden preoccupation with missing housemaids peculiar?"

"Perhaps." He shrugged. "Perhaps not." He turned his head so that he was looking at her directly. "I think, at the very least, it is worth a try."

"Why would you do this? Miranda is nothing to you." She swallowed hard and removed the last bit of her pride. "I'm nothing to you."

One of his eyebrows arched. "Does someone have to mean something to a person in order to do the right thing for them?"

His voice had turned haughty. In that moment, he was very much the wealthy society gentleman. His arched look, combined with the dizzying emotions running through her veins, caused her own voice to become painfully sharp. "I don't know, Mr. Armstrong. I would usually say yes. Because though I might have been aware of all sorts of dangers women faced in the big city, until it was my sister I feared hurt, I never did anything. Do you often make it your business to help others?"

He looked away first. "No. But I want to help. And once more, I think you need my help. Let someone help you, Rosalind." Lowering his voice to a mere whisper, he added, "Let that someone be me."

His words were dizzying. The offer was tempting.

But more than that was the feeling for the first time that she didn't have to be alone any longer. If she accepted his offer, she would have someone to discuss her suspicions with.

"Rosalind, now that I know, I fear I am already involved. I'm going to try to help you, with or without your approval. You might as well give in."

He was right. It wasn't like she had much of a choice. She could either give in gracefully or perpetuate the myth that she was strong enough to do this on her own.

"Thank you, Mr. Armstrong. I will appreciate any assistance you may give me."

The faintest of smiles hovered on his lips. "I am glad you've seen things my way. Now, when is your next afternoon free?"

"Not for almost a week."

"I'll try to find a way to see you at Sloane House. And don't fear, Rosalind. I will be nothing but proper at all times."

The reminder of how precarious her job situation was made her stand up and back away. "Until then," she said before turning and walking away.

And though the afternoon sun shone on her back, she had the strangest feeling that it was Reid Armstrong's concern that was warming her insides.

CHAPTER 10

Unwilling to stop himself, Reid watched Rosalind walk back to the Sloane estate, bypass the front door, and walk to what must have been the servants' entrance. Not for the first time, he reflected that the somewhat utilitarian dress should have detracted from her beauty. It was plain and loose fitting, so different from the current ladies' fashions. Most women of his class were wearing bright satins and taffetas decorated with cords of ribbon and yards of lace.

But Rosalind looked as fresh and quietly pretty as many of the women of his acquaintance. Of course, the beauty he was thinking about wasn't the result of fine textiles and ingenious design. Instead, it radiated from within.

This was not the first time he'd thought about her—or his attraction to her, he realized—since first meeting her at Sloane House. He'd found himself thinking of her at odd times and in odd places. He'd be speaking to one of the women at his church and he would notice the fine dusting of freckles on her nose . . . just like Rosalind's. Or he'd overhear a person's voice on the streets, the way they lengthened their vowels, and he would think they sounded like Rosalind.

He wasn't sure what his preoccupation with her or his need to help discover what happened to her sister meant. All he knew was that there was a voice inside him that proclaimed she was important. Perhaps it was his conscience?

Maybe it was God, gently reminding him to do good works?

"Armstrong? I say, Armstrong, is that you?"

Startled from his musings, Reid turned in surprise. Almost as quickly, he attempted to hide his dismay. It was Eric Newhouse, one of his classmates from Lawrenceville, but unlike Douglass Sloane, Reid felt no sense of obligation or gratitude toward the man.

"Hello, Eric," he said. "I haven't seen you in ages."

"I've been on the continent. Doing my tour before I settle into the family business." He chuckled. "Unfortunately, it only lasted a year. You know how that goes, though."

Reid actually did not know, but there was no reason to share that. Eric had been born into almost as prominent a family as Douglass had. Reid, who had not, was instead his parents' calling card into high society.

"It's been several years since we matriculated. Have you stayed here in Chicago this whole time?"

"I have. I'm running my father's business with him." Reid was pleased he could say the words without even flinching. When was he ever going to come to terms with his father's failing health?

He tensed, half waiting for Eric to ask him about his father's state of being. Most everyone knew he had tuberculosis and was ailing. In addition, many feared that Reid Armstrong would never be the man his father was—and weren't shy about saying so. Many did not know he had now also started his own business.

But instead of going that route, Eric simply looked him over like he was an unusual specimen. "Ah, yes. I had heard that you chose to go right to work." Eric's voice had turned cool. "Well, it seems to have done you no harm. Your success has been creating quite a stir in some circles. Congratulations on your success."

"Thank you. I have much to be thankful for. I feel blessed beyond measure."

The words, so honestly stated, drew an obviously uncomfortable breath from Eric.

He fidgeted a bit, and even went so far as to take a step backward, giving them each some distance from the other. "So, I'm on my way to see Sloane. I imagine you are doing the same. You two always were thick as thieves," he added languidly. "Are you leaving or about to enter?"

"As a matter of fact, I have just taken my leave." Reid decided Eric could discover for himself that Douglass wasn't receiving visitors.

"It's lucky that our timing coincided. We seem to have missed each other at some of the debutante balls."

"Yes. It's been good to catch up."

Eric glanced at Sloane House. "It is, however, unlucky for me that I arrived just as your tête-à-tête with that fetching girl finished." His voice lowered, becoming oily. "I would have liked to have made that one's acquaintance."

Only living for years in a boarding school, pretending he was one of the crowd, kept Reid's expression impassive. "I'm sorry, I don't know what you mean."

"Oh, I believe you do," Eric said in a light, joking way. "Was I mistaken, or were you sitting on this bench a few minutes ago?" He held up a hand, laughing off any reply Reid might have attempted. "Don't answer that. We both know you were. Actually, it looked like you were having quite a fine time flirting with her. Who is she? A maid in one of the houses nearby? I looked away and didn't see where she went to."

Reid could have cursed his naïveté. Had he really imagined their conversation wouldn't be noticed? "I was speaking with a lady—"

"No offense, but she was no lady, Armstrong." Eric's gaze hardened. "Don't even try to deny it. Her gown was only something one of the lower classes would wear. And there is only one reason a woman of her class would be in this part of Chicago. No one with eyes would mistake her to be anything else."

While Reid stood stoically, Eric chuckled to himself. "She's a pretty thing, I'll give her that. How is she under the sheets?"

This was beyond any sort of decency. Straightening to his entire six-foot-two height, Reid looked down his nose at Eric. "I beg your pardon. Sir."

Eric laughed. "Sorry, chap. I should have remembered that you still possess far too many of those bourgeois, middle-class sensibilities. You don't date and talk, do you? Of course, it wouldn't be an actual date, and you very well might not have been talking about anything at all . . ."

Reid knew Eric was baiting him. He also knew enough to realize that any protestations he made would be duly noted. His words would be used as gossip and as fodder for bored conversations in the best drawing rooms. Next thing he knew, his imagined transgressions would be exaggerated and shared and joked about. And eventually, regarded as the truth.

Before long, it would reach the ears of one of the Sloanes. And then Rosalind would be fired.

And that was the best scenario. Eric could also use his protesting as a way to subtly blackmail him at a future time or merely use it as a source of amusement among their circle of friends. The result of that, of course, would tarnish Rosalind's reputation, and perhaps even cause her to be the recipient of several lurid offers.

And since he was now very aware of how much she needed the job, he merely smiled. "Enjoy your afternoon, Newhouse," he said with the slightest of bows before turning the opposite way on the street.

Eric paused as a new thread of respect flew into his words. "It seems you've become a bit shrewder over the years, Armstrong. I must admit that I'm surprised. And impressed."

Reid kept walking, but that brief exchange had served him well. He'd just been reminded that cruel gossip could be born and spread at the drop of a hat . . . and that it could spread twice as quickly as gossip some might deem "innocent."

He wasn't going to be able to meet with Rosalind anywhere publicly again. Of course, meeting in private had its own set of cruel consequences. If he wasn't careful, it wasn't going to be ribald rumors or gauche innuendo that ruined her reputation. No, it would be his inability to constantly remember that they were never alone and always being observed.

It was a pity he hadn't remembered that a half hour earlier.

CHAPTER 11

And so that, dear family, is what I have discovered so far.

Rosalind wrote at the bottom of her long, somewhat rambling letter.

I now have an idea about Miranda's life here at the Sloane estate, and I am acquainted with most of the servants with whom she worked. I also know when she disappeared. But I have no idea why she did so. That is the most disturbing aspect of my efforts. Sometimes I am so close to making progress, but then the reality of how much I do not yet know threatens to overwhelm me and I begin to doubt myself and your belief in me.

Holding the nib of her quill lightly over the paper, she wondered if she should mention anything else.

She flexed her fingers, happy that her palm didn't hurt so much anymore. It had been three days since she'd broken the china, injured her hand, and talked to the handsome Reid Armstrong on the park bench. Three days since she'd felt the first ray of hope that she was going to be able to discover what had happened to her sister.

But she didn't dare mention any of that. Her parents would only worry, and there was no real news anyway.

Picking up the nib again, she wondered if she should mention how distant and sometimes cruel Veronica could be. Or how Douglass had been kind to her, but she still felt a bit apprehensive whenever she was in his presence.

And what about Reid? Should she mention how she had given in and told him her whole story? Speaking to him had been against her better judgment and had been the opposite of their wishes to keep her investigation as private as possible.

She ached to give them hope, but at the same time, she knew better than to give them such a gift. Hope was one of the Lord's blessings, that was true. But in other ways, hope could be the very work of the Devil. It permitted a person to believe that their imaginations or dreams could actually be true.

She had certainly found herself experiencing several moments like that. She'd spy something in Mr. Armstrong's gaze that seemed to be far warmer than an impersonal glance to a maid. Or she'd be ironing one of Veronica's delicately light linen nightgowns and she'd imagine what it would be like to go to sleep in such luxuriousness.

Finally, she'd be dining in the servants' hall, eating leftovers from the family's dinner, and she'd catch herself wishing for more steak or fish or velvety smooth custard. All of those things had been foreign to her when she arrived and would become distant memories when she returned to Wisconsin.

And sometimes, particularly in a time like 1893, mere years away from the new century, Rosalind feared their class-filled society could only do damage to the souls who were not prepared to understand their place in it. At this time and place—especially in a city like Chicago—it was imperative that people knew their place. Workers weren't treated well in the factories. But strikes and fires did little to change things. All they really did was delay the inevitable and cause loss of job or harm to those who stood in the way of progress.

Whether she had become philosophical or only dared to let her family live in the dark for as long as possible, she ended up simply signing her name as she always did.

With love, Rosalind

Then she sealed her letter and carefully set it aside to be posted before she changed her mind.

She was going to have to take more risks and push herself harder. She was going to need to leave the mansion more often, talk to strangers, and ask more pointed questions. Otherwise, she feared she would never fulfill her promise to her family.

Worse, she would never learn the truth.

And if that happened? Well, that would be unconscionable. Her sister was impetuous and beautiful. She was willful and bold—and perhaps a flirt around men she'd met in Chicago.

But that was who she was, not the reason for her disappearance.

In her heart, Rosalind was sure someone had preyed on Miranda. Or convinced her to do something she should not. And even if Rosalind didn't feel comfortable learning about some of the things Miranda might have done, even if she didn't really want to know the worst secrets about her sister, she could always bear that herself. All the family needed to know was what had happened to Miranda. They didn't need to know every single detail. Actually, it was probably best if they never knew.

This new knowledge gave her a sense of security. Made her feel a bit more at peace. When she'd left home, she'd merely been acting as an arm of her family. She'd come to Chicago at their bidding, determined to make them proud by doing what they asked.

But now, especially after speaking with Mr. Armstrong, she realized that this had become her mission. It had also become her goal and her priority. It no longer mattered what her parents wanted her to discover or what would make her siblings proud. She wasn't proud, but she felt this new resolve deep in her bones. And once more, she knew it was the right thing to do as well.

With that in mind, she slipped her letter into her purse and decided then and there to start afresh. Cook had asked her to go to the farmer's market again that afternoon. She would use the errand as an opportunity to talk to everyone she could. Perhaps she could even make the acquaintance of a maid from one of the neighboring houses. She'd seen quite a few girls doing many of the same errands she did.

Who knew? Perhaps she would even finally stop and chat with the flower seller on the corner and ask if she'd ever seen Miranda. It was worth a try. She was stronger, braver than she used to be. She was different now.

An hour later, when she walked out onto the streets of Chicago, Rosalind's newfound resolve wavered. As she hesitated outside the servants' entrance, Jim, that laconic man about trade who had been so chatty weeks ago, approached.

"Hello, Rosalind," he said in a friendly voice. "Name's Jim. We spoke in the kitchen a couple of weeks ago."

"I remember." She stood still, not quite sure what to say next.

Then, like a lightning bolt hitting her, she remembered the promise to herself. So she forced herself to smile and promote conversation. "What brings you out to the house today?"

He looked delighted to be asked. "Ah, you know. This and that. Big houses like this always need something done. Today, I was up in Master Douglass's suite. Some of the woodwork needed refinishing and such."

"Had something happened to it? An accident, perhaps?"

Jim chuckled. "What an imagination you've got." Stuffing his hands in his pockets, he rocked a bit back on his heels. "I'm not one to say what might have been causing destruction in Master Douglass's rooms, but I have a feeling it might simply be time. Time can do much damage, don't you know." He paused. "Or perhaps a pretty young thing like you don't know."

"I seem to be learning about time and aging with the best of them," she said lightly. "And I must be off to post this letter."

"You going by yourself?"

"Yes. I'm getting quite good at navigating my way around the city. At least this part of the city, that is."

His expression turned grim. "Have a care now. There was another story printed in the *Tribune* about the crime rate going up, on account of the fair and all."

With vigilance, she shook off her unease. And reminded herself that they'd all been worried sick about Tilly, but she hadn't been hurt at all . . . only in love with a soldier. "Don't worry about me. I'll be fine. Good day, Jim."

He tipped his hat. "And to you, too, Miss Rosalind."

His ungraceful antics made her chuckle. And their conversation had given her a small feeling of success too. Perhaps visiting with people was easier than she imagined.

In no time, she purchased all the items on Cook's list, making an effort to converse with vendors and other domestics. However, it was no use. The market was unusually busy and crowded. No one had time for idle talk.

Resolving to try again another day, she posted her letter, then, after riding the grip car back to Michigan Avenue, walked slowly back to the mansion. The sun was shining and the air almost cool. A faint breeze was in the air, making the usual stagnant city air almost smell fresh.

She stopped and lifted her face to the sun. It was a perfect moment. One to savor.

"A flower, miss?"

The melodic voice beckoned her. Rosalind turned, noticing the flower girl not much older than her, the one she had been planning to talk to. She had set up shop on the corner, an open box of daisies, chrysanthemums, and carnations at her feet.

"No, thank you. I'm only a maid, you see." Holding up her canvas tote full of cucumbers, peppers, and tomatoes, she added, "I'm afraid I don't have much use for flowers."

Some of the hope in the girl's eyes dimmed. "I suppose not."

Rosalind realized that many people who were on the way to the Sloanes' probably passed the girl.

And that got her to thinking that maybe, at long last, Rosalind had found someone who could give her some information.

"Who usually buys your flowers?"

The girl's manner became defensive. "What concern is it to you?"

Rosalind held up a hand, a sign of defeat. "It's nothing, I promise. I'm just curious, that's all. They are really beautiful."

The girl dimpled as some of her reticence eased. "I had violets and four roses, but a gentleman picked them up for his ladybird a couple hours back."

"So it's the gentlemen who buy most of your flowers? The ones who live in these houses? Not ones who merely work around here?"

The flower girl took a moment to ponder that. "It depends, I suppose. Some men buy them for their mistresses or girlfriends. Every so often I sell blooms to a man who's in trouble with his wife, though. Then he's buying everything I got." Her eyes lit up with mirth. "One evening, a gentleman bought everything I had, on account of his wife being upset with him for forgetting their anniversary."

"Ouch."

She chuckled. "I told him if my flowers won't do the trick, nothing will."

Rosalind smiled back, liking the idea of someone's big problem being a forgotten anniversary. "Have you worked on this corner very long?"

"Longer than I'd like. Almost two years."

Excitement welled inside her. "Then you probably recognize many of the people who live and work in the area."

"I do." She nodded slowly, gazing at Rosalind with a new suspicion. "Why are you chatting with me all of the sudden?"

"What do you mean all of the sudden? Have I been rude to you?"

"Rude?" The woman looked at Rosalind askance, as if she'd just sprouted horns and started speaking German. "Listen to you, acting like you're worried about my feelings. I'm a flower girl, not one of the swells living here and squiring their ladies!"

"What did you mean, then?"

Her cheeky expression turned a bit hesitant. "I meant, why are you asking me so many questions all of the sudden?"

"No reason. I, uh, was just curious about some things . . ." Her voice drifted off, hoping that the girl wouldn't ask her to explain much more than that. If she pushed her, Rosalind didn't know what she would say next.

Luckily, however, the girl didn't seem too put off. "Well, usually I would say that you walk by me all furtive like, like you're afraid your own shadow is going to catch hold of you."

Rosalind was embarrassed. She had no idea that was how she appeared. "I'm rather new here. At first, I think I was scared of my own shadow. I guess I didn't realize I was so noticeable."

"Maybe not to everyone. But I stand here a lot, you know. And sometimes I don't have many customers."

Remembering her vow, Rosalind pushed a bit for information. "I moved here from Wisconsin a few weeks ago. You might think this is silly, but at first, I was afraid of everything here."

"That's not surprising at all. Chicago is a big place, and with the World's Fair being here and all? It's gotten bigger every day, and that's a fact. When I first got here, I was scared to death of them trains. I was even certain I was going to get run over by one of them trolley cars."

"I did the same thing." With a self-conscious chuckle, Rosalind added, "I mean, I still do."

"You'll get the hang of the grips. Everyone does."

"Where do you hail from?"

"Indiana." She looked Rosalind over, and for the first time Rosalind realized that the girl wasn't looking at her with contempt or through superior lenses. Instead, it was with a good dose of envy. "How did you manage to get hired on right away at one of the big houses?"

"I'm not sure," she fibbed. "I went to the employment agency on the same day one of the families had just requested a new housemaid.

They sent me right over." At least they had after she told her tale about her mother wanting her to work for the Sloanes.

"Lucky, that. It must be something, living in one of those big houses and working for one of those fancy families." A thick longing was in her voice.

It was on the tip of Rosalind's tongue to admit that it wasn't so wonderful. The work was hard, and she spent much of her days trying to move silently around four people who thought little of her. But she also had a room at night, enough food, and some level of friendship with some of the other girls in the house.

"Why did you leave Indiana? Why did you come to Chicago?"

The girl frowned. "I read in the paper that there were going to be a lot of jobs, good-paying jobs, for women who wanted to work at the fair. I'd been working as a maid-of-all-work for a family, but had to quit when I fell in love, because the family didn't like their help socializing none. Then, well, my boyfriend started having a real hard time finding work in South Bend. A terrible time. He said he weren't going to marry me unless he could afford it, so I got a wild hare and decided to come to Chicago for a spell and surprise him by bringing back a good amount of money home."

"Your parents let you go?"

Some of the honesty in her eyes shuttered. "My parents don't care what happens to me as long as I don't burden them. Plus, like I said, I'd been working in a house for a few years by then."

"And did you get work at the fair when you arrived?"

"Well, I arrived here along with a slew of other females desperate for work and a bit too ignorant to know better. The group of us got a couple of rooms at a rickety boardinghouse, then appeared at the address listed in the paper."

She rolled her eyes. Managing to look both embarrassed and

contemptuous, she said, "I discovered soon enough that there was only one way to earn the money the papers had been talking about, and that was on my back."

Rosalind was surprised, but not as shocked as she would have been just a few short weeks ago. "What did you do?" she whispered. "Start selling flowers?"

A pained look entered the girl's gaze before she diverted her eyes. "Listen, I don't know you, and I certainly don't understand why you're asking me so many personal questions. But I think I'm done answering them."

"I'm sorry. I didn't mean to offend."

"I've got to sell these flowers. Otherwise I'll be out here a lot longer than I had intended." Her voice hardened, layering a thick shell around herself that assured Rosalind that she wished that layer to be impenetrable. "Leave me be."

Before Rosalind knew what she was doing, she pulled out a nickel. "I'll take a nickel's worth."

The girl looked at the nickel and was obviously judging it against the last bits of her pride. The look made Rosalind embarrassed for them both.

The girl paused, then shrugged and held out her hand. "A nickel's worth three carnations, miss." Her voice was clearer now. Subservient.

"I'll take them—if I can know your name."

The girl looked stricken. And for some reason, on the verge of tears.

For a moment, Rosalind was sure the girl was going to refuse her, to turn her back on Rosalind and hold on to her pride, whatever that was still worth.

Then, with great reluctance, she held out her hand. "It's Minerva."

"My name is Rosalind. Thank you for talking to me. It was nice to talk to someone from a small town, like me." She handed over the coin, then took the three worst-looking carnations, imagining that taking them and not the nicer ones might help the girl some.

After she took the flowers, she paused, half expecting Minerva's gratitude, or smile. Anything to prove to her that they had become more than strangers.

But Minerva had already turned her back. She was walking toward a trio of young gentlemen, her steps suggestive. "You handsome gentlemen be needin' some flowers today?" she said, her voice thicker. Huskier.

When the men stopped and chatted a bit, Rosalind continued on her way, wondering if she'd just been taken in by something as blatantly fake as Minerva's ploy to the men.

Perhaps the flower girl had seen she was an easy mark and had said whatever it took to get her sale. Because standing out on street corners, hawking flowers to strangers in all kinds of weather, was difficult.

Rosalind realized that everything was all a matter of perspective. She'd been feeling a bit sorry for herself working in the mansion because she'd become almost inanimate. Almost a nonentity. But she'd only thought that because she hadn't imagined anything worse.

Minerva, or whatever her real name was, had certainly known worse, and was living it at the moment.

Yes, it was indeed time to stop dwelling on her problems and begin looking for answers. And, to an extent, looking for happiness in her situation. She had to do anything it took to find her answers. And then, with either her sister or her sister's story in her heart, she would go home. Back to Wisconsin.

And before she knew it, Rosalind knew her experiences here would soon fade away into her past. Like a train's departure, her time as a maid at Sloane House would be gone in a flash.

Almost forgotten.

CHAPTER 12

"Where have you been?" Nanci demanded the minute Rosalind walked through the servants' entrance.

Looking around the area, she noticed at least seven people all working frantically. Some were polishing silver, others ironing table linens. Even Jerome was pulling out handfuls of white tapers and examining them for flaws. Every person looked upset and more than a bit ill-tempered.

For a brief second, Rosalind worried that she had something to do with everyone's attitude, but for the life of her, she couldn't imagine what she could have done. "I went to the farmer's market and posted a letter. Why?"

"Because things here are at sixes and sevens," Mrs. Abrams said in a thoroughly exhausted tone. "Mrs. Sloane has decided to host a dinner this evening for twenty-two. Mrs. Pullman is even supposed to be here."

"What?" Even she knew the Pullmans were one of the wealthiest and most influential families in the city. It was their name on the train cars, after all. If that was the case, then Mrs. Sloane was bound to be even more exacting than ever. Mrs. Abrams and Mr. Hodgeson too.

Rosalind could almost feel the sorry-looking carnations wilting in her hand, in company with her dismay. Nanci grabbed the flowers with one hand, tossed them carelessly on the top of the key cabinet, then pulled Rosalind forward with the other.

"Wait a moment," she protested. "I wanted to put those in water."

"Water isn't going to help those blooms," Nanci said with a disparaging glance. "All that matters is this dinner."

She was put out enough to raise her eyebrows to that. "All that matters?"

Nanci deftly ignored her sarcasm. "To make matters worse, Mrs. Sloane wants six courses. And all the stops pulled out too."

"Why?"

"Well, if Mr. Pullman's presence isn't enough, rumor has it that Mr. Eric Newhouse will be here too. Mr. Newhouse is Veronica's best chance for making a match, you know. He just returned from the continent and is looking very dapper indeed." Lowering her voice, she added, "It's also been hinted that his parents want him to settle down soon. They've told him to pick a bride and set up a home as soon as possible."

"My goodness. Does Veronica love him?"

Nanci grabbed a towel and handed it to Rosalind. "How should I know? I doubt anyone has been discussing love, anyway. That has nothing to do with it."

"I suppose not."

"Mrs. Sloane wants to make sure he sees Veronica at her very best before Mr. Newhouse begins to mix with the rest of society again."

She lowered her voice. "And most especially before he sets his sights on Eloisa Carstairs."

"Who is she?"

"The most sought-after girl this year. She's beautiful, well mannered, and terribly rich. Her family even owns another home in Florida."

Rosalind was amazed. "How do you know all this?"

Nanci sniffed. "I listen."

Cook looked up from her dicing and glared. "All of these fancy people entering the home means that you'd best put on a fresh apron quick-like. I'm going to need you to help me clean the pheasant and the trout—well, as much as you can with your hand like it is."

She could clean a bird, no problem. Growing up on a farm had given her plenty of experience with that. But fish were another story. Impulsively, she said, "Nanci, want to help me with the fish?"

"Of course not! I'm needed upstairs in ten minutes. Mrs. Sloane wants Veronica to try on several gowns. That means I'm going to have to help her get them all on, put away all the ones that won't do, and then help her dress her hair." With a grimace, she added, "Most likely, I'll be mending a rip or tear too. Miss Veronica never has met a seam or a stay that she hasn't tried to pull apart."

Now thinking she got the better job, Rosalind hurried to Cook. "I'll slip on a fresh apron quickly."

Emma glanced at her from the pile of sterling spoons she was polishing. "You'd best redo your hair too. If Mrs. Abrams sees you like that, all windblown, she'll have your hide."

Cook made a motion with her hands. "Go, girl. Don't tarry neither. We've got too much to do."

Rosalind did as she was told. Running up the servants' stairs, she stepped as quickly as she could up the dim corridor, turned down a hall, and then the moment she got into her room, slipped on one of the two aprons she'd been given when she'd started at the home. Taking Emma's advice, she smoothed back her curls, twisted them neatly, then finally pinned the coil at her nape. After she pinned on her cap, she flew back down the hall.

A few moments later, she was scampering down the stairs again, then almost tripped when she found Jerome standing at the landing. He was lazing against the wall, one of his elbows resting on the balustrade, just as if he were a man about town instead of a footman.

Even more disconcerting was the fact that he was smoking a cigarette. A wispy line of smoke snaked up around him like a sheer length of fabric. But what caught her off guard was the fresh look of interest in his eyes.

"Where were you this afternoon, really?"

"I went to the farmer's market. As you know. You were sorting candles when I arrived, after all."

He waved her comment off impatiently. "What else?"

She didn't know what he meant. More importantly, she didn't want to know. Hoping she was only imagining trouble where there was none, she took another step down, moving to the side as she did. "Please let me by."

But instead of moving to the side, the footman stood straighter, looking as immovable as one of the city's tall skyscrapers. "In a minute." His smile was a bit cooler than it had been a few days before, his eyes a bit more calculating. "Perhaps I need a favor before I move."

Watching as he inhaled, then blew out another whiff of smoke, she blinked, suddenly nervous. "I'm sure I don't know what sort of favor I could possibly grant you."

A flash of humor appeared in his eyes. "I can think of all sorts of things."

Her pulse quickened. "I don't know what you mean." Suddenly worried about being alone with him, at his mercy, she cleared her throat. "I must go. Cook is looking for me. She'll give me the worst jobs if I'm late."

A hand stretched out. Wrapped itself around her forearm. "Don't worry," he murmured. "I'll let you go. In just a moment." He leaned forward, bringing with him the aura of tobacco and a deep masculine scent tinged with a faint hint of lime. "You've been a busy girl, haven't you?" he whispered. "First, I seen you talking in the hall with Mr. Douglass himself. Then, just a few days ago, all sorts of people watched you sit on the bench in the park with none other than Mr. Armstrong. The two of you looked so cozy too."

Yet again, Rosalind wished she had been more circumspect. And though she ached to remove her arm from his grasp and retreat, she began to wonder if he was the one who had done something to her sister. Perhaps this was a pattern of his? "Why have you been watching me?"

"It's hard not to watch you and wonder. After all, very few women in your situation take so many chances." He exhaled a last bit of smoke before snuffing the end of the cigarette under the toe of a well-polished shoe.

Then his eyes narrowed. "So . . . what I want to know, what I am so very curious about, is why you are meeting with all these men. Why are they seeking you out? What are they offering you, Rosalind?" Then his lips curved upward. "And what does it take to make you say yes?"

She was shocked. And frightened. And . . . and late! "They are offering me nothing. And furthermore, my conversations are certainly none of your business."

"They could be. Or do I have it all wrong?"

"I have no idea what you mean."

"Of course you do. You must. All I am saying is that there's no need to set your sights up to men so high above your station. You know you mean nothing to them, after all." He leaned closer. "If you're a lonely girl, you only have to look right here."

"You shouldn't be speaking of such things."

"Why? No matter what you might tell yourself in the dark, or in those gentlemen's company, you're no lady, Rosalind."

"Let me pass."

"In a moment," he said again. "You still haven't told me why you were talking to Mr. Armstrong. Or did he just happen to see a maid and decide to pass time talking about the weather?" Jerome's eyebrows waggled. "Does he do this a lot now?"

She hated the leer. Hated that they'd been seen and now were being talked about.

Hated that she knew without a doubt that she was going to have to see Mr. Armstrong again. Even if it compromised her reputation, she couldn't dare to not use all of his influence and contacts to uncover what had happened to her sister.

That reminder made her voice harder. "Let me pass."

"Not yet. I still have no answers," he said softly. "Everyone is wondering what he did to break down some of those chilly walls of yours and actually give a man the time of day. What did he do? Or is it that he is wealthy?"

"It was nothing." She was frightened now. Jerome was not backing off, which meant that she was at his mercy for however long he wished to speak.

Frantically, she prayed for the sound of another pair of footsteps on the stairwell or the echo of voices from the servants' hall. But only silence surrounded them. No one would hear her if she cried out. No one would know how terrified she'd become.

Using the last of her willpower, she said, "Cook is going to be wondering what happened to me. I really must be on my way. Now."

But he ignored her pleas yet again. "You mustn't act so shocked. It's not like things like this don't happen all the time."

"They do?"

"Of course they do. You should know that from Nanci."

Rosalind didn't want to hear another word about her roommate. "What happens to other people is certainly none of my concern."

He reached out and ran one finger down the crease in her sleeve. "You know, there was once another girl here who acted a bit like you. She was quiet. Kept to herself." He shook his head. "Acted so shocked about most everything." He paused. "But one day that changed."

"Of whom are you speaking?"

"Miranda." He grinned.

The mention of her sister's name created a new sense of urgency inside her. At another time, on another day, she would have tried to figure out what Jerome meant. But now all she wanted to do was get away.

"If you do not step aside, I will report you to Mrs. Abrams. I will tell her and anyone else who would care to listen that you made terrible, lewd suggestions."

"Is that all?"

"Oh no. I'll be sure they know that you accosted me on the stairway."

He drew back as if burned. "Hold now."

She continued, eager to make a jab of her own. After all, she had so little to lose where he was concerned. If he did his worst, he could very well ruin her or ruin her reputation. Neither was acceptable. "I assure you, I will. I have nothing to lose."

"What makes you say that?"

Now that the tables had been turned and he was the nervous

one, she went on the offensive. "Did you have something to do with Miranda's disappearance? Is that why she left in such a hurry? Jerome, did you compromise her? Ruin her? What did you do to her? Where is she?"

"I had nothing to do with her going off." His eyes were wild now. Worried and doubtful.

"So she just left?"

The stillness between the two of them continued for seconds. The air felt thicker, the tension heightened. For the first time, she felt that everything she was going through was going to be worth it. After all.

Then they heard the faint pounding of soles upon steps. Someone else was in the passage. He stepped to the side with a sarcastic bow. "As you said, you are late. Please, don't let me keep you further."

And as the footsteps grew louder, Rosalind knew she had no choice but to hurry back to the kitchens. And hope that she didn't get in trouble for once again taking too long to do her job.

CHAPTER 13

Sitting in his mother's elegantly appointed private receiving room, Reid watched her quietly go through the steps of pouring him tea.

He had no desire to drink any. All he really wanted to do was sit in the shade outside, sip a cool glass of lemonade, and remember every word of his latest conversation with Rosalind. Even a day later, the desire to remember each word, each expressive movement of her face, pulled him like little else had in recent memory.

The pragmatic part of him said that it made sense. After all, much of his day was made up of meaningless exchanges about little of importance.

His chat with Rosalind had been anything but that.

"Reid?" his mother prompted.

He realized she'd been holding the fine china teacup out for him for far too long. He took it and then took a sip of the strong East India tea. "Thank you."

She sipped her own, which was liberally laced with cream and sugar. Then she looked at him directly. "Now that the niceties have been taken care of, perhaps you could talk to me about what is bothering you."

"Pardon?"

"Oh, for goodness' sake, son, do not play dumb. You've spent much of the last ten minutes gazing into nothing. Something has caught your interest, and just like when you were a lad, nothing is going to take it off your mind until you are good and ready."

He was mildly embarrassed to be so transparent. "I had no idea I still harbored so many childish qualities."

Her eyes lit up. "That, son, is the very reason you need to confide in me as soon as possible." With a triumphant smile, she rested her teacup back in its saucer, set them both down on the table, then folded her hands on her lap. "Now, you may begin. I am listening."

Reid was mildly taken aback. Though he and his mother had spoken about his schooling, his work, and his father's health, they'd certainly never crossed the line into his personal problems.

"I'm not sure how to begin. Or what to share," he said honestly. Did a gentleman dare burden his mother with a story like Rosalind's? Or should he be more thoughtful of her delicate sensibilities?

"Reid, whatever it is, it can be dealt with. With God all things are possible, you know. Begin at the beginning, of course."

"What I have learned is not fit for delicate company, Mother."

Her eyebrows arched. "Since when have you decided that I am too delicate to face reality?"

He was discomfited. "Well, now—"

"And why, exactly, have you decided to start determining how much I need to know about things?"

"Mother—"

She cut him off yet again. "And, for that matter, whatever happened to you simply telling me your news?"

"Well, this story . . . it is rather disturbing, I fear."

She leaned back and rearranged her skirts. "Ah, I see. So you fear I may be shocked? You're concerned that I might faint? Be scandalized?"

As a matter of fact, he was becoming rather shocked by their present conversation. "I fear this might trouble you unnecessarily. I don't wish to cause you any sleepless nights. Or undue stress. You have quite enough of that in your life at the moment."

"Because of your father."

"Yes. Of course I mean because of Dad."

After once again picking up her teacup, she sipped slowly, her eyes closing in pleasure for a brief moment. Then they focused squarely on him. "I beg your pardon, Reid, but I'm afraid you have me confused with some other ladies of your acquaintance."

"Pardon?"

"You must have forgotten that your father and I have not always lived here in the midst of all this glamour and superficiality. At one time, we had a perfectly normal existence in South Bend." She raised a brow. "Do you remember our home? It was within walking distance of the train tracks."

He felt himself color. "Point taken."

"I hope so. Now, I spent my morning listening to a group of women wax poetically about flower arrangements. I spent two hours in the salon getting fitted for gowns. I also bought a new hat, one that has a profusion of fake gardenias on it. Please tell me something worthwhile."

"Yes, ma'am." After debating briefly about what would be the best way to begin, he decided to tell her all he knew. "This story begins, I suppose, with my meeting a maid at Sloane House. Her name is Rosalind."

A flash of wariness—and, dare he think, disappointment?—appeared in her eyes. "Yes?"

"I met her a couple of weeks ago. Veronica and Douglass were talking to her. She's new, you see."

"And?" Reid could see she was both disappointed and a bit bored. It was obvious that she had no desire to hear some gossip about a maid.

"And I must admit that she is a beautiful young woman. I, um, haven't been blind to that."

Interest sparked in her eyes. "Oh?"

"Yes, she has brown curly hair and blue eyes. Trim. And the kind of complexion most young ladies of our acquaintance would be most envious of."

"She sounds lovely."

"Oh, she is." He sighed. "But, Mother, that is not why she has been on my mind."

"Reid, come to the point."

"I will be happy to, but the story has happened to me in a roundabout fashion. And because of that, I feel forced to tell it to you in the same way." He held up a hand to cut off any further protestation. "Suffice to say that I have discovered she is no ordinary maid. She is here under false pretenses."

"Which are?"

"Her sister, who goes by the name of Miranda and worked at Sloane House as well, went missing. Rosalind is there to discover what happened to her."

"I hate to disappoint her, but she might be on a fool's errand. Many women have tales of heartbreak and woe. They are jilted by a lover or merely get homesick." Looking a bit more optimistic, she added, "There's also the chance the sister did what many women everywhere do when they are off on their own. Sometimes, when a young lady is out of the watchful eye of her family, she does the unthinkable."

"Which is?"

Her eyes sparkled. "She falls in love and gets married to a man of her choice."

He chuckled. "Touché. But . . . don't you think if something good had happened to Miranda she would have written to her family?"

"Perhaps. Or perhaps not. Sometimes the woman might not want to hear her family's criticism. A woman's heart is a fragile thing, you see."

Reid blinked. Frankly, he was taken aback by his mother's flowery words. He'd had no idea she was such a romantic! "But they are not of society, Mother. They are farmers in Wisconsin."

She smiled slightly. "Just because the family isn't society and doesn't live in a large city, it doesn't mean they don't care about the choices she makes."

"Sorry. Yes, of course you are right."

She shrugged off his apology. "No, please forgive me. Here you are, telling me Rosalind's story, and instead of listening I seem to be doing my best to give her story my own ending. What does she intend to do?"

"She's determined to keep asking questions and sleuthing." He couldn't help it. He had to smile. "She's determined to save the day, Mother. I find her goals both terribly laudable and extremely sad."

"Is that what you told her?"

"Of course not. I told Rosalind I'd help as much as I could."

"You were concerned about giving her false hope?"

"Mother, I know you think this is a fool's errand, but my heart goes out to her. Besides, she is a nice girl. She hasn't been poisoned by the city yet. I'm afraid if I don't reach out to help her, she is going to be prey for some other man of her acquaintance whose motives will not be as upstanding as mine."

She gazed at him a long moment. Then, at once, her expression softened. "I think you are doing a brave thing, son. And a kindness that she will always remember, whatever the outcome. I am proud of you."

He inclined his head, a mocking expression on his face, for they both knew he'd done nothing yet to be proud of. "Thank you."

"You'll keep me informed if you find any information—or if I, too, can help?"

"You, Mother?"

She looked chagrined. "I have to admit that my interest in Rosalind's investigation far surpasses my latest goal."

"Which is?"

"Finding you a wife, of course." Her smile sparkled now. "Of course, lately that has seemed to be my own fool's errand. Actually, at the moment I fear that finding a missing maid might be far easier than finding the perfect wife for you. You are proving to be a rather difficult man to bend to my will."

Thinking about the parade of debutantes in whom he had no interest, he inclined his head. "I fear you may be right about that."

―――

Three mornings later, Rosalind gaped at Nanci. "I don't understand," she said. "Why on earth would the family be giving us tickets to see the fair again? You know how expensive they are. And an unexpected day off too."

Nanci pointed one leg out and straightened her black stocking. "You might be the type of girl to look a gift horse in the mouth, but I certainly am not. Mrs. Abrams handed me the two tickets and said they were for the two of us to use today. So you had best get out of that black dress and into your best gown."

Rosalind grinned at Nanci's statement. The last time they'd gotten paid, Nanci had tried to get her to keep a portion of the monies and buy a more flattering day dress. Though she'd been tempted to do the same, so far she'd resolutely sent the majority of her paycheck home each Friday. Any monies she did keep were for emergencies.

Her family had sent her here to discover Miranda's whereabouts, and, of course, assist her as best she could. She would never spend those precious dollars on a new gown, even though she had to admit that the idea of wearing a new dress with leg-of-mutton sleeves did spark a bit of longing deep inside of her.

Returning to the present, she watched Nanci adjust her bustle, then step into a lovely gown in a deep cerulean blue. What was the right answer? Did she accept the ticket and accept the day off without question? Or did she dare ask the housekeeper about it?

"Rosalind, you have no choice in the matter. If you don't accept the gift, you are going to look very ungrateful. Now, come help me button this."

Rosalind stepped behind her and efficiently began fastening the long row of buttons. "I suppose you're right," she said.

"I know I am." When all twenty-eight buttons were fastened, Nanci opened up a box and pulled out a beautiful bonnet with feathers the exact shade of her dress.

Rosalind now felt completely green with envy, and was completely curious as to how Nanci could afford such an ensemble. "Where did you get that dress? And that hat? Did your family send you funds?"

Nanci shook her head. "Of course not. It was a gift." She smiled slightly. "Now, let's go. I want to make the train."

Nanci not only had been given two tickets to the fair, she also had obtained money for them to take the South Side Rapid Transit train. This time, instead of standing for an eternity with other service workers and tourists on a trolley, they were sitting in comfort as the elevated train sped its way to Jackson Park.

In no time at all, they were walking among the multitudes, fixing their eyes on the White City in awe. And just like last time, the crowds were from all walks of life and many nationalities. Foreign tongues mixed with more familiar ones at just about every corner. Ladies in their finery were escorted by fine gentlemen in their top hats. Children in their perambulators and nannies and older men and women mixed with tourists from almost every country in the civilized world.

Their voices, combined with the heavenly aromas from the various restaurants and street peddlers, provided an experience Rosalind knew would be increasingly hard to describe to her family.

But just as she was about to suggest they go to the Women's Museum, Nanci tugged on her sleeve. "Let's go to the Ferris wheel."

"But you are afraid of it, remember? That is why we gave away our tokens."

"I changed my mind. Now I would fancy a turn on it, I think."

From every corner of the fair the Ferris wheel loomed above them. It was an amazing feat of technology—and, Rosalind privately thought, of ingenuity too. But that said, she was more than a bit frightened to even stand near the structure, never mind think about riding on it.

Embarrassed to share her fears, she concentrated on the one Nanci would most likely understand. "A ride on Mr. Ferris's invention is fifty cents! I could never afford such a thing."

"You don't have to be able to afford it." With a broad, triumphant grin, Nanci opened her purse and pulled out one crisp dollar. "I had a surprise for you!"

Now her suspicions had increased tenfold. "Nanci, where did you get all of this money?"

This time, Nanci didn't even attempt to pretend she had no secrets. Instead, she smiled sweetly. "That's for me to know and you to find out."

Rosalind yearned to take Nanci in a corner and demand she tell her what was going on. But of course this wasn't the time or the place. Instead, she followed Nanci through the crowds, entered the midway, and proceeded to the Ferris wheel.

Rosalind's stomach knotted as they waited in line, eventually stepping into a metal cage with almost sixty other people. After the cage was snapped shut, an operator moved the switch, and they lurched toward the sky.

Over and over, the wheel stopped while people were let on and others were let off. And then they lurched even higher into the sky. Some people in their company gripped the sides and peeked out through the mesh in wonder. Others laughed and joked. One poor woman fainted when, apparently, she realized she was afraid of heights.

While Nanci grinned and seemed to enjoy each second, Rosalind felt her mind drift. She was more concerned about how Nanci had gotten her new dress and hat and the Ferris wheel tokens than exploring the wonders surrounding her.

When they finally stepped out of their carriage thirty minutes later, Rosalind was ready for a seat on a bench and perhaps a tall glass of lemonade.

But Nanci had other plans. "We must go," she blurted.

"Where now?"

"Wooded Island."

Rosalind stopped. "Why there?" As far as Rosalind knew, there were only the Japanese buildings and a series of rose gardens there, and woods and trails that led to nowhere. Rumor had it, many fairgoers went there to escape the crowds. "You'll find out," Nanci answered over her shoulder. "But hurry. We are almost late."

Late for what? Rosalind ached to ask but decided not to press. Nanci's voice had a thread of anxiety in it now.

Then, just as they turned toward Wooded Island, Rosalind's heart sank. At last she understood the reason for the tickets. For the dress and hat and the sudden day off work.

There in front of them both stood Douglass Sloane. He was looking at his timepiece, scowling, then abruptly raised his head and stared. Lines of irritation in his forehead smoothed. His stance relaxed, his gaze sharpened. And as he slowly smiled, one dimple appeared.

And Rosalind felt a tinge of fear.

Then her heart raced when she saw who he was standing with. None other than Reid Armstrong.

Mr. Armstrong's expression was the complete opposite of Mr. Sloane's, however. Instead of relief, he wore a look of trepidation and worry. Only when their eyes met did another emotion enter his features—reluctant humor.

This time they were not going to have to pretend to meet unexpectedly. They weren't going to have to scheme to devise a private meeting. No, this time they would stand together in plain sight.

Rosalind didn't know if that made her feel relieved . . . or even more apprehensive.

CHAPTER 14

"Nanci, how did you know Mr. Sloane and Mr. Armstrong were going to be here?"

"A little bird told me." She beamed before lowering her voice. "I'm going to tour the fair by Douglass's side. You may keep company with Mr. Armstrong."

"Thank you for letting me know," Rosalind said sarcastically.

As if she finally was aware of Rosalind's trepidation, Nanci blushed. "I do hope you are not too vexed with me. I didn't dare tell you what the plans were. Think of how upset both Mrs. Sloane and Mrs. Abrams would be!"

Rosalind imagined that only she would recognize the irony of being worried about both a great society lady *and* her housekeeper.

Then Nanci looked troubled. "Rosalind, will you be all right with being alone with Mr. Armstrong?"

"I suppose I'll have to do my best." Secretly, she was thanking her lucky stars and the Lord's many blessings. Ever since Jim and Jerome had made snide comments about seeing her with Mr. Armstrong, Rosalind had been harboring many doubts about how she was going to be able to be seen with the man and keep her position in the house.

This occasion was a boon, for sure.

She said nothing else to Nanci as they greeted the men. Douglass seemed to eye her a bit too long, but quickly turned his attention to Nanci. Holding out his arm, he said, "You look fetching."

"I hope we aren't too late?"

"It's not a problem." Turning to Reid, Douglass said, "I'm going to escort Nanci privately for a while. I'll meet you here in two hours?"

Reid barely had time to nod before Douglass walked with Nanci toward one of the scenic trails.

Rosalind watched their figures fade into the distance before she walked to Reid's side. "I'm curious. Did you know Nanci and I were going to be here?"

"I did not." His voice was harsh.

"I didn't either. I didn't know you were going to be here until I saw you standing here with Mr. Sloane."

Looking vaguely uncomfortable, he looked back at the trail where the other two had now disappeared. "Douglass is intrigued by Nanci."

"She is a beautiful girl."

He eyed her closely. "Nothing will come of their liaison. I hope she realizes that."

Rosalind was worried too, but loyalty to Nanci made her defensive. "I believe she is past the age of being naive about such things, Mr. Armstrong. I don't know much about being a servant in a large home, but I have come to the conclusion that no maid has delusions of marrying the young master of the house."

"I pray you are right. I would hate for your friend to get hurt."

"I think a lot of the shine wears off when one launders another's clothing, Mr. Armstrong."

The muscles in his jaw twitched, but he said nothing.

"Well, it seems as if we have two hours to explore. Is there anywhere you'd like to go?"

She shrugged. "The Fine Arts Palace isn't too far. Shall we go there?"

"That would be fine." He started in that direction, walking slowly so she could keep up, but otherwise with no concession to her.

At first she worried about what people would think about the two of them being together, but she promptly forgot about her reservations. The other visitors seemed to be far too entranced with the wonders of the fair to give Rosalind and Reid more than the most cursory of glances.

After they walked up the marble steps and into the grand building, Reid guided them to a gallery on the left. Then, as he stood in front of a collection of Italian Renaissance paintings, he asked, "Have you discovered anything new?"

"Well, I met a street vendor, a woman." Briefly she told him about the flower girl Minerva. She told him she had seemed particularly observant, but, of course, Rosalind didn't know her well enough to pry for more information. "I'm going to visit her again as soon as I can. Perhaps we can develop a friendship."

"That is a good idea, Rosalind," he said as he guided her into another one of the one hundred forty rooms. She looked around with interest, enjoying the sights, but truly unable to think of anything other than their conversation. "There is one other item I should probably mention."

"What is that?"

She scanned the area around them and saw that most people were ignoring them. However, one or two ladies were watching her converse with Reid with curious expressions. That made her even more aware of the need to tell Reid about her conversation with Jim as well as relay Jerome's snide remarks. She did so as quickly as she could.

To her amusement, Reid was incredulous. "I am a gentleman. I would never set my designs upon you."

"Yes, sir. But unfortunately, my reputation is not quite as stellar. Everyone would believe that I had designs on you."

"What would you like me to do to repair your reputation?"

"Nothing at all. If you make too much of a fuss about our innocent relationship, it will only cause more speculation."

"But still, I hate to think of you being subjected to such things."

"Mr. Armstrong, don't forget, my sister has gone missing. I fear she's been subjected to much worse than gossip and speculation."

"I suppose you're right." He cleared his throat. "We should probably start walking back now. Take my arm."

Noticing the ladies' continued interest, she whispered, "Mr. Armstrong, for our affiliation to continue, you mustn't be so familiar with me."

"Beg pardon?"

"You need to treat me like a servant, Mr. Armstrong," she murmured. "People must suspect nothing about our conversations." She tilted her head toward the ladies in a meaningful way.

He glanced behind him, sent the ladies a decidedly cool appraisal, then turned back to her with yet another glacial stare. She would have giggled if their cover wasn't so important.

When they walked out into the sun again, Reid smiled at her. "Never has two hours gone by so quickly."

"I feel the same way."

"I will be attending a meeting in a home just down the street from

Sloane House. Douglass won't be there. I thought I would bring up your sister's name to see if it raises any suspicions."

"Do you really think someone will remember a maid?"

"It's worth a try. I feel certain that someone knows something about what happened to Miranda. Sooner or later, we'll discover who that person is."

She liked that he used the word *we*. "I hope so."

As they meandered back toward Wooded Island, they passed a street seller selling glasses of lemonade. Reid purchased two of them. She sipped gratefully, then smiled. "It's delicious. Thank you."

He smiled softly. "Your enthusiasm is a delight to behold."

She met his gaze, feeling something special and meaningful between them again. She hated to imagine it was anything other than a mutual need to help another person. But she felt so alone in the world that she was willing to grasp at most anything to keep her spirits alive.

She felt her neck and cheeks heat. Embarrassed about her feelings, she looked toward a trio of benches just on the edge of Wooded Island. "Oh, thank goodness. There's Nanci," she said, waving a hand in her direction.

Nanci, however, merely gazed at her with an empty, glassy stare. Mr. Sloane was nowhere near.

"I wonder what happened to Mr. Sloane," she mused. But as they got closer to Nanci, Rosalind had a dark suspicion that something terrible had transpired with her friend.

Reid followed her gaze, then stiffened and muttered something under his breath.

When they reached Nanci's side, Rosalind saw that her eyes were tear-filled, her hair was slightly mussed, and her lips were swollen. After catching Reid's gaze, Nanci tucked her chin in obvious embarrassment.

Reid cleared his throat. "May I escort you ladies back to Sloane house?"

Abruptly, Nanci got to her feet. "Thank you, but I believe we will be more than fine on our own."

"Are you sure?"

"Positive."

Reid flashed a concerned look at Rosalind. "Is that what you want?"

She didn't know what she wanted, but she felt she needed to follow Nanci's lead. Nanci needed her—and her trust. "Yes, Mr. Armstrong. Thank you for your company and for the offer, but we will be fine."

He hesitated, then tipped his hat and walked away.

Standing next to Nanci, Rosalind reached for her hand. "Tell me what you would like to do."

"Leave here. Leave Chicago." She raised a brow. "Leave my life?"

"Nanci, what in the world happened? Why are you crying? What happened to Mr. Sloane?"

She swiped at her eyes. "Not here." She circled her arm through Rosalind's and tugged. "Let's go to the Women's Building."

"All right," Rosalind said, though she privately thought that sounded like a terrible idea. "If you are sure that is what you wish to do. Do . . . do you know where Mr. Sloane went?" she asked again.

"Douglass? Oh yes. He went away." She leveled her gaze on Rosalind. "You see, he only came to explore the island. Now that he has? He couldn't get away fast enough."

"Nanci, if he acted inappropriately—"

Nanci turned to her, disdain heavy in her eyes. "What don't you understand? We are not part of the Michigan Avenue crowd. We will never be part of society. No matter how much we might smile or how attractive the gentlemen might think us, we're nothing."

Rosalind flinched. "We are more than that."

"Not where it counts." Glancing around them, Nanci's voice filled with enmity. "At the end of the day, Rosalind, we are merely two girls who bow and scrape to their betters because we are very lucky to have jobs."

"Yes, of course, but—"

"How can we even seem ungrateful? Haven't you heard that people are going hungry?"

Anger for the situation, anger for Nanci's deriding comments, fueled her temper. "So why did you agree to meet Douglass then?" Rosalind asked pointedly. "If you know Douglass will never think of you as more than a servant in his house, why did you spend time alone with him?"

Nanci shook her head slowly, as if she couldn't understand Rosalind's naïveté. "Because I'm not dead. Yet."

Nanci's words shook Rosalind to the core. And they set off a spark of questions. "Is this what happened to Miranda? Did she get too close to Douglass and he abused her?"

Nanci jerked her head to the side. "Why does it always go back to Miranda? Why do you even care?"

"Because someone should."

Nanci's eyes flashed fury. Then, little by little, her expression eased, as if she, too, had just realized how wrong it was for a single girl to disappear and no one to lift a finger to find her.

"I don't know if she was ever with Douglass," she said finally. "Maybe she was."

"Do you think he had anything to do with her disappearance? Do you think maybe he made her leave?"

Nanci's eyes widened as she considered that possibility, and then she shook her head. "No."

Though they were walking at a fast pace, Rosalind didn't dare leave their conversation. "Why not?"

"Because he doesn't work that way. Douglass Sloane is an indolent gentleman. He can be amusing and wicked and great fun. But he knows one thing more than anything else: his legacy is the Sloane name and the home that has housed generations of his ancestors. He knows what he has to do to keep it."

"And what is that?"

"He must marry a society girl who will increase the family's wealth and place in society. For him to get one of those debutantes, he must keep his reputation on this side of respectable."

"In other words, he can be bad, but not too bad."

"That is exactly it," Nanci said bitterly. "He can do most anything . . . as long as he doesn't get caught."

They were almost at the Women's Building now. Rosalind knew that once the conversation ended, there would be no opportunity to open it again. Unlike hers, Nanci's life was destined to be in the grand house. "If he's so worried about getting a real lady for a wife, I don't understand why he would treat you so poorly."

"Why?"

"Well, he must know you could complain to Mrs. Abrams. Or even to his mother."

Nanci glared at her, then pulled her to a grassy section of lawn on the left of the building. "I'm only going to say this one last time, Rosalind, and I hope you hear what I'm saying at long last. Girls like you and me do not count. If we complain? We will get fired."

Rosalind felt her skin pale. "And Douglass knows that."

Nanci sniffed before turning around and stepping up the white steps into the building. "Not just Douglass," she murmured over her shoulder. "Everyone. Everyone knows this."

"Don't say a word about this to anyone, do you hear me? If I ever hear that you did? I promise, I will never forgive you."

Rosalind nodded. Then, feeling miserable, she followed Nanci into the Women's Building.

She had a feeling she had just lost her only real woman friend in Chicago.

CHAPTER 15

Four days later, Rosalind was still worrying about Nanci. Her friend and roommate was having trouble sleeping. More than once Rosalind had been awakened by Nanci's crying out in her sleep.

The mornings, however, were a different story. Every time Rosalind tried to talk to Nanci about her nightmares, Nanci would deny that anything was wrong. Even though she now had dark smudges under her eyes and little appetite, she refused to discuss what had happened with her and Douglass during the two hours they were alone.

Coming from a large family, Rosalind was a firm believer in discussing problems. Keeping secrets was never a good idea, especially if they festered over days and weeks. And now, other people were starting to notice Nanci's short temper and lackluster spirit.

Finally Rosalind couldn't take it anymore. They were in Mrs. Abrams' sitting room mending stockings and sheets. When Rosalind looked over and saw Nanci's large, uneven stitches, she knew she was going to have to redo them.

"Nanci, why don't you close your eyes and rest for a few minutes while I redo that seam?"

"There is no need to redo anything. My work is fine."

Rosalind pointed out the obvious. The material around the seam was gathered in an odd spot. In the condition it was in, not even the lowest scullery maid would wear the stocking. Certainly Mrs. Sloane would not.

"You know this isn't good enough."

"Well, now. Aren't you just the perfect lady? What have you decided? That because you have struck up a conversation with Mr. Armstrong, you now have every right to boss me about?"

Rosalind was completely taken aback. "I'm trying to help you. Can't you see that?"

"I was doing just fine before you entered the house. I will be that way long after you leave too."

"Why would you think I'd be leaving?"

A true wariness entered her eyes. "No reason."

Setting the stocking she was darning to one side, Rosalind said, "What really happened between you and Mr. Sloane at the fair?"

Nanci paled. "That is none of your concern."

"I think it might be. You're making mistakes that I could be blamed for."

Nanci sniffed. "Everything that goes on in this house is not your business. In fact, it would be better if you kept your nose out of other people's business entirely. The sooner, the better."

"Why?"

"Because if you don't, you might just find yourself out of a job. Or gone."

"Gone?"

The flicker of unease Rosalind had started to feel grew stronger.

To stop her hands from shaking, she clenched them into tight fists. "Nanci, you know a lot more about Miranda's disappearance than you've let on, don't you?"

"Why are you so fixated on that girl? She isn't the first girl in Chicago to have gone missing. You hardly batted an eye when Tilly left."

"I cared about Tilly. Besides, we all discovered Tilly got married."

"Then care about Miranda enough to stop mentioning her name."

"I can't."

Nanci jumped to her feet. "Why on earth not? You didn't even know her."

Rosalind bit her lip. Though everything inside of her warned her to keep silent, her heart couldn't seem to do that anymore. "I did," she finally said. "I do know Miranda."

Nanci slowly turned back to her. "What are you talking about?"

"Miranda is my sister," she whispered.

"What?" The last bit of color tingeing her cheeks faded to white. "Is that why you came here? To Sloane House?"

Rosalind nodded. "I have to figure out what happened to her. When she first got here, she wrote us all kinds of stories about the house. About the Sloanes." She waved a hand. "About all of you. But then her letters got shorter, her stories more evasive."

Nanci's shoulders tightened. "And then?"

"And then we heard nothing. One week passed. Then two. Three. Then we were all so concerned, my father traveled out here and talked to the police."

"What did they say?"

Remembering the haunted expression on her father's face when he came home after that painful trip made her want to cry too. "They laughed at him. They said that she'd probably run off with some man. Or that she didn't want to be found. They disparaged her character, making my older sister sound like no better than an adventuress." Picking up another stocking, she wrapped it around her opposite hand. Tightened it until it hurt. "Don't you understand why I'm here, Nanci? Don't you understand why I can't simply give up and walk away? I know in my heart that something happened to her. I feel it."

"It would be better if you gave up. You . . . you might find out things you don't want to know."

"I don't know that I would."

"I do. Miranda . . . she was no saint, Rosalind."

"Why would you say that?"

"I have my reasons."

"What are they?" Impulsively, Rosalind reached out for her. "Nanci, what do you know?"

For a moment, Nanci looked like she was about to divulge a secret, but then only shook off Rosalind's touch. "Now that I know why you've been asking, I'm going to tell you something that you need to never forget."

Her breath hitched. "What?"

"Accept that there are some things you'll never know. Accept that she is gone. Stop asking questions and accept it."

"I can't do that."

"You're going to have to. There are things happening in this house that you are either too oblivious to notice or refuse to see."

"Like what? And who are you referring to? Do you mean someone on staff . . . or someone in the family?" Thinking quickly, she said, "Did Miranda hurt someone's feelings or something? Or did someone suspect her of something worse? Nanci, some of her last letters hinted that she'd begun to be afraid. Who do you think she was afraid of?"

"I don't want to be cruel, but perhaps it would be best to simply accept the fact that your sister is gone. There's nothing you can do to bring her back. Trust me, sometimes you have to simply forget."

"You don't know what you're asking. I can't simply forget my sister."

Nanci glanced at the stocking she still held, then tossed it on the floor with a look of disgust. "If you refuse to listen to reason, I hope and pray you will keep me out of it from now on."

"Why? What are you so afraid of?" Grasping at straws, she said, "Are you afraid of someone here finding out who I am and that I haven't given up? Are you afraid of Douglass finding out?" When Nanci closed her eyes, Rosalind pushed further. "Are . . . are you afraid of Douglass?"

"Leave Mr. Sloane out of this. And while you're at it, you should probably never speak to Mr. Armstrong again either."

"Reid is going to help me. We've become friends."

"I promise you, he is not your friend." After peeking out the doorway, she said, "Besides, Veronica has her sights set on him, even if her mother prefers Mr. Newhouse. If Veronica even thinks that you could be a rival, she will make your life miserable. She enjoys that."

"I could never be a rival. And besides, how would she ever know I was talking to him? Are you going to tell her?"

"Don't be so naive. I'm not the only person who has eyes and ears, Rosalind. And I'm sure not the only person in this house who has noticed that you are way too curious for your own good."

With one last disparaging look, she walked out of the room.

Feeling as if she'd just run for blocks, Rosalind breathed heavily as she watched Nanci's departure. She felt uneasy and afraid. And, unfortunately, as if there were now even more questions to answer and worry about.

Every time she thought she had gone two steps forward, it seemed that she was destined to take another four steps back. Picking up the pair of scissors, she carefully started removing Nanci's stitches. Maybe if she found some control, things would start to get easier. Maybe if she could begin to trust herself, she could actually do something that would help Miranda.

Twenty minutes later, Mrs. Abrams popped her head in the room while walking by. "Rosalind, I thought Nanci was going to help you with the mending. Where is she?"

"Um, I'm not sure. Perhaps Miss Veronica needs her."

Mrs. Abrams sighed. "Probably so. Our young lady has a big evening tonight. The Uptons are having a ball and Veronica needs to look her best."

Walking into the room, she casually picked up the pair of stockings Rosalind had just repaired. "These look very nice, Rosalind. You do very good work."

"Thank you, ma'am."

"When you finish, go to the conservatory to see if the girls there need help dusting." She paused, seeming to realize that it was a bit out of the ordinary to keep heaping chores on Rosalind's shoulders. "You don't mind, do you, dear?"

What could she say? "Not at all."

"Good. It's best to keep busy here, I've found. If we're busy, it keeps us on our toes. And out of trouble."

"Yes, ma'am," Rosalind replied. But as she gathered her basket of needles and thread, she wondered why Mrs. Abrams had felt the need to remind her of that.

Had something new just happened? Or was she afraid that Rosalind would discover that something unfortunate already had?

CHAPTER 16

Eloisa Carstairs was everything Reid Armstrong's family had ever imagined a perfect prospective bride could be.

Slim and elegant, perfectly attired and perfectly mannered, Eloisa was the epitome of society, the personification of all that was genteel and good. If Reid made a match with her, his parents would be thrilled. Blessed with golden hair and eyes the color of pale aquamarines, she was the picture-perfect beauty they had hoped for him when they'd sent him to expensive schools and later moved to their spacious house along Michigan Avenue.

Reid knew this. He imagined Eloisa knew the same thing as he carefully pressed his lips on her gloved hand.

But their alliance was proof that not even a perfect match equaled attraction or desire. In short, though they did share a slight friendship, it seemed they would never claim anything more.

"It's a pleasure to see you again, Miss Carstairs."

"Indeed. It has been some time. Since the Griffins' soiree, I believe." Reid knew she was referencing that so he would understand that their time together had been remembered.

"I remember our waltz well," he replied, doing much the same.

Her lips curved into a kind, warm smile. Her eyes, on the other hand, kept searching his face for something more. Something that suggested deeper emotion was a possibility. He felt much the same way. But after the briefest of pauses, he inwardly sighed. And Eloisa took a small step backward.

He wished this was easier. He would love nothing better than to find his perfect match and be done with it. Then he could go about his life. But so far, the only woman who had stirred anything resembling longing or desire was a maid in the Sloane household. He imagined much of her attraction had less to do with her blue eyes and mahogany hair and more to do with the mystery surrounding her.

Perhaps.

"Miss Carstairs, would you do me the honor of saving a dance for me this evening?"

"Of course, Mr. Armstrong. I always enjoy dancing with friends." She smiled at his grin, both of them signaling that they understood where the other stood. Then her eyes widened as she glanced just beyond his shoulder. Her chin lifted and her whole posture became more contained.

"Veronica."

"Hello, Eloisa." Veronica inclined her head regally, as if she was the one with the higher social status, when in fact most in the room would consider them equals. "I couldn't help but admire your gown. Dear."

"You are too kind." Eloisa's smile turned brittle as she fingered the pale gold gown. It was extremely flattering, and even Reid's untrained eye knew it had to have cost a small fortune. She turned to him. "Mr.

Armstrong, please excuse me. I just remembered that I had told my mother I would check in with her at this time."

"Of course. May I escort you?"

"Thank you, but no. I will be perfectly fine." Eloisa turned away without a backward glance.

"Now we may breathe easier." Veronica chuckled as she closed the gap between them. As she watched Eloisa melt into the glittering crowd, she murmured, "I do hope you appreciated my timing."

"Timing?"

"Well, I looked over here and saw the two of you standing still and straight. Like wooden soldiers." She pressed a smooth palm on his black evening coat. "I had no choice but to try to rescue you from what had to be an uncomfortable conversation."

"I had no idea that you harbored such concerns over my happiness."

Her eyelids lowered. "You would be surprised, I think."

Reid looked at her a little more closely. As always, she was exquisitely attired. Though some would, perhaps, cast doubts about her beauty or her habit of looking a bit too cynical, no one would ever make the mistake to presume that she wasn't always dressed in the first tiers of fashion.

"You look as lovely as ever, Veronica. I do like that color blue on you. What is it? Indigo?"

"Sapphire." She shrugged. "I never was one to choose to fade into the woodwork."

"It isn't merely the blue of your gown that makes you stand out, Veronica."

Her lips parted before slowly smiling.

Beyond them, couples were dancing in the ballroom. The eight-piece orchestra's beautiful strains of a waltz by Strauss created an otherworldly effect. As Reid looked at the crowd, scanning the participants for familiar faces, he noticed Veronica's eyes flicker with a trace of longing. That look gave him pause, and for the first time, raised his impression of her. "Would you do me the honor of this dance?"

Pleasure, quickly masked with brittle hauteur, filled her expression. "I didn't know you danced, Reid."

"I have learned all the necessary steps. And I do promise I'll do my best not to step on any toes."

She held out one hand. "I could never refuse an offer like that."

He guided her through the throng of gentlemen and ladies, standing stoically as Veronica stopped often to say hello to acquaintances. Then he carefully wrapped one hand along her small waist, held her hand with his left, and guided her into the masses.

When he looked down on her face, he realized that he'd never been so close to her—not like this. And that she smelled like jasmine and fresh gardenias, a tantalizing combination.

Her gray eyes, for once, didn't have the cold, calculating edge that usually rested in their depths. Her full lips held a small smile.

She looked, for lack of a better word, sweet.

"Mr. Armstrong, you dance divinely. You'd best look out, you know."

"And why is that?"

"Because the other ladies present are sure to notice what they've been missing and will be batting their eyes shamelessly at you now."

"I'll try to prepare myself to be mobbed."

She laughed. The sound was gay and sweet—again, so different from her usual brittle demeanor. He curved his hand a little more securely around her waist. She allowed him to ease her a few inches closer.

For the first time in their acquaintance, he imagined kissing her.

Pressing those soft lips against his own. Tasting her sparkle. Holding her in an intimate embrace. Without her usual edge, she seemed almost desirable.

It was a revelation.

As if she read his thoughts, her skin flushed. "Reid, you are staring at me as if I were a stranger."

"Am I being rude? A thousand pardons."

"Oh, I'll only need a dozen of those." Her smile warmed as she tapped two fingers on his shoulder. "Do tell me, though, what is on your mind."

"I was merely thinking about how life continually surprises me."

"Oh? In what way?"

"I had thought I'd known almost everything about you, but then you've managed to surprise me this evening."

Thick lashes shadowed her gaze. "I can only hope it's been in a good way?"

"I can hardly answer that and still remain a gentleman."

The orchestra finished the last movement, bringing their dance and their conversation to a stop. Reid suffered from a momentary loss. He had liked being with her.

"May I escort you to your next partner?"

"You may escort me off the dance floor. You are ever the gentleman, Reid."

He guided her to the side of the room, where the air was a little quieter. "I suppose I will see you soon. Whenever I call on Douglass."

She tilted her chin up. "Is that the only reason you come to Sloane House, Reid? To see my brother?"

"Not at all. He is not the only Sloane who has captured my interest."

She nodded her head, accepting his gallant words, just as she accepted that he'd practically had no choice but to utter them. "Of course."

He was charmed. Perhaps she was the right woman for him. Maybe God had been simply biding his time, tempting him with housemaids until Reid was ready to accept a lady like Veronica.

Seeing the open French doors, he was just about to ask her if she'd care to take a stroll on the balcony when she spoke again.

"I'm so glad we spent some time together, Reid."

"The pleasure was all mine."

A smile teased her lips. "The truth is, I've been a bit worried about you of late."

"Oh?"

An eyebrow arched. "I'm referring to your recent faux pas."

"Which faux pas was that?" he teased. "We both know I've had many such incidents."

Her voice lowered, turning almost slick. "Douglass told me that you had the poor taste to be seen with our newest maid. In broad daylight. That was poorly done, Reid."

And in a flash, he was aware of her true colors all over again.

He hated that she was speaking of things that were none of her business, that she was speaking of a woman who likely delivered her coffee or pressed her dresses as someone less than worthy of notice.

"You are speaking of Rosalind, I presume?"

"Oh. Is that her name?"

"Your behavior is shameful, Veronica. I would have expected a lady such as you to know better than to gossip about a maid in her household."

"I would have expected a gentleman such as you to not be seen escorting maids around public expositions."

"Is that the problem? That I was seen?"

Now her gaze was disdainful. "We both know it was a problem. It raises questions about your character."

"My character."

"Indeed. It is all very low-class. Honestly, Reid, if you are having some little romp with a maid, you should at least take care to be a bit more circumspect."

"To protect my reputation."

"And mine."

It was on the tip of his tongue to point out that her brother had been at the fair with yet another maid in the house. That it was rumored he'd taken advantage of many maids in his employ. But that would be neither gentlemanly nor proper.

He also was tempted to ask why she even cared. But if Douglass had told her about him being with Rosalind, there must have been a reason.

Though he was almost positive that the two of them had nothing to do with Rosalind's sister's disappearance, he knew he couldn't ignore the opportunity to ask a question or two.

"The Columbian Exposition is a dangerous place, as is Chicago right now. The papers are filled with stories of women from the country going missing. I would have thought you would be relieved to hear that I was taking the time to escort one of your servants."

"I am sure the servants are used to fending for themselves, Reid."

"But not all of them have fared so well. I mean, haven't you lost a few maids lately?"

"Tilly ran off with a peddler. Or perhaps it was one of the workers at the Exposition? I don't exactly recall."

"And Miranda?"

Her lips pinched. And, if he was not mistaken, her luminous skin paled the slightest bit. "I am unclear why you know so many of our staff's names. And why you seem to be so intimately acquainted with them."

"That is unfair, Veronica. We both know that Miranda's disappearance has caused a bit of unease for your mother. She told me about the maid's mysterious disappearance herself."

Veronica blinked. "One cannot always be certain about my mother's sentiments."

"All I know is that she was concerned."

"Perhaps she should have also told you that we heard rumors that Miranda had been seen keeping company with a number of men. Obviously her morals left much to be desired. It is not my fault she left. And it is certainly not my brother's, either."

It was time to retreat. Veronica was obviously feeling confrontational. If they weren't careful, it would cause notice.

"I do beg your pardon, Veronica. I don't know why I decided to bring up such an unsavory topic."

"I don't know why either. Just when I imagine you are everything my family has ever wanted for me, you become tryingly bourgeois."

"It's my humble roots, I'm afraid. You can clean me up and teach me to dance, but I'm afraid I am still the same man."

"I am finding your company tiresome, Reid. Good evening." She turned away and brushed into the crowd. He folded his arms across his chest and watched her disappear.

For a moment he had been caught up in a dream. For a moment he had imagined that he could form a relationship with someone like her. But once again, reality had set in. And he realized that no matter how hard he tried, Veronica Sloane and most of her peers held little interest for him.

It was inevitable now. Sooner or later, his parents were going to be sorely disappointed.

CHAPTER 17

With a smooth turn of the knob and then a well-placed shove with her hip, Rosalind was able to enter Veronica's room almost silently. Feeling rather proud of herself, she balanced the morning coffee service in her arms and crossed the room.

Below stairs, it had become something of a joke to see who could convince her to deliver the breakfast trays. Rosalind had made no bones about the fact that she would rather do almost anything than carry the heavy, burdensome trays up the steep flights of stairs—even stand over a hot ironing board and press scores of linen napkins. She had a great fear of dropping one in the main hall in front of any of the family.

However, today's duty could not be pawned off to another. All eight bedrooms in the home were occupied in preparation for the dinner party the Sloanes were hosting for Veronica. Nanci had heard that Mr. and Mrs. Sloane expected a proposal soon, and they were bound and determined to present both themselves and their daughter in the best light.

But besides that, Cook said that for some reason Veronica had specifically asked for Rosalind to take up her tray. Not that she had any idea why.

Now, taking a peek at the bed, she was shocked to see Veronica wide awake. She was staring at her with a venomous expression.

Taking a deep breath, Rosalind quickly put the silver tray down on the desk. Then, taking care to keep her expression blank, she spoke. "May I pour you coffee, Miss Veronica?"

"You may."

As quickly as she could, Rosalind turned over the cup, poured the coffee, added cream and sugar as Veronica preferred it, then brought it to her bedside.

Veronica was sitting up in bed now, staring at her with a cool expression. Unlike times before, she held out her hand for the cup and saucer.

All Rosalind wanted to do was to get out of the room as fast as possible. "Will there be anything else?"

"Oh yes." Veronica set the cup down after taking the smallest of sips. "You can explain to me why you have chosen to make your life so difficult."

"Pardon me, miss?"

"*Pardon me?* Ah, but you have become so refined for a Wisconsin farm girl, haven't you?" When Rosalind's eyes widened, she laughed softly. "Yes, I've done a little bit of research about you."

"Why?"

"Because, for some unknown reason, you have decided to make yourself my rival." Her voice dripped sarcasm. "Now, why is that?"

Rosalind would have given almost everything she had to be able to leave the room right then and there. She was confused. But more than that, she was truly frightened. She was at a complete disadvantage, and both of them knew it.

All she could do was say anything she could to assuage Veronica's fears and leave the room without doing damage to her position in the household.

"Miss Veronica, we both know that I am only a servant."

"Yes, we know that's all you actually are. But it has come to my attention that you have been overstepping yourself." She picked up her cup and sipped again, just as if they were friends sitting together in a tearoom. "I heard you went to the Exposition with both my brother and Mr. Armstrong."

Rosalind was so flustered, she spoke without thinking. "I didn't go there with them. I only happened to see them there."

"So you don't deny the rumors?"

"No. But nothing happened." Not with her, at least.

Veronica laughed softly. "Of course nothing happened. Nothing happens to housemaids—at least not anything of consequence." Her expression became hard. "Actually, in the grand scheme of things, you are nothing."

The words hurt. She didn't care if they were likely true in Miss Sloane's world. "Miss Veronica, I only saw Mr. Sloane and Mr. Armstrong by chance."

"Were you by yourself?"

"I cannot answer that."

Veronica sighed as if Rosalind had just disappointed her greatly. "I'm going to be perfectly frank with you, though I have no idea why. Currently, I am at a point in my life where I must obtain a proposal and be married. My parents expect it, and everyone in our circle of acquaintances does as well. If I don't marry soon and well, I will become a laughingstock." She fastened a hard gaze on Rosalind. "I don't intend for that to happen."

"I see."

Veronica shook her head. "No, you most definitely do not. My brother has slowly been developing the most unsavory of reputations. More and more, his circle of friends has been filled with men and women with those same disreputable characters. *Almost* everyone, that is."

After taking another sip of coffee, she continued. "For some reason, Douglass's reputation has begun to slowly diminish mine. Men who once saw me as a candidate for marriage now turn away when they see me approach." She looked directly at Rosalind. "All except for Reid Armstrong. For some reason, he feels loyal to my brother. And, consequently, loyal to me."

Rosalind ached to agree that Reid was a man of honor. But, of course, how could she say a word? Instead, she stood there, standing almost at attention as Veronica drained her coffee cup.

"Rosalind, for some reason, Reid is not only aware of you, but he has taken the time to know your name. Now it seems he is willing to be seen publicly with you. If you want to keep your job, you will not continue this association. I will not be tied to a man who is known to have liaisons with housemaids."

"But . . . I have done nothing untoward."

"Even if you have not, it wouldn't matter. You would lose your position if people thought you did."

The threat was there, as clear and true as if Veronica had said it out loud.

And though she felt threatened, she couldn't help but defend herself. "I have done nothing to be ashamed of."

"It doesn't matter. If you continue to do *anything* that causes Reid to speak to you or even acknowledge your existence, you will suddenly be out of a job with no recommendation."

As Rosalind continued to gape at her, nearly paralyzed by fear, Veronica continued. "I will accuse you of stealing, I think. Maybe even something worse."

"W—worse?" Rosalind sputtered.

"It's simple, Rosalind. I am Veronica Sloane. You are simply one in a long line of unsuitable maids."

Rosalind's throat went dry as she began to have a very good idea about what happened to her sister. Miranda must have caught the eye of one of Veronica's beaus. Veronica had noticed and gotten her fired. "You . . . you've done this before, haven't you?"

Veronica's eyes turned cold. Then, to Rosalind's shock, she held out her cup and saucer for Rosalind to refill.

Bitterness coursed through her as she did as bid, then handed the cup and saucer back to Veronica. "Will there be anything else, miss?"

Veronica eyed her carefully, seeming to examine every hair and inch of her. As if she liked what she saw—Rosalind's obvious fear— she smiled. "No. I think that will be all. For now."

Seething, Rosalind turned away.

"And, Rosalind?"

She paused. "Yes?"

"Tell Cook and Abrams that I have no desire for you to bring me my morning coffee again. I definitely do not like starting my day with you at my side."

"It will be my pleasure to pass that on, Miss Veronica," she said before escaping. Out in the hall, she leaned against a wall and willed herself to stop shaking.

Something had just changed. Everything had just gone from bad to worse.

Knowing her days at Sloane House were numbered, Rosalind began to jump at any chance to escape the confines of its walls. Now she accepted any errand as an opportunity to ask grip car drivers, market vendors, and even newsboys about Miranda. Cook found much amusement in her change of heart and began to seek Rosalind out for any errand that needed to be done.

After seeing Minerva two days in a row at the same spot, she began talking with her. On the fourth day, she pulled out the daguerreotype of her sister and showed it to the flower girl.

"There is a resemblance, that's true," Minerva said after taking a cursory look at the photograph.

"She is my sister. Almost a year older. Do you by chance ever remember seeing her?"

Minerva glanced at the picture again, this time closing her eyes for a few seconds after staring at it hard. "Well, I'd be lying if I said I remembered her, though I do seem to recall a woman looking much like her walking this way a time or two."

"Thank you for that." But no matter how hard she tried to conceal her thoughts, she knew her disappointment was evident.

Minerva looked at her kindly. "I'm proof that a gal can try not to be found. Don't despair, if you're thinking the worst. Sometimes a woman simply finds something she'd rather do. Or receives a better offer."

"Is that what happened to you?"

"Obviously not." She jutted up her chin a bit. "But I'm still alive, so that says a lot. Things could be worse."

"Yes, I'm starting to realize that sad fact. Things can always be worse."

"Get on with you now. You're going to attract attention, standing here with me. And it won't do me any good either. I've got flowers to sell."

Discouraged, but feeling a bit braver, too, Rosalind walked to some of the other street sellers and showed them Miranda's daguerreotype. Most took a hard look at the photo when Rosalind told them that the woman pictured was her sister.

But no one had any information for her.

Rosalind was about to feel discouraged until she remembered that Chicago was a very big city. It would be too much to hope that one of the few street sellers she talked to would not only recognize Miranda but have useful information too. All she could do was persevere and hope and pray that her determination would soon pay off.

Later that afternoon, Nanci cornered her in the laundry. "What in the world are you doing, going out and about so much?"

"Nothing."

"That's not what it looks like. I saw you talking to that flower girl, showing a picture. What were you doing?"

"I was showing a daguerreotype of my sister."

"So you're bound and determined to not give up your search? Even though I've warned you time and again that doing so is a mistake?"

"I can't give up."

"If you don't give up, you had better start wishing for eyes in the back of your head. You're going to get harmed."

"Why would you say that?"

Immediately, Nanci clammed up.

Rosalind jumped at the sliver of hope. "You know something about Miranda, don't you?"

"I've said more than once that I don't."

"No, I think you do. I think you know a whole lot more than you are letting on."

A momentary weakness flooded Nanci's expression before she visibly tamped it down. "All I know is that you're playing with fire. And the way you're doing things? Never taking no for an answer? It's going to cause you pain. And I can promise you that I won't lift a finger to help you."

Rosalind was disappointed. She'd really hoped that Nanci had become a friend. But whether something had happened between her and Douglass the other evening—or whether she was afraid to help Rosalind with her investigation—it was obvious that there was a chasm between them that was widening day by day.

"I hear you."

Nanci shook her head. "Just stop what you're doing and concentrate on your life here—or go back home. I promise, things could be worse. Things could be a lot worse." She turned away before Rosalind could comment on that.

Hours later, she was delivering a freshly pressed grown to one of Mrs. Sloane's guests when she practically ran into Reid. He grasped her shoulders. "Careful," he said in that kind way of his. "You almost ran me down."

"I'm sorry, sir." She gestured to the pale peach dress she was holding. "I was attempting to deliver this too quickly."

"Do you need some help?"

"Of course not." Worried that someone might spy the two of them talking, she edged away. Needing him to drop his hands—and wishing she could always have him by her side. "I'd best go . . ."

"Not yet." He reached out again, this time placing his hand on her bare forearm. Then, to her disconcertion, he kept it there, warming her arm . . . and to her shame, her insides. "Tell me how your search for your sister goes."

"I've discovered nothing new, though I have a feeling Nanci

might know more than she is letting on." Briefly, she also told him about how she'd started showing street merchants Miranda's picture.

"That was another good idea." He smiled at her encouragingly. "I had an idea too. How about I accompany you to the police?"

"I told you. My father already went there once. They laughed at him."

"No offense, but sometimes the police must pick and choose which cases they try to solve. They might put a bit more thought into saying no to me."

"Thank you, sir. I would be so grateful if you could do that."

He smiled. "*We*, right? I wouldn't think of going without you."

"And where would that be?" a voice called out from behind them.

Only then did Reid's hand fall. Rosalind turned around with a deep sense of foreboding. "Miss Veronica. I . . . I was just returning Miss Livingston's gown."

Veronica's lips thinned with a barely controlled fury. "Is that what you were doing? Because it sounded to me like you were doing something far different."

Before Rosalind could say a word in her defense, Reid spoke. "Come now, Veronica. Aren't you being a bit dramatic? There was nothing more going on here beyond a small conversation."

"I am a lot of things, Reid. However, naive is not one of them." As she turned to Rosalind, her voice lowered. Turned malicious. "I believe I warned you about what would happen. If I were you, I'd try to act surprised when it did." She turned and walked away.

And Rosalind realized that she'd just made her very worst mistake. "I'd best be on my way, sir."

Reid's eyes narrowed and he reached out again, like it was taking everything he had to not pull her close to him. "Wait a moment. It sounded like she was threatening you. What did Veronica mean?"

Oh, the temptation was there. She ached to give in to every weakness she had and tell him the truth, reveal that she was close to being out of work and a place to live.

But then she noticed just how incredulous he was. He really had no concept of what it meant to be completely at another's mercy. And for some reason, she was in no hurry to dispel his confusion. Besides, there was nothing he could do anyway. The very last thing her reputation needed was for him to show a real regard for her.

Carefully, she removed all expression from her face, turning it into a mask. "That was nothing you need to worry about, sir."

He gripped her arm. "Rosalind, the truth, now."

"No, now I must see to my job." Pasting a smile on her face, she murmured, "I have a dress to deliver, you see."

Only after she delivered the dress, walked down the hall, and finally was walking upstairs to her room did she let herself react to Veronica's words. With shaking hands, she wiped away the two tears that had dared to slip from the corners of her eyes. At last, something at Sloane House was now abundantly, beautifully clear. She would soon be out of a job.

The only question was when . . . and what she would do next.

CHAPTER 18

When Reid was twelve, he lost his brother. Calvin had come into the world four years after him, and though Reid would like to say he had welcomed his baby brother with open arms, that would surely be a lie.

From the time Calvin had been old enough to walk, he'd been determined to tag along after Reid. Reid had no choice but to accept his brother's company. However, he did his best to ignore him.

As the years passed, Reid came to notice something: Calvin was everything he was not. Whereas Reid was known to be impatient and selfish, Calvin was always willing to give of his time. In addition, ownership meant nothing to Calvin. He shared his toys, his food, his time, his attention with whoever needed it. Their little sister, Beth, two years younger than Calvin, adored him. She merely tried to stay out of Reid's way.

By the time Calvin was eight, there were many things about him of which his family could be proud. He loved sports and excelled in them. He was handsome too. Their mother used to say that Calvin's looks would garner them all nothing but trouble.

In fact, on more than one occasion, Reid remembered thinking that his brother had been gifted with a great many blessings in life. So many that it was sometimes hard not to be jealous. And Reid probably would have been jealous, except for the fact that Calvin did have one substantial flaw. Calvin was a liar.

Oh, not in a bad way, of course. What eight-year-old did terrible things? But he was the person who would never admit to being tired, or hungry, or in pain. He was always *fine*. Always.

He died because he hadn't admitted that he was sick.

For two days, he kept his illness to himself. He stayed in his room and pretended to study his readers when he was actually sleeping.

Beth was the one who noticed that Calvin's face was suspiciously flushed at dinner. Reid, of course, hadn't noticed. He'd been too pre-occupied with his friends and a certain girl who was inordinately fond of wearing blue ribbons in her hair.

When Beth mentioned Calvin's bright red cheeks, his mother took a better look at her younger son and noticed his glassy eyes. When she pressed her hand on his forehead, she realized Calvin had a high fever. A doctor was called. And that doctor confirmed that Calvin had contracted the influenza.

A panic arose in the house. Beth was sent away to stay with cousins. Reid—much to everyone's surprise—refused to leave his brother's side.

For the next twenty-four hours, he cajoled and bullied Calvin to drink the medicines and submit to cold baths to bring down the fever. His brother had done it all without complaint, but there was an acquiescence in his eyes that told Reid much. He accepted that there was no hope.

Finally, late the next evening, long after their parents had fallen into an exhausted slumber and the nurse had done the same, Calvin finally told Reid the truth.

"I'm going to die."

"No, you're not," Reid had countered. "And you'd better not say any of that again or Father is going to whip your behind." That had been their father's constant threat, though he'd yet to make good on the promise.

But even that reminder hadn't made Calvin smile. "No, Reid. I know I'm going to die soon. I've been talking to God and his angels for days now. They say I don't have much more time here."

Reid hadn't bothered to waste time pointing out that angels definitely did not talk to little boys about trips to heaven. Instead, he'd done his best to sound like their father. Stern. No-nonsense. "You listen to me, Calvin. You need to tell those angels that you're not ready to go. Promise them anything, Calvin."

"I already have. But they've made some promises too." With a stare that was far more mature than his eight years, Calvin spoke again. "The angels have promised to look out for you. They say you're destined for great things."

It had been all he could do to will the tears not to fall. "You are the family's hope, not me."

"That is where you are wrong." Calvin coughed, the effort racking his body. A flash of pure pain entered his eyes.

Reid helped him sit up, patted his back softly. "We don't need to talk about this anymore. You're supposed to be resting."

Calvin shook his head and glared. "No. No, Reid, I've gotta tell you this. The angels told me that you are going to make Mom and Dad real proud. Beth is going to depend on you. You're going to be real rich too."

"Calvin—"

"Listen," Calvin whined in a voice that was very un-Calvin-like. "You are going to do everything, Reid."

His brother's voice was so sure, his gaze so direct, Reid didn't have the heart to refute his words any longer. "If you believe it to be so, then I will do my best to do you proud."

"No, Reid. You have to *promise*. Promise you will do those things. All you have to do is promise."

"All right. I promise." Of course, what he didn't add was that he would have said anything for Calvin to lean back and rest.

Calvin had smiled then, a pure, angelic smile. It almost made Reid believe in angels after all. He coughed again, allowed Reid to pat his back and help him sip water, then he closed his eyes. He died an hour later.

That last conversation with Calvin was both Reid's best and worst memory of his childhood.

After that awful time, he'd tried harder to be patient. More generous. He looked after Beth more. He tried harder in his lessons. He tried harder in a hundred ways. And to his consternation, much of what Calvin had predicted would happen, did. He had a good life.

But now, as he walked down the front steps into the Sloanes' main drawing room, he realized that though he'd done much good, he'd still retained some of the selfish ways he had been born with.

Douglass Sloane was not a man Reid ever wanted to emulate. He'd symbolized his parents' hopes and dreams in the social realm, and Reid also knew that he owed him a great debt for his assistance in boarding school. But in the past year, his flaws had started to outweigh his strengths. He'd become increasingly degenerate and increasingly cavalier in his treatment of other people, especially women. His drinking had become constant, his pranks and amusements had become darker and more lurid.

Most of their original group had begun to distance themselves from Douglass, and Veronica was bearing the weight of those consequences. Men were wary of being associated with Douglass and therefore refused to even dance with her.

After a time, Veronica's softness had faded. Now, her desperation for an ideal match had given her a hard, almost lethal edge. Her tongue was cruel, and because of that, her beauty dulled. Little by little, she'd become a source of amusement for many of the women in their circle of friends. Meanness and pettiness did not garner much compassion for a person's flaws.

Now, as Reid watched Douglass, who was currently surrounded by a group of men who wouldn't have even gained entrance into the Sloane mansion two years ago, Reid knew it was time for him to break his ties with the family too.

Calling Douglass and Veronica Sloane friends was going to harm his sister's debut into society. And because he'd long ago promised Calvin, Reid knew he would do whatever it took to prevent anything to mar Beth's coming out.

It was time to leave.

Douglass looked up from the conversation he was having, caught his eye, and beckoned him forward. "Armstrong, are you going to simply stand there like a statue, or are you going to join us?"

"Pardon me." Right then and there, he knew this would be his last evening in the mansion. After tonight, he would distance himself.

Stepping next to Douglass, he greeted the other men with civil, if somewhat cool greetings. Douglass noticed his lack of enthusiasm. "Come now, gent. This is no way to treat family."

"What are you talking about?"

"My sister, of course." Douglass grinned at them all. "We all saw you dancing with her at the Upton house."

"One dance does not make an alliance," Reid countered lightly. "Though, of course, your sister is both charming and lovely."

The other men guffawed, making Reid flush. He had, perhaps, flowered a bit too much praise on Veronica.

"She is attractive, but has the disposition of a viper," Douglass retorted. "Though, perhaps, that will make her interesting to bed."

Douglass had just crossed the line. The other men froze, but said nothing.

It would be easiest to merely do the same. But, at last, Reid knew he could no longer hold his tongue. "I don't find your comments amusing. In fact, they're rather reprehensible."

Douglass looked mildly uncomfortable. "Reid, I fear your plebian roots are showing. Yet again. Come have a drink."

Reid was considering what to do next when he spied Veronica in the shadows of the hallway, close enough that she had to have heard her brother's caustic joke. "Excuse me," he murmured, then turned away.

Douglass chuckled. He apparently had seen her now as well. "See what I mean, gentlemen? He's smitten!" Reid let the comment fall behind him.

"Veronica, are you all right?"

She regarded him with a cool disdain. "Are you referring to my brother's penchant for announcing my charms?" She was prodding him to bring up the shameful comment, whether to embarrass him or her brother, he didn't know.

Suddenly, the evening was too much. Witnessing Veronica's treatment of Rosalind. Listening to Douglass's rude and tasteless words—and now Veronica's determination to pretend Reid was the one at fault because he'd had the nerve to actually refer to them.

"I do believe it's time I left. Please convey my regrets to your mother."

"Do you really have to leave us, Reid?" The words were banal but infused with a double meaning.

He ignored it. "I do. It's for the best, I think." He, too, could speak in half-truths.

A new acknowledgment, and, perhaps, respect, flooded her expression. "I see."

He turned before each felt it necessary to exchange simple words that held too much meaning. He left the room before Douglass caught sight of him and thought to wonder about his actions.

From the moment he departed the hallway, Reid felt lighter than he had in years. It was as if with that one decision, he had chosen to change the course of his life. Best, it was his decision for himself. Not out of obligation or guilt.

He strode across the Italian marble entryway, past the Chippendale credenza, past the exquisitely carved grandfather clock. Last of all, he passed Nanci, dressed in a freshly pressed uniform, looking pretty and formal in black and white. Her eyes widened as he passed, but she didn't say a word.

Just as he didn't acknowledge her.

He opened the door without the assistance of the footman and then quickly closed the door behind him with a smart click.

At long last, he had left Sloane House.

Looking around, he noticed that haziness had filled the early evening air, most likely from the increased number of trains in the city. It was thick with fog and smoke and the faint scent of trash and debris.

Just a block away a somewhat bedraggled flower girl was hawking roses to passersby. And Reid realized that the air had never smelled so sweet. He promptly bought a dozen roses for his mother. He had a feeling they would brighten her day immeasurably. And, perhaps, make Calvin pleased.

That was something, he supposed.

CHAPTER 19

She was late.

After running past a sneering Jerome and a disapproving Mr. Hodgeson, Rosalind darted to her room and hastily put on a freshly starched apron. Seconds after that she winced at her reflection in the mirror, then bit her lip as she took down her hair and hastily pinned it up again. She'd just pinned her cap on her head when Mrs. Abrams walked to the doorway.

"Ah, Rosalind. There you are."

"Yes, ma'am?"

Mrs. Abrams scanned Rosalind's form, taking in everything in one fell swoop, from her precariously pinned cap to her apron to her black boots, which were sorely in need of a shine. Her gaze softened before turning resolute.

"Mrs. Sloane would like to have a word with you. Come with me, please."

The request almost took Rosalind's breath away. Not trusting her voice, Rosalind silently followed the housekeeper through the maze of servants' rooms, through the thoroughly scrubbed dining area, along the narrow, windy hallway that led to the wine cellar, the silver room, and the laundry. A few servants paused as they passed. Some looked away; others stared at her with expressions of disbelief and disappointment.

Rosalind's stomach knotted as she prepared herself for the worst. Obviously, she was about to be let go. She only hoped and prayed that she would get a day to make other plans before she had to leave the estate.

As they walked up the steep flight of stairs to Mrs. Sloane's private study, Rosalind figured she had nothing to lose by asking Mrs. Abrams for information.

"Do you know what this is about, Mrs. Abrams?"

"I do."

Her voice was clipped, and those two words were filled with enough censure that Rosalind knew it would be pointless to ask another question. Obviously, she was not going to get any immediate answers.

When they entered the study, Rosalind saw that Mrs. Sloane sat at her desk, carefully penning letters. Mrs. Abrams practically stood at attention, waiting to be acknowledged.

"Yes, Abrams?" the lady finally murmured.

"I have brought Rosalind, as you requested. Is now still a good time for you to speak to her?"

At last Mrs. Sloane turned, her gray silk gown rustling with the motion. She studied both Rosalind and Mrs. Abrams, then nodded. "I suppose this is as good a time as it will ever be." As she crossed the room, she gestured toward a pair of upholstered chairs. "Please sit down."

Rosalind followed Mrs. Abrams' lead and took a chair, perching on the edge of the floral fabric.

Mrs. Sloane sat down as well, neatly arranging her skirts. After a lengthy pause, she looked at Rosalind with a vague expression of distaste. "I'm afraid there is no easy way to do this. It has come to my attention that you are suspected of stealing from my home."

It was all Rosalind could do to keep from gaping. "Beg pardon?"

"It would be best if you went ahead and told us the whole story instead of denying it," Mrs. Abrams said. "Lying will only make your situation worse."

"Ma'am," she sputtered. "I mean, Mrs. Sloane, I promise, I have never stolen anything from you, never taken a thing from this house." The words tumbled out faster. "I have never stolen anything in my life."

The housekeeper clucked her tongue. "Are you sure you are not mistaken?"

"I am positive! What have you heard?" Turning to Mrs. Sloane, Rosalind added, "Ma'am, what have you heard? What is it that is being said I stole?"

"Rosalind," Mrs. Abrams reprimanded. "Watch your tongue."

"I'm sorry. But I really have no idea . . ."

Mrs. Sloane's voice turned pained. "My daughter said you delivered her breakfast tray the other day. Is that true?"

"Yes, ma'am." She didn't understand what that had to do with anything.

"Veronica said she was asleep when you entered, but awoke long enough to watch you pocket one of her combs after you laid her tray on her desk."

"Her comb?"

"Veronica has, or rather had, a pair of tortoiseshell combs. Each is inlaid with silver and decorated with a spray of amethysts. They are not only very dear, but they have extreme sentimental value. They were a gift from her grandmother on her sixteenth birthday." Smoothing a hand down one of her sleeves, Mrs. Sloane murmured, "I'm sure you can understand how upset she was to discover one missing."

"Yes, ma'am. I can see that. But I did not touch them!" She stood up. "I promise, when I last delivered her tray, she was awake. I poured her not one but two cups of coffee."

"You will sit back down," Mrs. Abrams barked.

Rosalind did as she was told, but she felt as if every muscle in her body had turned to stone. After a moment, the housekeeper turned to Rosalind and asked, "Are you certain about this?"

"I am more than certain. I am positive. I would never steal from Miss Veronica or from anyone in the house. I need this job too much to do anything like that. Plus, that is not who I am. I am not a thief." Turning desperately to the housekeeper, Rosalind said plaintively, "Ma'am, you know how much I dislike delivering trays. I'm always afraid I'm going to drop one. Or not be able to open a door with my hands full. I wouldn't have even delivered the tray except that Cook said that Miss Veronica had specifically asked for me to take it up."

Mrs. Sloane looked taken aback. "I must admit that your story does sound very convincing."

"It is the truth. I'm afraid Miss Sloane is mistaken."

"Rosalind!" Mrs. Abrams hissed under her breath. "Remember your place."

Mrs. Sloane looked from one of them to the other, then seemed to make a decision. "Please wait here. I am going to get Veronica and see if we can make some sense of this story."

After she left, Rosalind pressed her hands to her eyes and tried to will them not to tear up. No good would come from crying. But she truly was scared. Beside her, the housekeeper seemed terribly agitated.

"I promise I didn't take anything," Rosalind pleaded. "I swear to you, if something is missing, it's not my doing."

"Why would Miss Veronica make up such a tale?"

Rosalind ached to tell everything she knew about Reid and Douglass and even Nanci. But that felt wrong. She didn't want to betray anyone else's confidences, especially since most of what she knew was based on rumor.

"I don't know," she said at last.

Mrs. Abrams pursed her lips, looked at Rosalind worriedly, but said nothing more.

A scant ten minutes later, Mrs. Sloane returned, followed by Veronica and Nanci. After a deep breath, she stood in front of Rosalind and folded her hands behind her back. "It seems there has been a slight misunderstanding."

Unable to stay seated, Rosalind slowly stood up once again. To her dismay, her legs were shaking. Though she had feared she would be dismissed, she was discovering that the idea of being fired and the actuality of losing her job and place to live were two different things. She was beyond frightened.

Unable to meet Mrs. Sloane's gaze, she held on to the armrest of the chair in hopes of steadying herself and stared at the floor. "Ma'am?"

"When I entered my daughter's room just now, Nanci was there, arranging her hair. And it seems the other comb was in a dresser drawer."

"In a drawer?" Rosalind cast an incredulous gaze on Veronica. Veronica was staring straight ahead. Mrs. Sloane now looked contrite.

"Well, um, it seems that Nanci recalled seeing it when she put away some of Veronica's stockings. The comb was not lost at all. It must have fallen in the drawer accidentally. I fear this has all been a silly misunderstanding."

A silly misunderstanding? Veronica had not only lied about her taking the comb, but she'd lied about what had happened in her room when Rosalind had given her the tray. Her mother had been ready to dismiss her without a recommendation. Mrs. Abrams had been content to accept the story and hadn't been going to do anything at all.

However, it seemed that she was expected to deal with the consequences without a word or an apology and go on her way.

"Thank you, ma'am," she said softly, feeling the irony in every pore.

Rosalind didn't dare look Veronica's way. She did glance at Nanci, though. But to her surprise, Nanci looked just as distant as the other women in the room did.

Mrs. Abrams stood as well and brushed her hands against each other as if the last half hour had sullied them. "I am glad this little confusion had a happy ending. Will that be all, ma'am?"

"It is. I am sorry for taking you two away from your duties."

Feeling as if she was in the midst of a storm, Rosalind meekly followed Mrs. Abrams out of the room and down the hall. Only when they were on the servants' stairwell did she say anything. "Mrs. Abrams, did you believe Veronica when she told her mother I'd taken that comb?"

"It didn't matter what I believed."

"But I hadn't done anything wrong. Veronica was lying. And Mrs. Sloane didn't even apologize."

"Why should she? She is the lady of the house, and it seems as if it was an honest mistake."

Not ready to give up her indignation, she blurted, "Veronica made up the story."

Mrs. Abrams turned on her heel. "Listen to me, girl," she said, impatience lacing her tone. "Over time, you will find that there might be a great many things the family does that you might not agree with. That is the drawback of being in service. You learn far too many secrets about a family. But our place is certainly not to judge."

Though she knew she was letting her temper get away from her,

Rosalind couldn't hold back the onslaught of words. "But if Nanci hadn't found the comb, I would have been fired without a reference."

"That is true."

Rosalind stopped. "But what would have become of me then? I wouldn't be able to get another job. I would have been forced to live on the streets."

"That is why you must always make very sure that your conduct and demeanor are beyond reproach." A thread of impatience tinged Mrs. Abrams' voice then, as if she had seen something very important and she was frustrated by Rosalind's inability to see it. "Rosalind, it is time you understood that you must be on guard at all times. Stop running late. Stop taking so many risks. Stop talking to Mr. Armstrong. Become worthy of the job you hold." She paused, then wagged a finger. "And most of all, remember that there is no one in this house you can trust."

That sounded overly dramatic. Gathering her gumption, Rosalind raised a brow. "You mean to say I can't even trust Mrs. Sloane herself?"

"No one," she whispered before turning away, leaving Rosalind with even more questions and feeling as if she'd already lost something valuable that she'd never get back—her reputation.

Hours later, when she was brushing out her hair, Rosalind turned to her roommate. "Nanci, I truly am so grateful that you found that comb. Thank you so much."

"I certainly didn't do it for you. Miss Veronica needed the second comb for her hair."

Rosalind smiled, sure her friend was joking.

But if anything, Nanci only looked more sullen. "Rosalind, since you've been here, you've done nothing but start trouble. You're not a good fit, and I'm not the only person here who thinks so. The truth is, I wouldn't have been sorry if you'd been asked to leave."

"That's a terrible thing to say."

"It may be hard to hear, but it's the truth."

Rosalind searched her friend's face. "Nanci, won't you ever tell me what happened with Douglass?"

The skin around Nanci's lips tightened. "I have no idea what you are talking about."

"Come now. We both know that something happened on Wooded Island. If you'd like to talk about—"

Nanci cut her off with a scowl. "Rosalind, I might have once tried to be your friend, but we are not friends now. You've brought a lot of havoc into my life. I'll be civil to you, but let me be clear. I no longer want to converse. You should know that I've talked to Mrs. Abrams and asked to share a room with someone else as soon as possible."

Too hurt to reply, Rosalind turned away and climbed into bed. Minutes later, Nanci extinguished their light, blanketing their room in darkness. For a brief selfish moment, Rosalind ached to give in to self-pity and let the tears form. Everything was going so poorly and her parents and brothers had put their faith in her.

Now, more than ever, she was completely alone.

Dear Lord, she prayed. *I don't know what to pray for that you don't already know about. You know I have tried everything I can think of to discover Miranda's whereabouts. But every road seems to bring me to a dead end. Now I am at my wit's end. I've alienated everyone, and it's obvious I'm completely alone. I simply don't know what to do any longer.*

She was just about to close her eyes when she realized something very important. She wasn't alone. She wasn't alone, and she never had been.

No matter what happened with her mission, no matter what happened with her position at Sloane House or with Nanci, with her search, or even with her beginning friendship with Reid, there was One who was always there.

Just as he was for Miranda.

Little by little, the tension in her shoulders eased and a smooth sense of peace covered her. Grateful, she felt tears sting her eyes as she drifted off to sleep.

Unaware when Nanci got up and walked out of the room.

CHAPTER 20

For the last few weeks, instead of sending the majority of her money home to her parents, Rosalind had kept half. She felt bad about that. She knew her siblings needed new shoes and clothes and her parents had lots of bills to pay.

But a sixth sense told her it was important to keep some money aside for a rainy day. Her situation at Sloane House felt too precarious to not be prepared for any sort of problem. Yesterday's events only reinforced that.

With some of the portion she kept, she bought another ticket to the fair. She also hid some cash in the lining of her boot. If she suddenly did get dismissed, she didn't want to be worrying about how she was going to eat or find shelter. At least not immediately.

━━

Rosalind went to the World's Fair on her next day off. This time, she didn't mention where she was going to anyone. Things had gone from bad to worse with Nanci, and though no one had actually said anything, Rosalind felt a shift in everyone's attitudes toward her—as if she hadn't been completely innocent when Veronica claimed she'd seen her steal her tortoiseshell comb.

After paying the entrance fee, she went directly to the Manufactures and Liberal Arts Building. It was not only the largest building, but also had the distinction of being the only structure that held booths from almost every state and country present at the Columbian Exposition. Rosalind figured if Miranda had gotten mixed up with someone at the fair, there was a good chance that someone in that building might have seen her.

She was wrong.

In fact, three hours later, she was regretting her decision. She'd forgotten that thousands of people visited the fairgrounds every day, and during that time, exhibitors were busy talking to visitors. No one had time to scan the crowds and look at women.

Still, she tried. Over and over, she interrupted conversations, asked for help, and explained that her sister was missing. But no matter how many people she showed Miranda's photograph to, no one recognized her sister. In fact, the only response she'd gotten had been lewd offers.

After a pair of workers from the Ireland cubicle followed her for several minutes, Rosalind left the building. Outside, the air was warm and humid. Almost stagnant.

She left the fairgrounds in a haze of disappointment. She was running out of ideas for whom to contact about Miranda, but she was not eager to rush back to Sloane House. But she stepped on a trolley and took it back toward Michigan Avenue.

By now she was familiar with grip cars and was even more used to the ebb and flow of big-city life. Now she had a better sense of whom to avoid completely. In addition, she'd begun to be invigorated by the noises and sights of Chicago. She was intrigued by the many people from different backgrounds, amused by the way everyone—no matter what economic level they were on—was able to mingle and meander together. An energy was present that didn't exist in the countryside of Wisconsin.

After helping a very scared tourist on the trolley with directions, Rosalind realized she'd come full circle. Now, instead of avoiding crowds, she sought them. Instead of only looking to associate with people just like her, she was finding joy in meeting folks who were far different. She was worlds apart from the shy, timid girl who'd arrived at Sloane House with only a hope and a prayer of discovering what had happened to her sister. Somehow, some way, she'd come into her own.

And she was grateful for that, she realized. Even if she still failed in her efforts to discover what had happened to Miranda, she was thankful for the opportunity to grow as a person. So few people had been given opportunities like the one she'd received.

She traveled a quarter of an hour, then hopped off the trolley and stepped into a candy store. Giving in to temptation, she bought a small bag of peppermints. After popping one in her mouth, she decided to avoid the street car for a bit and walk to Sloane House.

The peppermints kept her happy as she strolled down one block, then two. Just as she crossed another intersection, a fight broke out on the street.

It began in an instant, with the force of lightning. First there was calm, then within seconds a noisy fray broke out. Fists began to fly, curses were screamed, clothing was torn. Within seconds, the altercation that had started between two men quickly turned into a noisy brawl that encompassed at least twelve ruffians.

Rosalind became frightened as the fight grew more violent. She noticed other women, men, and children taking great care to move far out of the fight's perimeters. Thinking that was the right decision, she darted into the first open door she saw, the open door to a beautiful stone church.

The entrance loomed like the first sign of hope she'd been aware of in ages. The cool vestibule felt like a long-forgotten hug, easing her muscles. Encouraging her to relax, gently reminding her to take time to pray.

As her eyes adjusted to the dim light, she walked slowly inside, becoming aware of the strong sense of peace that surrounded her, melding in with the dim light, infusing her senses with the scents of incense, candles, and lemon oil.

Her pulse seemed to slow as she breathed in deep. A few fortifying breaths eased her soul.

And then she heard the music.

A choir, made up of an odd assortment of forty men and women, was practicing in the front of the church. Each person held a red leather hymnal in his or her hands. Some were older, some looked to be barely out of school. By their clothing, it was apparent that they came from all walks of life. However, their faces were united in the joy each felt by their combined voices.

And what harmonies, indeed! Rosalind closed her eyes and let the melodious mix of voices float over her. They were singing an old hymn, "How Great Thou Art." It was a familiar song, close to her mother's heart. Her mother had sung it more than once while cooking in the kitchen by herself.

Rosalind had always thought she knew the hymn and was familiar with the way it made her feel. But everything she knew was a sad comparison to the purity of the choir's voices as they melded like the voices of angels.

She was mesmerized.

Sitting down on the first empty pew, she eased back against the worn oak, took comfort in the solitude.

The voices rose in the last chorus, held the last notes for countless seconds, then finally faded. After the last note rang out, the stark return of silence seemed too dark in comparison.

"That was pretty good, everyone. But that last little bit needed some work, don't you think?"

Rosalind opened her eyes and listened incredulously as the choir director played a few bars on the organ. "Do you hear the difference? Yes? No?"

The choir members made a variety of disparaging noises. Some looked the way she felt, as if it was difficult to outdo perfection.

Smiling broadly, she entertained herself with watching the members struggle to keep their opinions to themselves as the director continued, admonishing them for not practicing enough, for not staying on beat, even for not enunciating more clearly.

A few people in the choir noticed her amusement and grinned back at her, seeming to enjoy the novelty of having a kindred spirit on their side in the audience.

And then she caught one man's eye and her heart skipped a beat. There, in the middle of this mismatched choir run by a temperamental director, stood Reid Armstrong.

The moment he recognized her, his expression changed from vaguely amused to concerned. After murmuring something to the man on his left, he walked down to see her.

"Mr. Armstrong. Beg pardon, Mr. Armstrong!" the director called out.

Reid stopped. "Sir?"

"Beg pardon, but you have not yet been dismissed."

"I'm sorry, Deacon Thomas," he said with a little bow. "But there is someone in the audience I must speak with."

Deacon Thomas looked over his shoulder in surprise, spied her, then smiled. "Is that the way of it, then? Well, don't tarry too long, sir."

A few of the older women tittered as Reid kept walking.

Rosalind felt her face heat. For a moment she considered standing up, but then fearing that it might draw even more attention their way, she stayed seated until he scooted in next to her.

"Rosalind, what a surprise! Are you okay? Is something wrong?" he asked, each word tumbling over the next. "How did you know I was here?"

"I didn't! There was a fray outside. The crowd got rather big and rowdy quickly. I darted in the church to escape."

Looking concerned, he reached out for her gloved hand. "Did anyone accost you? Were you hurt?" Gently, he placed her hand between his own.

Even through her glove, she could feel the warmth of his touch. "N—not at all."

Noticing her stammer, he leaned forward, bringing with him his scent of balsam and cologne. "Are you certain?"

How could she ever reveal that it was his touch and concern—and not the noise of a crowd—that had her on pins and needles? "I am perfectly fine."

Afraid he would notice how affected she was by his touch, she gently pulled her hand away and straightened her spine a bit. "Anyway, I entered the church for my safety. But it was your chorus of voices that drew me in. You all sounded lovely."

"I'm afraid our esteemed director doesn't quite agree."

She thought about that. "I have never been part of a chorus, of course, but I imagine that being exacting is every choir director's job."

"I fear you are right." He looked at her sheepishly. "I am ashamed to say that sometimes we egg him on. Getting him on his high horse can be quite fun. He is usually the quietest of men."

She nodded toward the man speaking to the group. Deacon Thomas kept looking over at Reid in an irritated way. "Unless you are agitating him on purpose, I think you should return to your place. He is missing you."

"I will. And what will you do?"

"Oh, I'll check outside in another moment or two. If the brawl is over, I'll go on my merry way." She leaned forward. "I have the whole afternoon off. Three more hours."

"Then I insist you stay for the rest of the practice and allow me to walk you home."

She knew, of course, that she felt too happy about his invitation. It wouldn't do for her to get any closer to him. Especially when she considered Veronica's threats. "I'm not sure if that is a good idea."

"Please reconsider. It's rare that we are away from the many prying eyes and ears at Sloane House. Plus, we have many things to discuss." His face became shadowed. "Some things have happened recently that you might not know about."

Thinking of Veronica accusing her of stealing and Nanci's refusal to talk about what had happened between her and Douglass, Rosalind nodded. "I, too, have news."

"Mr. Armstrong?" Deacon Thomas called out, his voice now tinged with impatience. "Do you intend to return to us anytime soon?"

"Yes, Deacon," Reid said after a quick wink in her direction. "I am sorry for the disruption." He scooted off the pew and trotted back to his place in the choir.

Rosalind couldn't help but smile as she leaned back and watched him take his place. He really was the most wonderful of men. Kind to her, recklessly full of fun with deacons. Suave and debonair with the ladies and gentlemen of his station.

As she realized that one day he would find his wife among those ladies, she felt a bit deflated. It would be so nice to imagine that their alliance could continue for years and years. Oh, she certainly didn't entertain any hopes that everything that kept them apart would suddenly not matter. She was too much of a realist now to ever think that.

But she did like to think that they'd become friends of a sort. Simply put, she enjoyed his company, and she had a feeling he felt the same way about hers. But once her mission was concluded, their alliance would fade. No bride of his would understand a friendship with another woman.

And even if she did, it certainly wouldn't be the same. They would have lost their reason for being friends. Before long, their conversation would falter into meaningless comments about the weather and the state of their health.

And their former friendship would be merely something she recalled with a slight, surprised skip of her heart. Wondering if she'd simply imagined their alliance was something more than it ever was.

Perhaps she was even doing that now?

The thought gave her pause and embarrassed her. As the deacon raised his hands and led both the organist and the choir into another hymn, Rosalind scooted a bit farther into the center of the pew where the light from the open doorway didn't skim her skirts. Where she could sit in the shadows, alone with her thoughts.

Desperately hoping that Reid wouldn't be able to discern her thoughts from where he stood.

CHAPTER 21

Reid couldn't help but continually glance toward Rosalind. Sitting by herself in the middle of a lonely pew, she looked more fragile than ever.

And, he realized, beautiful.

Wearing a smart-looking bonnet instead of the usual servant's white cap, her dark mahogany hair shone against the dark wood behind her. Her simple dress, devoid of lace, bric-a-brac, or beadwork, emphasized her slim figure.

It took everything he had to stay on task and keep his attention on the choral director's directives and the complicated musical score they were learning. Still, he fooled no one.

"Who is the lady?" Andrew Biltmore whispered when the deacon was correcting the sopranos' stanza.

"Merely a friend."

"Surely she is more?" he said, lowering his voice. "She came to your rehearsal, after all."

"She's here by happenstance. There was a ruckus outside. A few men started an argument and several others joined in. She stepped inside for safety, then was drawn in by our music."

Andrew looked like he was torn between skepticism at the story and gratification about their chorus bringing in an audience. "It's your lucky day then." He grinned. "Where did you meet her? At one of your many parties or dances?"

Reid shook his head. Andrew was a junior lawyer in a small legal firm. Not of his social class. While he was socially acceptable, he wasn't part of one of the families that attended the balls. He was certainly nowhere near Douglass Sloane's social status, or Reid's for that matter. But that said, Andrew was quite a bit beyond the servant class.

And that meant Andrew would be shocked and not a bit dismayed to imagine that Reid was courting a housemaid. Young men generally hoped to marry up, after all. Reid instinctively knew Andrew wouldn't understand a mere friendship between them, either. And to betray Rosalind's confidence was unthinkable.

Luckily, Deacon Thomas didn't give them any further time to speak. He raised his arms and had them begin the last section of the hymn from the very beginning.

Forty minutes later, the deacon dismissed the group, they said their good-byes, and Reid was escorting Rosalind down the busy street. Horses and their carriages trotted by, their clip-clopping hooves mixing in with the jangle of the trolley bells in the distance.

"You are a wealth of surprises, Mr. Armstrong," Rosalind said with a smile. "I would have never imagined you as part of a church chorus."

Reid was used to the comment. He'd known when he joined the choir that his choice of activities would be questioned, but he'd found that his enjoyment of the group far outweighed any negative comments. However, he was still interested to hear her reasons for the statement.

"What surprised you? My singing in a church or the company I was keeping?"

"Both." She paused, obviously choosing her words with care. "I had no idea you could sing. And while I don't see myself as an authority on the upper classes, I didn't imagine church—or church functions—were seen as important."

He pondered that as he kept to her right, taking her arm as a pair of unruly boys scampered down the sidewalk on her left. "I'm a Christian," he said at last. "It's as much who I am as the color of my eyes or the fact that I'm left-handed. My mother is very devout. She raised me to have the Lord in my life. I'm grateful for that."

"And your father?" she asked as they paused at an intersection.

He thought about that. "His faith is important to him as well, though I must admit that he was never one to openly embrace his faith. Usually it was just an understood thing."

Determined to get to know her better, he looked into her eyes. "What about you?"

"Me?"

"Yes. It's only fair that you get to have your share of questions," he teased. "Were you raised with religion?"

"Yes, but it wasn't so formal. We have a community church, but it takes over an hour to get to it. Living on a farm as we do, my folks couldn't always take off so much time, not even on Sundays."

"You mean to say that your animals haven't heard of a day of rest?"

She chuckled. "Oh, they've taken the resting part to heart. They just haven't come around to thinking that we need to take time off too." She shook her head in mock sorrow. "No matter how much I've talked to the pigs, they still want to eat every day."

His lips twitched, enjoying her humor. "So what do you do instead?"

"We have church at home. My father reads from the Bible. We pray together. We talk about our week and our dreams. Talk about where we see the Lord calling us."

"That sounds nice," he murmured, meaning it. "I like the idea of making things simple."

"It is simple, but it is certainly nice too." She smiled. "One of the benefits of growing up in a large family is that there are a lot of us to contribute to any discussion. Sometimes we agree. Sometimes we don't. But no matter what, those moments together in our family room? When we're all seated and discussing the Lord's Book? It brings us closer together."

"You've been blessed."

"I think so." Glancing at him, she added, "But there is something awe-inspiring about sitting in a pew and listening to a choir. It was beautiful."

"I'm rather new. I've only been there a year. But I do like it. As you noticed, our choir is made up of all sorts of people."

"Mainly middle-class folks?"

"Yes."

"And that doesn't bother you?"

"Not at all. My roots are firmly middle class. Besides, I like knowing all sorts of people." He smiled, hoping she'd realize he included her in that group.

She smiled back at him then, just as a group of four schoolgirls walked by. Their chatter was loud and their need to stand four-across made it necessary for Reid to pull Rosalind close to his side, almost against the plastered wall of a bank building.

With that step, she was so close that he could smell the faint scent of lemons in her hair.

His hand curved around a trim waist that felt only slightly corseted.

Surprised, she gazed up at him. Her lips were slightly parted, her eyes beckoning him. If they were alone, he knew he'd be tempted to kiss her.

Which, of course, would be a terrible mistake. No matter how much he enjoyed her company, nothing more personal could ever erupt between them. Definitely nothing romantic.

All he was doing now was helping a friend in need. Being a Christian. Nothing less.

Because there could definitely be nothing more.

Rosalind soon discovered that not only had her walk with Reid been observed by some of the other servants, but apparently, according to Mrs. Abrams, it had also been commented upon by one of Mrs. Sloane's acquaintances.

Less than an hour after she returned, she felt the effects.

At the servants' table that evening, everyone from the scullery maid to Mrs. Abrams herself treated her with a bit of disdain. By the time they had finished the main course, Rosalind was feeling stung and more than a bit defensive.

"Mr. Armstrong merely walked me back. That is all," she said for the third or fourth time. "As I've told you all, I darted into his church to escape quite a ruckus."

Nanci sniffed. "Don't you sound all high-and-mighty now, needing a fine gentleman to accompany you on the sidewalks."

Cook cast a sharp glance her way. "Getting a bit above ourselves, are we, Rosalind?"

Emma raised a shoulder. "Maybe he's sweet on her."

"Of course he is not," Rosalind protested. "Mr. Armstrong was merely being kind."

Jerome scoffed as he pulled over a dish and helped himself to a heaping portion of raspberry trifle. "Swells do that sort of thing with their ladybirds. If that's what you are, you should just say it. You wouldn't be the first girl to compromise herself for a bit of fun."

Rosalind didn't need a mirror to know that her face was now beet red. "I have not compromised myself. I've done nothing wrong."

"Well, your behavior has once again become suspect," Mrs. Abrams said. "I'm afraid I'll have to speak with Mrs. Sloane about this."

Rosalind felt heat leave her body and become replaced with what felt like ice. She turned her head, hoping to catch Nanci's eye. But Nanci was as determined as ever to ignore her. She had gotten up, poured herself a cup of coffee, and was now leaning against the door frame. Distancing herself yet again.

Rosalind knew she was now truly, completely alone. She sat without speaking another word until Mr. Hodgeson excused the table. After taking her dishes into the scullery, she escaped to her room, glad that it was still technically her day off.

She read a book she'd borrowed from the home's library off and on for the next hour, half waiting for Nanci to enter their room. But as the hours passed, it became apparent that Nanci was in no hurry to spend any time with her at all.

Rosalind wondered what Nanci was doing. Was she spending time with the other women servants? Or was she attending Veronica?

Or was she spending yet more time with Douglass even though Rosalind was still sure he had hurt her that day at the fair?

Rosalind hated that such things were even going through her mind. But that was what she'd been reduced to, she decided. She was afraid and running out of time. When the housekeeper spoke to Mrs. Sloane, Rosalind knew she would be let go.

At last, she closed her eyes and willed herself to go to sleep.

Early the next morning, Rosalind rose, noting that everything around her still looked the same. She was startled to see that Nanci's bed was already neatly made. Rosalind didn't recall her roommate returning during the night, but she also realized that she'd slept like the dead.

Checking the simple clock on their shared chest of drawers, Rosalind winced. She'd awoken ten minutes later than usual! Nanci probably had dressed in a flash and was already going about her duties.

Not wanting to be thought of as neglecting her duties, too, Rosalind dressed as quickly as she ever had, then hurried below stairs. After a quick breakfast eaten in silence, she prepared trays for Cook, then was sent to clean the main parlors. Next, she helped with a dozen other tasks, all the while feeling the other servants' judgmental eyes on her.

It was almost a relief when Mrs. Abrams summoned her to another meeting with her and Mrs. Sloane. She walked behind the housekeeper, keeping her eyes on the floor in front of her so she wouldn't have to see anyone's expression as they passed.

At last they arrived at Mrs. Sloane's private drawing room. "Mind your manners today, Rosalind," Mrs. Abrams cautioned.

"Yes, ma'am." Oh, she would watch her tongue. But she also realized that she now had very little to lose. Already she was being judged for her actions when she knew that in truth she hadn't done anything wrong. Slowly, she raised her head and stood a bit straighter.

"Mrs. Sloane, I've brought Rosalind in," the housekeeper announced.

"So I see. Both of you, please come in and sit down," Mrs. Sloane said. Her voice sounded strained. Perhaps a little aggrieved too.

Feeling more than a bit confused, Rosalind sat.

After a sigh, Mrs. Sloane said, "Rosalind, it has come to my attention that you have continued to push the boundaries of acceptability. Definitely below the expectations of this household." Staring hard at Rosalind, she paused. Obviously, she was waiting for Rosalind to protest or defend herself.

Rosalind said nothing, though. She was feeling rather tired of defending herself to both Mrs. Sloane and the other servants in the household. She was also becoming weary of being told to act in an acceptable way while both Douglass and Veronica were allowed to behave so poorly. Though she wasn't the green, naive girl she'd been when she first arrived at the house, it still smarted a bit to be on the losing end of such a double standard.

Mrs. Sloane raised her brows at Rosalind's silence, cleared her throat, then spoke, her voice even darker and more disapproving. "Under normal circumstances, we would be asking for you to leave. Unfortunately, I'm afraid that isn't going to be possible."

"Why?" Rosalind asked.

The housekeeper intercepted Mrs. Sloane's answer and answered with a sigh. "It seems that Nanci has left us. Being her roommate, we were hoping you could shed some light on her disappearance."

She leaned forward, completely jolted. "What? Was this planned?"

"Did she not share any of her plans with you?"

"No, ma'am. I'm afraid we haven't been talking too much. We had a falling out."

Both women sent Rosalind looks that signaled they weren't in the least surprised. "When did you last see her?" Mrs. Sloane asked.

"Last night at the servants' dinner."

"She didn't come to your room last evening?"

"She hadn't by the time I went to sleep."

"And this didn't alarm you?" Mrs. Sloane looked incredulous.

"I thought maybe she was attending Miss Veronica late last night.

Sometimes we catch catnaps in the servants' sitting room while wait-ing to be called to help undress hair or prepare bedrooms."

She didn't dare add that she'd wondered if Nanci could have been with Douglass for at least part of the night. It didn't seem in character for Nanci, but certainly stranger things had happened in the house, and more than one footman told tales of helping women slip out the door in the early morning hours.

"I see," Mrs. Sloane murmured, though it was obvious she didn't believe her.

Mrs. Abrams studied Rosalind. "And what about this morning? Do you really mean to say that you didn't see her at all?"

"I woke up about ten minutes late, and noticed right away that Nanci's bed was neatly made."

"And did you remark on it to Cook? To anyone downstairs?"

"I'm afraid I did not." Nerves threatened to get the best of her. Her hands started to shake a bit. Not wanting the other women to see how affected she was by Nanci's disappearance—and by their disdain—Rosalind clasped her hands tightly together.

When she caught her composure, she said, "I assumed that Nanci had risen before me and had gone to do her duties. As I said, we had a disagreement and had been avoiding each other."

"Before I went to fetch you," Mrs. Abrams informed her, "I went to your room and inspected it. Her clothes have been removed. She must have packed up her things in the middle of the night."

On one hand, that gave Rosalind a bit of relief. Surely Nanci wouldn't have packed a bag if she'd been in danger. But on the other hand, she thought about Douglass and the way Nanci had looked at him—at least before the incident at Wooded Island. Was she— still?—so smitten that she would do anything he asked of her . . . even become his mistress?

Her imagination continued to run wild. Perhaps someone from the fair had lured her away. Perhaps at this very moment Nanci was trapped in an impossible situation, just waiting for someone, anyone, to help her.

"Do you think she is all right?" she blurted. "Should we ask the police to become involved?"

"We shall do no such thing," Mrs. Abrams said sharply.

"But she could be in danger."

The housekeeper's gray eyes flashed. "You are forgetting yourself, Rosalind."

Rosalind knew she was stepping out of bounds. But there was still that knowledge that Nanci was the only person in the house to whom she'd told her suspicions about Miranda. Had Nanci said something to the wrong person? "I am merely concerned about Nanci."

"I understand your concern, but I am afraid it is misplaced." Mrs. Sloane raised a reprimanding brow. "A missing housemaid, especially one who has packed her bags, is certainly no reason to set up an alarm to the authorities. Besides, what would we say, exactly? That she left without telling us good-bye?"

Rosalind tucked her chin. Afraid again of acting the fool. "I just don't want anything to happen to her. That's all."

"What we must concentrate on now is you," Mrs. Abrams said sharply. "As Mrs. Sloane stated previously, we would ordinarily ask you to leave immediately. However, since Nanci left without notice, we cannot spare you."

Rosalind felt her throat tightening, though whether it was in relief or fear of her future, she didn't know.

"I don't think you understand. Be assured that just as soon as I hire a replacement and ascertain she is acclimated to the household, you will be given your notice. Your days here are numbered, Rosalind."

"I—I understand." She was eager to leave the room, eager to fig-ure out what happened to Nanci. But then she remembered Minerva, standing at the corner selling flowers. And she knew what she had to do.

"If there was a woman interested in the job, could she simply knock on the door for an interview?" She glanced back and forth between the two women.

Mrs. Sloane deferred the question to Mrs. Abrams with a nod.

The housekeeper thawed a bit to answer. "We'll be using a place-ment agency. But we might also place an ad in the paper. Lately, the agency hasn't been sending us the best of candidates. Why do you ask?"

"I have met a woman who used to be a lady's maid."

"And?"

"And . . . I would hope that you might give her a chance."

"Your tenacity knows no bounds, Rosalind." The housekeeper shook her head. "We will absolutely not start meeting with stray women you've met."

"Please! She's nothing like me. She might be a good fit. I simply thought that perhaps she could apply."

"She may apply, Rosalind," Mrs. Sloane allowed. "But I will point out that a reference from you would not be the best idea."

"Yes, ma'am." Without waiting to be excused, Rosalind stood up and walked out of the room. She was tired of following rules that didn't apply to everyone. Tired of living in fear. Tired of worrying about her future.

Actually, she was just plain tired.

CHAPTER 22

For all her good intentions, Rosalind had no opportunity to run to the corner to discuss employment with Minerva. She also had no time to do any investigating about Miranda's or even Nanci's disappearance. Whatever the reason for Nanci's departure, it had created an enormous amount of work for the remaining staff at Sloane House.

Nanci had been extremely talented at arranging Mrs. Sloane's hair. Because neither she nor Veronica wanted Rosalind dressing their hair, Emma and Emily had been asked to do it. This, of course, necessitated that other servants perform the usual duties of the parlor maids.

And because Mrs. Sloane had been more vocal than usual about the disruption in the house, Mrs. Abrams had felt obligated to double check everyone's work. Like a game of dominoes, her actions determined everyone else's behavior. Her stress made her usually clear directives jumbled and disjointed. That, in turn, had set both Cook and Mr. Hodgeson off.

And because those leaders felt out of sorts, their instructions to the rest of the kitchen staff, coachmen, and footmen turned clipped and impatient. They barked commands, scolded over minor accidents, and everyone's tempers rested on increasingly short fuses.

For those two days, the house—a stressful place on the best of days—had begun to feel like an extremely luxurious workhouse. None of the servants had time off. Nerves continued to fray, tensions rose, and more accidents happened. And because everyone needed to point a finger at someone, Rosalind was their favorite target.

Dora had not been shy about telling everyone who would listen that she was sure Rosalind's falling out with Nanci had fueled her departure. Jerome gossiped to anyone who would listen as well.

Knowing there was nothing she could say to turn their opinions of her, Rosalind kept to herself as much as possible. For those two days, she worked silently and as efficiently as she could. But more chores and duties than she would ever have time for were heaped on Rosalind's slim shoulders.

Ironically, the hard work and tense atmosphere were improving her domestic skills. Rosalind could now clean a fireplace and lay a new set of logs faster and more efficiently than almost anyone in the house. She could also iron dresses perfectly, lay out breakfast trays expertly, and put a room to rights for guests in a matter of minutes.

She could tell her improvements had been noted but had also been viewed with a type of resignation with which one might imbibe medicinal syrup. It was appreciated, but not enjoyed.

In the midst of all the drama and isolation, one person did make an effort to befriend her. To her dismay it was Douglass Sloane.

At least once each day—sometimes more—he sought her out and spoke to her kindly. To her shame, she found herself looking forward to these visits, sometimes even enjoying his company. She tried to tell herself she shouldn't say a word to him. That he likely had something to do with Nanci's disappearance and perhaps even her sister's disappearance. But even though there were countless reasons to avoid him, she still found herself talking to him when he spoke to her, a smile on his handsome face.

"Rosalind, you are the proverbial busy bee these days. Are they even letting you sleep?" he'd asked just a few hours earlier. She'd been walking back to the kitchens after delivering a coffee service and tray of pastries to Mrs. Sloane's study. "Every time I turn around, I see you walking to and fro with a purpose."

"It's because I have been walking purposefully, sir," she quipped. "Your household is a busy place."

He leaned against the wall of the narrow hallway. With his body positioned like that, and his direct gaze seeming to prevent her from looking anywhere else, Rosalind at last felt like she counted, like someone was paying attention to her and she was worth something.

"Are they working you too hard, dear?"

The endearment caught her off guard. "No, sir."

"Sir? It's Douglass, remember." His voice softened. "Is there anything I may do for you? I would be happy to ask Mrs. Abrams to go a little lighter on you."

"Please don't." She knew—even if he didn't—that her days at Sloane House were almost at an end. As soon as Mrs. Sloane could replace her, she would.

Before she knew what he was about, he reached for her hand and held it between his own hands. Neither was wearing gloves, of course. And her rough skin with the chewed cuticles and short nails looked even more frightful than they usually did. "Your hands . . ." His voice drifted off as he inspected them.

Standing across from him, so close, she felt the first flicker of unease, and the realization that once again, she'd been such a fool. Of course she'd been happy for his attentions because she'd been so lonely.

But that didn't change the fact that there was something dark and almost sinister about him. Something that made a lump in her throat ache and all her senses wake up and take notice. He was a dangerous man.

A dangerous man wrapped up in a beautiful, desirable package. But still, she was afraid of him.

He didn't let go of her hand. Still staring at it, he ran one finger along her knuckles. "Have you figured out yet what happened to Nanci?" he asked.

His voice was deceptively casual. Unnervingly direct. Though he still hadn't met her gaze, she felt his regard as intently as if he was staring straight at her. When she said nothing, his grip tightened. It didn't hurt, but she would have a difficult time freeing her hand without pulling hard to get it free.

"Are you going to answer?" he murmured in that easy, silky way he spoke. "Or attempt to ignore me?"

Apprehension hit her hard. His question felt like a test of sorts. It was obvious that he was waiting for the right reply. Waiting for her to tell him what he wanted to know.

If only she knew what that was.

"I don't know anything," she answered at last.

He raised his chin. Stared at her. His eyes were dark and cold. Sharp, like a reptile's.

"I do."

"Sir—"

He ran his hand up her arm, finally digging his fingers into the soft skin right above her elbow. "It's Douglass, remember? Now, why don't you tell me what's been going on in that pretty head of yours."

"Sir, the truth is that we . . . Nanci and I had a falling out. She wouldn't speak to me about you," Rosalind said in a rush. "I asked her about what happened between the two of you at the fair, but she wouldn't tell me."

"So you were curious? What, exactly, did you want to know?"

She felt her body tremble. With her arm in his tight grip, she knew he felt her tremors too.

A new light entered his eyes. It looked a bit like amusement, a bit like pleasure.

She had no choice but to answer. "Only if she was okay. And if she was in love with you," she improvised quickly.

He dropped her arm. "She was not in love. Not with me, anyway. But surely you had to have known that."

"I knew nothing. She refused to say a word."

"Were you jealous of her happiness?"

Happiness? She shook her head. "No, sir. I—I just was worried about her. That's all."

"So many women leaving our house. First Miranda, then Tilly. Now Nanci. I wonder who will be next?"

She was scared. Frightened. But she couldn't back down now. "Douglass, d—did you know Miranda well?"

It was as if he'd been prodded with a stick. He stepped back in a hurry. "I knew her well enough."

"Do you know what happened to her?"

A line formed between his brows as he studied her a bit more closely. "I gave Nanci funds to leave. To go back to her family," he said, suddenly changing the subject back to Nanci.

"You did?"

His lip curled in distaste. "She was in a family way, it seems." He sighed. "I suppose it couldn't be helped. Anyway, I gave her funds and she left. We, uh, both decided it would be best if no one else knew. Now this secret is your burden too. But of course if you tell, you'll ruin her reputation forever, and that would be such a terrible thing." He paused. "Don't you agree?"

"Yes, yes, sir."

Almost imperceptibly, his posture relaxed. "I'm so glad we understand each other now. Do be careful of your curiosity, Rosalind. It killed the cat, you know." And then he turned and walked away, his gait slow and leisurely.

She, on the other hand, felt as if she could be wrung out, she was so caught off guard by their conversation. All she wanted to do was run to her room and scream out her frustration and cry out her self-pity.

Instead, she did what was expected and walked briskly down the hall and into the kitchens. Cook was waiting for her, arms over her chest, her face flushed with disapproval. "We all have work that must be done, Rosalind. Your lollygagging is hurting all of us." With a disdainful look, she added, "Do you even care anymore?"

"Of course I care."

"Then what do you have to say for yourself? What took you so long to deliver the tray?"

"Nothing. I have nothing to say anymore." Seeing a stack of clean linen napkins, she picked them up. "I'll go press these now."

Cook looked a bit taken aback, then with a more curious gaze, she nodded. "Yes. Do that."

As she walked away, Rosalind realized that she had no more tears to cry. Well, that was something, she supposed. But although she now knew what happened to Nanci, she still had no idea what had happened to Miranda.

Why was Douglass willing to tell her about Nanci but avoided talking about her sister?

CHAPTER 23

It wasn't until late that afternoon that Rosalind had time to run out to the street and look for Minerva. Not only did she hope to help out the flower girl, but she felt that her presence at Sloane House could only help the rest of the servants. Everyone was so exhausted, their nerves so frayed, any new addition to the staff could only help the strained circumstances inside the house.

To Rosalind's relief, Minerva was standing at her usual corner, her box of flowers lying on the ground next to her feet. Both the chrysanthemums and Minerva looked a bit wilted. Rosalind wished she'd thought to bring her a glass of water.

Minerva's expression brightened a bit when she recognized Rosalind, but then she seemed to carefully tamp it down. Perhaps she didn't want Rosalind to think they'd actually become friends.

After pausing for a moment, doing her best to rethink what she was about to do, Rosalind strode forward.

"Hello, Minerva."

"Rosalind. Running errands today?"

"No. Um, actually, I came out here to speak with you."

"Is that right? Are you still looking for your sister?"

"I am."

"And how goes the search?"

"I haven't been too successful, I fear. Actually, I haven't accomplished much at all. It's been unusually busy at Sloane House, especially for the last couple of days. I only have a few minutes to be out here."

Minerva nodded like she'd suspected that. "Lots of folks coming and going from that house, and at all hours of the day and night."

"Yes, the family likes to entertain."

"Like I told you, sometimes it's best to accept how things are and move on. It's easier that way."

"I imagine so. Um, actually, since we're discussing change and such, I had an idea for you."

Immediately, the other girl's expression became guarded. "And why would you be thinking about me so much?"

"I've felt bad for you, standing on the corners, selling flowers in all sorts of weather."

Her chin lifted. "It's a reputable job."

"I meant no disrespect," Rosalind said quickly. "I only wanted to tell you that there is an opening for a housemaid at Sloane House that I think you should apply for."

Minerva's expression hardened, then she blinked, as if the words had just registered. Then she narrowed her eyes and stared at Rosalind a little more closely. "And why do you think I'd have a chance?"

"Nanci, my roommate, had to leave in a hurry. Her leaving has left the whole household in a bit of disarray. Mrs. Abrams, the housekeeper, and Mrs. Sloane herself are eager to find a replacement as soon as possible. Actually, they're so anxious that they are even willing to bypass going through a placement agency." Smiling as encouragingly as possible, Rosalind added, "You can simply go to the servants' entrance and speak to Mrs. Abrams today or tomorrow."

"It can't be that easy."

"I'm certain it is. Well, it is if you are so inclined. If not, then no harm done." She paused meaningfully, but mentally winced when she spied Minerva's look of scorn. Too tired to argue her point, Rosalind turned away. Her current situation was hard enough without being subjected to barbs from Minerva too.

She'd taken three steps when Minerva's voice rang out.

"Wait!"

Surprised, Rosalind turned. "Yes?"

"If I did go to Sloane House, what would I do? What would I say?" Though Rosalind thought she was trying to hide her real feelings, hope lit Minerva's eyes. Awkwardly, she ran a self-conscious hand down the front of her dress. "And what about my clothes? I'm sure your Mrs. Abrams will see that my appearance has much to be desired."

Rosalind looked at her critically. "I don't think you need to worry too much about your dress. It's clean, modest, and neatly mended. Besides, if you are hired, you'll be given a uniform. All I would do is smooth back your hair neatly. And be prepared to answer a lot of questions about your experience."

"I have a lot of that."

She smiled encouragingly. "Then you should be fine. Or at least you'll have as good a chance as anyone."

"Before you leave, tell me this. Why are you helping me? What do you get?"

"Nothing." Much less than that, of course. If Minerva worked out, then of course Rosalind would be out of a job. But to her surprise, her own needs and security didn't seem to be the only things that mattered anymore.

"Everyone wants something," Minerva pushed.

"I guess I'll get a feeling of satisfaction then. Even if I never find out anything about my sister, at least I would be able to help you. If you *want* to work in the Sloane House, that is."

"Should I tell them you sent me?"

"No. I haven't been a good housemaid, and that is putting it mildly. And now I had best get back." She'd barely walked two steps when Minerva called out to her again.

"Rosalind?"

She paused and looked over her shoulder. "Yes?"

"Thank you."

"You're welcome. I do hope you will apply, Minerva. It will be a good thing, knowing that you will be a part of a big house again."

She started walking again before she could say anything more.

When she got back into the house, Rosalind entered the kitchens and helped herself to a bowl of vegetable barley soup that Mrs. Russell had left simmering in a large crock on the stove. Other than a few nods, no one in the kitchen acknowledged her.

She was halfway done with her soup when a timid knock sounded at the door. Jerome answered. Right away, his usual cocky demeanor softened, giving Rosalind a hint that Minerva had wasted little time in taking advantage of Rosalind's news.

He turned to Mrs. Russell. "Cook, is Mrs. Abrams interviewing for Nanci's position already?"

"She is." After wiping her hands on her stained apron, Cook walked to the back door.

As Rosalind finished her meal, she heard Cook's somewhat

skeptical voice change just like Jerome's had. "Come on, dearie. And sit yourself down. Why don't you have some soup while Jerome here goes to find Mrs. Abrams, our housekeeper?"

Not wanting to run the risk of ruining Minerva's chances, Rosalind hurriedly washed her bowl and spoon and exited the kitchen. She passed Mrs. Abrams on the stairs. "Ma'am."

"Press Miss Veronica's dress for this evening," the housekeeper said crisply. "It has been set out on her bed."

Rosalind went to Veronica's room, got the dress, and headed to the laundry to do as she was bid. Down the hall, in Mrs. Abrams' private office, she could hear Mrs. Abrams and Cook chatting with Minerva. Their voices were kind, their questions easy and gentle. It seemed that they, too, had been just as struck by Minerva's beauty and her noticeable nervousness.

Shortly afterward, the housekeeper located Rosalind. "Did you iron the gown?"

"Yes, ma'am. It's hanging in Miss Sloane's wardrobe."

"Good." She cleared her throat. "I thought I might warn you that we have an applicant for the housemaid position. I think she might work out if Mrs. Sloane approves of her."

"Ah."

"She's a different type of girl than most of us, but I must say she seems most suitable. She speaks well and is eager to work hard. She looks like she's fallen on some hard times, but she has experience and overall she seems like she will fill the position superbly."

Rosalind waited, wondering what Mrs. Abrams was going to say next.

"I would like you to show her to your rooms and then let her put on your extra uniform for the interview with Mrs. Sloane. Let her use your mirror and pins too."

"Yes, ma'am." Rosalind wondered if the older lady had even considered how awkward it should have been for Rosalind to help prepare a woman to take her place. But perhaps she didn't care.

When she entered the kitchens again, Rosalind found Minerva surrounded by various members of the staff. All were either plying her with food, offering her suggestions for the interview, or telling her about themselves.

"Minerva, I am Rosalind," she said as formally as she could. She didn't want anyone to suspect that she had anything to do with Minerva's appearance in the house. "Mrs. Abrams thought I might be able to help you prepare for your interview with Mrs. Sloane."

Minerva stood up with a rush, her chair scraping the tile floor. Wincing at the squeak, her cheeks colored. "I am so sorry," she said to Cook.

"Don't you fret, now. We've all been in your shoes. And don't worry about your interview. Mrs. Sloane is always kind to applicants."

"Don't worry about her none either," Jerome said with a dark look Rosalind's way. "She won't be with us much longer."

Thankfully, Minerva said nothing at first as she followed Rosalind up the servants' stairs. When they were about halfway up, however, Minerva spoke—perhaps oblivious to Jerome's unkind remark about Rosalind from excitement at this new opportunity. "You never said how friendly the staff is. They feel like family, they do."

"I didn't think of it. Um, I guess I had assumed all staffs would be that way."

"No, Rosalind," she murmured. "Most of the time they're not that way at all."

CHAPTER 24

Those words echoed in Rosalind's head when she was summoned to Mrs. Abrams' sitting room at four o'clock and given an envelope with the last of her pay and a letter of reference. Though it seemed the housekeeper didn't have the heart to send her out without a letter of reference, Rosalind's cursory glance showed that it was barely adequate. Never again would she be hired in a grand house.

Feeling chilled, Rosalind folded the letter and counted the money. "Thank you. I'll leave first thing tomorrow morning."

"No, Miss Pettit. You will leave right now. Your time at Sloane House has come to its end."

While Rosalind stared at her incredulously, the housekeeper became even more businesslike. "I know the hour is getting late, but that can't be helped. Time stands still for no man."

Stunned and more than a little hurt that Mrs. Abrams was not even going to wait to see if Minerva did indeed "acclimate," Rosalind hurried to her room, changed out of her uniform, and threw what belongings she had into her carpetbag. As she hoisted it over one crooked arm, Rosalind realized she was leaving with quite a bit more than she came with. More importantly, she was leaving with a greater understanding of life and expectations and human nature.

As luck would have it, she passed Douglass Sloane as she left the house, and she set down her bag for just a moment to talk with him.

"I guess things didn't work out here after all. A shame."

Yet again his words were infused with multiple meanings. Now, though, she was able to reply with a bit of intelligence. "No, sir, it didn't. But everything wasn't a total loss. I learned a lot."

"Anything of use?"

"Yes, as a matter of fact. I learned a lot of information that will one day come in handy. And I realize a few important truths."

"Such as?"

"Well, I've learned to depend on myself. I've learned it is foolish to depend on anyone or anything."

He blinked. "Now that is harsh."

"I agree, sir. It has been very harsh. And more than a bit painful too. But I will survive. We all do."

"Some don't," he said softly. "Some don't survive at all."

She met his gaze and felt chilled all over again. Indeed, she had learned that too. Some in their midst didn't survive.

She picked up her carpetbag one more time, opened the door, and stepped out into waning sunlight. Wondering what would happen to her.

And a dark part of her wondered if it even mattered. She'd failed utterly in her goals. But most of all, she'd failed her sister.

———

"You have been avoiding me, Reid," Veronica Sloane said minutes after the fish course had been served in the glittering dining room where their group had gathered for yet another dinner party and ball at yet another fine house. "Do you have a reason?"

He had many, some that he could verbalize. Others represented only a myriad of mixed-up emotions he felt unable to share. Instead, it was more of a feeling that he was on the verge of making a complete change in his life, and a relationship with her—as he had decided the day he'd found Veronica in the Sloane House hallway shadows— would only complicate things, even if he wanted such a relationship. Was she really going to pretend no understanding had passed between them that day?

With care, he pulled apart his dinner roll and spread a small portion of butter on it. "We've all been busy, Miss Sloane," he murmured. "You most of all."

She smiled. "Listen to you! Those manners! Why, you almost sound charming."

He raised a brow as he popped the bread in his mouth.

Still ignoring her plate, she leaned a little closer. "Did you find that difficult?"

"Not at all," he replied lightly. He speared a thin portion of the sole and bit into it gratefully, thankful to have a reason to stop speaking with her. The fish had been poached in butter and lemon and practically melted in his mouth. He wished he had been able to savor it.

Impatiently, Veronica signaled that she was finished with the course. After a moment's pause, a servant briskly pulled the untouched dish from the table.

When her spot was cleared, she visibly relaxed. "My brother and I have a bet," she murmured. "We're wondering who you are avoiding. Is it me? Or is it Douglass? Or is it someone else in our home entirely?"

Reid decided to play along, not wishing to cause a scene. "I have no idea what you mean. As I said, I have been much occupied with other pressing engagements."

"No, you did not say that," she replied, her voice chilled. "You said nothing about engagements. Who has captured your attention?"

He didn't want to be difficult, but he also didn't want to have this conversation with her, especially not within the hearing of other people at the table. "Forgive me, but I am finding this conversation tedious," he said, a bit more loudly than was proper, risking causing a scene after all.

As he'd hoped, Veronica's shoulders stiffened and the lines around her lips whitened. But at last she did what he'd hoped she would—she turned to the person on her left and began conversing.

Eloisa was seated on his right. As he took another bite of fish, she leaned toward him. "That was a tad harsh, Mr. Armstrong."

"I know, and I am sorry for it." Rather, he was sorry she'd heard him.

She shook her head slightly, the movement making the diamond pins nestled in her golden coiffure sparkle in the candlelight's glow. "Oh, I didn't mean you should apologize for it. It was deserved."

There was nothing he could say to that without seeming more of a cad. "Tell me, how is your brother enjoying his European tour? My sister, Beth, seems to be enjoying her visit to Paris immensely." As conversational transitions went, it was poorly executed. Yet he gazed at her, hoping to convey without words his need to move on.

She didn't disappoint. Eloisa paused, then smiled graciously. "Currently, Thomas is in Italy. In Venice. Would you care to hear about his latest letter?"

"Nothing would please me more."

She began a somewhat amusing anecdote that involved her brother, a stray cat, and some unfortunate valet with an allergy. Looking at her pretty expression and her perfect manners, Reid breathed a sigh of relief. Eloisa was everything gracious and kind—the opposite of Veronica Sloane with her skeletal frame, caustic conversation, and harsh criticism of anything and everyone.

Hours later in the ballroom, Veronica strolled by with one of Douglass's more reprobate acquaintances. "Forgive me for embarrassing you earlier, Reid," she said. "I had only been wondering if you knew about our Rosalind."

"What about her?"

"She is gone."

Icy fear made his voice overly loud. "Has she gone missing?"

Veronica flinched while her escort looked mildly intrigued. "Gone missing?" An eyebrow arched. "Heavens, no. She was fired."

"Fired?" he barked.

"Have a care, Armstrong. There are ladies present," Veronica's escort cautioned.

Reid didn't care who heard him. "On what grounds?"

Veronica smiled so broadly, her top teeth gleamed in the glow of the candles. "For her poor behavior, of course. For some reason, she couldn't keep away from the gentlemen. It caused quite a stir."

She pursed her lips. "I don't think she'll ever learn how to be a lady." Then she smirked. "I'm sorry, I meant a lady's maid."

"Where did she go?"

All traces of amusement fled from her face. "Where does any woman go when she has little money, no friends, and no job?"

"That was practically a death sentence."

"It was hardly that." She sniffed. "But I do have a feeling she's wishing right now that she'd done a few things differently. I've heard the streets can be unkind to a woman on her own."

The man beside her grinned. "You should have sent her my way,

Veronica. If she isn't ugly I would have given her shelter. At least for an hour or two."

"Perhaps she found someone else to do the honors?" With another backward glance at Reid, Veronica circled her hands around the gentleman's arm and walked away.

Leaving Reid to stand in fuming silence. Thinking what he thought to be the worst . . . and then fearing things even worse than that.

CHAPTER 25

Rosalind spent her first night away from Sloane House in a small room in a cheap hotel five blocks from Michigan Avenue. Trying to find lodging so late in the day had been humbling. Walking the streets, carpetbag in her hand, had garnered her far more attention than she'd been prepared for. More than one man had lewdly propositioned her. Others had looked at her stuffed bag with a critical eye.

Rosalind had feared they were planning to either snatch it out of her hands or follow her into a dark alleyway. Just as bad, she knew she was wearing that same lost look she'd worn the first day she'd arrived in the city. And that expression, of course, was the altogether worst expression to have. It set her up for a great many dangers.

With each step, she was learning that though she'd had a great many experiences in Chicago, had thought she had grown into someone more confident, she hadn't really changed at all. She still felt lost and hopelessly alone.

Her first two attempts at finding lodging had failed horribly. One place was at full capacity and the other was not interested in housing someone like her. The landlady at her third stop must have seen something in Rosalind's expression that softened her mood, because she reluctantly rented her a room—for a full dollar over the advertised price. Rosalind had been so scared and weary she hadn't bothered to argue. Instead, she paid the fee, carried her bag to her room, and praised God that her room had a secure lock.

Now, in the early light of a new day, her mind was clearer and she felt a new resolve.

No matter how afraid she was, she couldn't leave Chicago without trying harder to fulfill her mission. She needed to discover what had happened to Miranda. And at this point, she needed to be willing to do whatever it took to achieve her goal.

That meant she needed to swallow her pride, find Reid Armstrong, and ask for his assistance. Knowing that she couldn't simply find his home and knock on the door because she didn't have his address, she went to the only place where she had a reasonable expectation of finding him and could wait for him safely—the church where she'd watched him sing in the choir.

After putting on her best dress, Rosalind pinned and smoothed her hair as best she could and carried her carpetbag down the narrow, rickety stairs. Even going down the stairs took some negotiating. There was no way she was going to carry her bag all over Chicago if she didn't have to.

She found the landlady in the dining room, serving coffee. "There you are," the woman said. "You going to be wanting breakfast? A quarter will get you coffee, toast, eggs, and bacon."

The food sounded heavenly, and the aroma reminded her that she'd missed dinner the night before. "Thank you." She took a seat at a small table in the back of the room.

A few minutes later, a young girl who looked to be no older than nine or ten brought out a dish of eggs and bacon and a large cup of coffee. Rosalind thanked her and dug in. The coffee was hot and rich, and the eggs and bacon were far better than she'd anticipated. When she was about halfway done, the landlady brought her a small plate filled with three slices of toast.

"Eat up, dear," she said in a kind, frazzled way. "You look like a strong wind could blow you away."

"It's very good."

Rosalind ate every last crumb. After all, there was no guarantee that she was going to have much luck finding Reid anytime soon.

When the landlady came by again, she asked, "Ma'am, could I leave my suitcase here for a few hours?"

"You don't want to spend another night?"

"I'd rather not if I don't have to. I'm on a strict budget."

"Where are you going instead?"

"I'm hoping to stay with a friend." When the woman's expression darkened with distaste, Rosalind felt her cheeks flush. She knew what she sounded like. Only women with bad reputations had no real lodging plans. Knowing she was about to be asking for Mr. Armstrong's charity didn't make things easier.

However, if there was one thing she'd learned during her time in Chicago, it was that far worse things could happen to a woman than a loss of reputation. Besides, soon she would be returning to Wisconsin and no one's opinion of her in Chicago would really matter.

"I have no desire to hold on to your bag indefinitely," she warned.

"I'll be back by five or six."

"I can't be guaranteeing that I'll have a room for you then."

"I understand." She stood up and grasped the handle of her worn carpetbag. "Where may I stow this?"

"Follow me." The landlady led her through the dining room down the hallway and came to a stop at a door that was marked with a sign that said "Private."

"I'll put your case in here. Until 5:00 p.m."

"Yes, ma'am. I'll be back by then. I promise."

After setting the suitcase inside the door, the woman walked her out. "I hope you know what you're doing, miss. Chicago is a dangerous place. Especially for green girls like you."

"Oh, I'm far less naive than one might think," Rosalind stated.

The woman rested her hands on generous hips and eyed her more closely. "You know what? I think that might be true. Best of luck to you today."

"Thank you." She smiled tightly, then strode out the front door. She had roughly nine hours to find Reid Armstrong and to try to convince him to help her—or get back there to pick up her belongings.

If it look longer than that to find Reid?

She was going to run out of both time and money.

Reid was in a panic. So much so, he'd broken down and told his father everything at his bedside that morning, right after visiting Sloane House and learning nothing from the staff about where Rosalind may have gone.

The moment everything was off his chest, guilt surrounded him. His father was ill. He likely had only a few more weeks to live. He didn't need to be burdened with Reid's problems.

But instead of looking wearier, his father looked almost rejuvenated. Reaching out, he clasped Reid by the hand. "Help me sit up, son."

Reid did as he was bid, fluffing pillows behind his father's back and trying to find a way to apologize at the same time. Finally, he said what was in his heart. "I'm sorry for burdening you like this."

"You're not burdening me, son. Actually, I think you might even be helping me."

"I don't see how that would be the case."

"Truth be told, for the first time in weeks, I'm thinking about something other than my pain and impending death."

Reid could barely hide his wince. "Father, don't speak that way."

"It's the truth, son. We know my days are numbered." He shook his head impatiently when he saw that Reid was preparing to argue that point. "Enough about me. Where do you think Rosalind is right now?"

"I have no idea. She could be anywhere. Walking the streets or in some cheap room." He lowered his voice. "At some man's mercy."

His father scowled. "Son, you're not thinking clearly. Stop letting your fears get the best of you and think."

"I have been thinking."

"Think harder. You're a smart man. At least, you used to be." He snapped his fingers. "Now, let's review everything you do know. Is she the type of woman to have already left Chicago?"

That was one thing he definitely did not need to ponder. "No. There is no way Rosalind would leave right now. Not without trying at least one more time to locate her sister."

"Good. It's about time you started using your God-given smarts. Now that you know that, where would she look? Who would she talk to? Who would she ask for help?"

Reid replied after thinking for a moment. "At first I was going to say she'd go to the fair, but now I'm not so sure about that. Rosalind told me she's already gone there several times without any luck." He paused, then said slowly, "Actually, Father, I think she would try to find me."

"Because you've offered to help her?"

"Yes," Reid said, finding talking out his thoughts to be beneficial. "And because I think she trusts me."

"Does she know where you live? Should we alert the staff that she might be stopping by?"

"I think that would be a good idea, though I don't believe she has our address." Mentally, he cursed himself. How could he have been so thoughtless?

"Where else would she try to find you?"

"Most every time we've spoken, it was at Sloane House. Of course she wouldn't find me there . . ." Then it came to him. "But the last time we talked, it was at church."

"You took her to church?"

Reid chuckled. "No." Briefly, he relayed the story of Rosalind getting caught in the fray on the sidewalk and entering the church for safety.

"That's it," his father said excitedly. "It has to be. If Rosalind is the woman you believe her to be, then that is the safest place for her. She'll go there because she trusts it. And she trusts you."

"Dad, I think you might be right."

"I'm certain I am," his father replied with a gleam in his eye. "Now, when you do find Rosalind, bring her back here. She can stay with us."

"I don't know if she'll trust me enough to come, but I'll ask."

"Do whatever it takes, Reid. I want to meet this girl, and you need to help her. My gosh, someone needs to help that poor child." Grabbing the bell by his bed, he shook it with a new vigor.

Looking a bit alarmed, Redmond, his father's longtime valet, appeared. "Yes, sir?"

"Go find Watterson. I need to speak with him. And you'd best call for Mrs. Griffin too." Looking spryer than he had in weeks, his father snapped his fingers. "Don't dally, now. We don't have much time."

After glancing curiously at Reid, Redmond nodded. "Right away, sir."

When they were alone again, Reid leaned back in the chair beside his father's bed and crossed his legs. "A lot of people would say that a mere maid's problems aren't ours. But instead of pushing her aside, you're offering to help her. You are a remarkable man, Father."

His dad grunted. "It's good you realized that before I'm gone."

"As a matter of fact, I've known that for quite some time."

"How long?"

"At least a few days."

His father chuckled. "At least it's not a recent development." Turning more somber, he added, "Seriously, as I've been sitting in this bed, I've had a lot of time to think about all the things I had thought were important. Ever since our financial situation improved, I wanted to be sure that you had every opportunity I didn't. I wanted you to be able to attend the finest schools, to be accepted in places that would never accept me."

"And that happened."

"Yes, but at what cost? I have to admit there have been moments when I've wondered if I've pushed you toward a life that was bright but meaningless. Beautiful but empty. To my regret, I wasn't even sure you should be part of that choir. I didn't think you would make enough connections there."

Reid knew he'd made the most important connection at the church—a connection with his Holy Father. "I've respected your wishes for me, but inside I knew I needed to be there. Maybe it was so I'd be there for Rosalind."

"That looks to be a very good possibility."

Further conversation was delayed by the return of Redmond, with the housekeeper and butler in tow. They stood at attention, their postures straight, their expressions worried and grim.

"You called for us, sir?" Watterson said.

"There is a very good possibility that a young woman might be calling at our house today."

"Yes, sir?" Mrs. Griffin asked. Only the slight inflection of her voice betrayed her confusion.

"If she does pay a call, I want you to invite her inside and make sure she doesn't leave. She will be here to see Reid."

The housekeeper looked indignant. "We would never turn away a lady. Even if she doesn't know it's not proper for her to be visiting a gentleman's home."

"This lady's name is Rosalind. Rosalind Pettit. She will most likely be dressed as a housemaid."

All three servants looked askance. "Yes, Master Reid," Watterson said.

His father cleared his throat. "No matter what she looks like, I want her to be treated with respect."

"She is a friend of mine, and she is in a bit of a difficult situation," Reid explained. "Actually, I wouldn't be surprised if she arrived at the back entrance." He paused, choosing his words with care. "Please treat her with kindness. Many people have not done so."

All three servants nodded, each one looking more curious than the last. Reid was tempted to tell them a bit more but decided against it. This was Rosalind's business, and he wasn't even sure how much her situation should become common knowledge.

When they left, he sighed and stood up. "Father, I'm going to take your advice and go to the church and wait."

"In the meantime, if she shows up here, we'll send word to you. I'll fill your mother in on the latest events as well."

"Thank you."

"Let's hope she reaches out to you, son." He nodded. "Indeed, you—and the church—are her best chances for survival."

Reid knew his father wasn't exaggerating in the slightest. As brave as Rosalind was, Reid knew she was really only a young farm girl on her own in the middle of a big city. Her innocence and the sense of betrayal she surely had to feel were a dangerous combination. It could even propel her to make some poor decisions. "I shudder to think about what will happen if she doesn't reach out."

"None of that, now. You need to stay positive. Focused. I will pray. If we do those things, I know we'll find her. And once we do that, we will all put our heads together and try to figure out what happened to her sister. And we will. I'm sure of it."

Reid was humbled by both his father's trust in the Lord and his hope for their success. Once again, he was reminded that he had a lot to learn to become the man his father was.

He only hoped there would be enough time to learn even more. He needed his father, just as he needed their Father in heaven. "Well, I'm off," he said. He marched downstairs, took his hat from Watterson, and strode out the door.

The moment he stepped outside, he was struck at just how bright the sun was shining. He blinked a bit, letting his eyes adjust to the daylight. Took time to look around him, take in the beauty of the morning.

Yes, the day was beautiful. The trees and shrubs surrounding their home were neatly trimmed and flowers bordered the estate like vibrant ribbons. Few people drove along the streets. It was almost quiet.

For once the air wasn't too hot or too humid, and the promise of fall was, perhaps, in the air. The winds their city was known for weren't gusting and kicking up dust and debris from the road. The air even smelled sweeter than it usually did.

Yes, all in all, it was a beautiful day. Beautiful in looks and in feel. It was a beautiful day to make a difference in someone's life.

With that thought in mind, he stepped down his front steps, turned right, and started walking to the church. He'd start there. If she didn't show, then he'd start exploring other places and other options.

All he could do was take one step at a time.

CHAPTER 26

Rosalind had been sitting in the same church pew she'd sat in before for an hour. For most of the time, she'd been completely alone. She'd passed the time by listening for footsteps and berating herself for not doing more to keep her job at Sloane House, telling herself she was ten times the fool.

Just like when she'd boarded that train in Milwaukee, determined to locate Miranda and bring her home safely, she'd been hopelessly naive.

Why had she cared whether Minerva had a bed to sleep in or not? Furthermore, why had she thought that she would have a chance of meeting Reid—or even anyone who knew him—at this time, on this day? The choir practice she'd stumbled upon had been later in the day, on another day of the week. She didn't even know how often they practiced.

She should have come up with a better solution. More importantly, she should have prepared better. She should have asked him where his home was, about his job. Asked him something of importance so if she did need him, she would be able to find him.

And, well, while she was at it, she certainly should have gone to the police station herself and asked about her sister, even though they had rebuffed her father. If they had no answers for her? She could have returned again and again until they took her seriously.

Instead, she'd taken the investigation into her own hands, even though she didn't know the city or the first thing about locating a missing person. Yes, she'd been ten times the fool.

After sitting for that hour, she was already coming to the conclusion that the only things she did have any more were hope and her faith. She started praying then. Her words were rusty at first, but little by little they began to meld together.

Asking the Lord to join her felt, finally, like the right thing to do—as if at long last she was doing something right. Every time she began to doubt and worry, Rosalind did her best to breathe deeply and let the scent of incense, lemon oil, and aged wood fill her soul. Each time, the cool air, mixed with the comforting scent and a sense of faith, soothed her.

Once soothed, she continued to pray for Reid and for her family and Miranda and miracles. Though she didn't always like to ask the Lord for help for herself, she asked him for strength and knowledge. For bravery and, finally, for peace.

She truly did need peace. Ever since she'd realized Miranda had gone missing, she'd lost a little bit of herself. At first, she grieved and worried. Felt a huge sense of loss. Then, after arriving in Chicago and taking the job at Sloane House, she'd begun to not only doubt herself but doubt others around her. Those negative feelings had slowly but surely chipped at her insides. Little by little, she'd stopped imagining the best in others and begun to treat everyone with suspicion.

Then, as she prayed, she slowly began to doubt even her own motives, fearing that she wasn't only looking for Miranda, but, in a strange, awful way, letting her worries transform her into something and someone she didn't even recognize.

It was time to move on. So she asked God to help her come to terms with her situation. If she was destined to mourn for her sister, then she needed to accept that and move on.

And then a funny thing happened. Her clenched hands eased. Her stiff shoulders relaxed. Gradually, her breathing slowed and evened. That was when she was almost sure that she heard the Lord speaking back to her.

She breathed deeply again and reminded herself that he'd been with her this whole time. It was time to stop doubting and to start listening. And he was telling her to remain where she was.

Because she didn't know what else to do, because she had nowhere else to go, she elected to listen. To be obedient.

Finally she was doing something right. Her body relaxed. Her mind eased. And in spite of everything that was so wrong, she fell asleep.

━━

"Miss?"

Rosalind started and rushed to sit up.

A heavyset man in a pew two rows away turned around. His gaze was serious and sad. "Forgive me, but you were here the other day, weren't you?" he asked. "When we had the choir practice."

She stared at him, distrustful, then realized that he might be the answer to her prayers. She nodded.

He looked pleased that his guess had been right. "You're Mr. Armstrong's friend, aren't you?"

She nodded again. "I came here today hoping to see Mr. Armstrong. Do you happen to know if he'll be by here today?"

He shook his head sadly. "Not to my knowledge. This isn't a practice day. And Mr. Armstrong doesn't make all the practices anyway. He's a busy man, you see."

She was crestfallen. "I was afraid of that."

"Is there something I could help you with?"

"Could you tell me his home address?"

"You want his address, miss?"

"I know it's out of the ordinary, but I must find him as soon as possible. It's terribly urgent."

He stared at her so long that she felt her stomach knot.

However, she looked directly at him. She had nothing to lose, and he was her only hope. It no longer mattered what kind of woman this man imagined her to be—most likely loose or pushy. After all, what other kind of woman would be sitting in a church, hoping and praying for help from a man she barely knew?

At last he came to a decision. "I suppose I could give you his address, though I do feel a bit odd about it." He scratched his trimmed beard. "I've never passed on a gentleman's address to a woman before."

"I've never asked for one before." She didn't add another word. Truthfully, there wasn't anything else to say. She needed an ally.

He stood up, pulled a fountain pen out of a pocket inside his jacket, then paused. Looking just beyond her, his face broke into a wide smile. "Well, would you look at that?" he murmured. "It looks like I was wrong."

"Pardon me?" She turned, then suddenly felt her heart flip over as a rush of emotions flooded her. "Reid." She stood up.

"Hello, Jackson," Reid murmured before directing all his attention on her. He strode forward, his gaze never leaving her own. His expression looked to be a cross between profound relief and unexpected joy. "Rosalind. Thank God."

She stepped to the aisle and met him. When he held out his hands, she grasped his with a mixture of pure relief and bountiful joy.

After squeezing her fingers lightly, he pulled her into his arms and held her close. "I've been so worried. So worried," he murmured into her hair.

With a sigh, he released her and smiled.

Rosalind smiled too. Her prayers had been answered. The Lord had listened to her and had looked out for her, first by that Jackson man and now with the one person she'd been praying and hoping to see. Tears flooded her eyes and slowly fell down her cheeks. "Oh, Reid, I don't think you'll ever know how happy I am to see you."

He pulled out a handkerchief and dabbed her cheeks. Looking at her tenderly, he said, "Actually, I do think I know, because I feel the same way. I've been worried sick."

"You have?"

"Last night Veronica told me you were let go. I questioned her, even stopped by the servants' entrance this morning and asked if anyone knew where you went off to. But no one had any idea. Ever since then, I've been a wreck, imagining the worst, hoping and praying to find you."

"They wouldn't have known. I had no idea what I was going to do when I left the house."

"That doesn't make me feel any better," he murmured as he clasped her hands in his.

She couldn't help it—she laughed. Enjoying his smile. Enjoying his touch. His hands felt so warm, so reassuring. Safe. "Seeing you here? It feels like a dream."

"Indeed. The very best of dreams." He squeezed her hands one more time before he dropped them. "Now, let's get you out of here. Are you hungry? Do you need anything?"

She felt so overwhelmed at the moment that she wasn't sure what she needed. But then she remembered her manners. She turned to the man who had been sitting with her. "I'm sorry, sir. I mean, Mr. Jackson. I didn't mean to completely—"

But he was gone.

"Reid, did you see where that man I was talking to went off to?"

"That was Edward Jackson. He's a shopkeeper who lives nearby."

"Well, he was about to help me. He was about to give me your address."

"Really? I didn't think he knew it," he mused.

"I was so grateful that he stopped to talk to me. I prayed and prayed for help, then both of you men appeared."

"I asked my father for advice. After going over possibilities, I decided there was a good chance you might come here because this is the one place you know I frequent with any regularity. I also left word with everyone at home to be on the lookout for you."

"You did all that?"

"I did. My father and I also gave strict instructions. If you showed up, everyone was supposed to ply you with hot tea and sandwiches until I came back."

She'd hoped and prayed he'd help her if she'd asked, but she had never imagined that he'd go to so much trouble. Not for a mere maid.

"As I said, I've been concerned about you." He held out his arm. "Now, come home with me. My parents are there and they want to help. Where are your things?"

"I left my carpetbag with the landlady of a little inn." She bit her lip. "I told her I'd be back for everything by five."

"I'll send a footman to retrieve your bag. Until you leave Chicago, you will be staying with the Armstrong family."

She was too desperate to do anything but accept his offer. "Thank you. I'll be more than happy to work for my room and board."

"Nonsense. You will be there as our guest, Rosalind."

"But, Reid, I am only a maid. You can't have me stay at your house as a lady. What will your servants say?"

"First of all, I don't care. And second? It seems the Sloanes have quite a reputation for running off servants. I have a feeling my staff might congratulate you!"

She couldn't believe he was joking. "If I stay, I'll gladly stay in an extra maid's room."

"No arguing. We wouldn't want this to happen any other way," he proclaimed as they stepped out of the dark church into the light of day.

Now that she wasn't shrouded with worry, she looked around and was surprised and pleased to see that the day was bright with nary a cloud in the sky. "It's a beautiful day," she murmured.

His lips curved upward. "Indeed, it is. The best of days."

Rosalind's first impression of Reid Armstrong's home was that it was much different than Sloane House. While Sloane House stood as imposing as a castle, its limestone bricks and multiple turrets, arches, and gables practically daring anyone to find a flaw, the Armstrongs' home was built entirely of wood. It reminded her of a giant farm-house, nestled among a variety of trees and shrubs and rolling hills.

It was a welcoming place.

While it was true that it wasn't all that grand-looking on the outside, inside, it was still impressive. Standing in the marbled tile entryway, she gazed at the mahogany banister and the trio of paintings decorating the wall to her right.

She saw the finely carved furniture and the thick imported rugs. The gas chandelier above them glittered, the crystals capturing the light from the upstairs windows and sending a myriad of bright colors flashing along the walls. Though she was no expert on fine furnishings, even she knew that the Armstrongs' interior could measure up to the Sloanes' in almost every single way.

Two servants were standing at the foot of the stairs, patiently waiting for instructions. After briefly meeting their gaze, she tucked her head down. There was no doubt in her mind that they would be sharing the news of her arrival with the rest of the staff. She could only imagine what they would say and what they were thinking about Reid's friendship with her.

"Erin and Benjamin, this is Rosalind, the woman I'm sure you have heard might be arriving. She'll be staying with us for a time. Rosalind, Erin is our parlor maid. Benjamin is my valet."

To Rosalind's amazement, both Erin and Benjamin greeted her with warm smiles. "We're glad you're here, Miss Rosalind," Erin said. "May I show you to your room?"

"Oh! Well, I . . ."

"I think I had better take things over now," announced a regal-looking woman who was walking toward them.

"Rosalind, may I introduce my mother, Mrs. Armstrong? Mother, this is Miss Pettit. Rosalind."

"Rosalind, welcome. Erin, go ask Mrs. Young to prepare a tray for our guest and bring it right into the drawing room." Erin curtsied and hurried off.

"Rosalind," Reid said, "we need to know where to retrieve your bag."

"My suitcase is at Mrs. Kingston's establishment. It is located just a block south of the transit station."

All three of them—the valet, Reid, and Mrs. Armstrong—stared at her in dismay.

"You stayed there last night?" Reid asked. "By yourself?"

"It was safe enough."

"The area is dangerous."

She didn't even try to pretend that she hadn't been worried or afraid. "It was the best I could do," she explained. "I was asked to leave Sloane House around four o'clock. One place was already full when I went there, and the next didn't want a person like me staying there."

"A person like you?" Mrs. Armstrong said.

Aware of Reid's valet still standing close by, she murmured, "It is obvious that I am not a lady, ma'am. Apparently to some, I am not even respectable."

"Let us not think anymore about that place," Mrs. Armstrong said briskly. "Benjamin, please go for the bag. You'd best take John with you."

"Yes, ma'am," he said before turning away.

Looking at her like she was more fragile than the most elegant china, Reid took her arm and led her into the drawing room. "Now, it's time for you to sit and relax. After you have something to eat and you freshen up, you can tell us all about your sister and what happened at the Sloanes'. All right?"

It all sounded beyond agreeable. With a weary smile she nodded. "Yes, Mr. Armstrong. That sounds just fine."

CHAPTER 27

Two hours later, after a much-appreciated opportunity to freshen up and after eating from a tray full of sandwiches and drinking two fortifying cups of hot tea, Rosalind told Reid and his mother everything she could.

For the most part, they listened without interrupting. The only time they spoke was when one of them asked to clarify her story or to ask her for her feelings about Douglass or Veronica.

At last, Mrs. Armstrong leaned back and shook her head in wonder. "My goodness, Rosalind. You have certainly had quite an adventure."

"Yes, ma'am."

"I want you to rest for a day or so and let the rest of us do a bit of investigating."

"Oh no, ma'am. I'm afraid I couldn't do that."

"I beg your pardon?"

"Though Reid, I mean, Mr. Armstrong, invited me to be a guest here, I couldn't stay out of charity. I'd really like to earn my keep."

"It's a big home, dear. There is plenty of room for you."

"No—"

"It would be a great service to us all if you could sit with my father, who is ill," Reid interjected smoothly. "Could you do that? He doesn't care for his nurse." His voice warmed. "If you could sit with him, help him get his meals, perhaps play cards or read to him from time to time? That would help us all immensely."

"Of course I would be happy to do that. But I could also work in the kitchens or help—"

"Definitely not," Mrs. Armstrong interjected. "My staff won't know what to think about you being down in the kitchens. In addition, I have a full staff at the moment. All the chores and duties are being covered."

Rosalind knew what Mrs. Armstrong said was true. As much as she ached to not be a burden, she also was now very aware of how a big household was run. Catering to her need to feel useful would not help anyone but her. It would actually disturb the well-run balance that already existed. "I understand."

"Good." She rose to her feet. "Now, let's get you settled in your room. I want you to rest for a bit now, and then Reid will take you to his father's room and introduce you."

"Yes, ma'am."

Reid stood up as well. "I'm very glad you are here, Rosalind. I'll knock on your door in an hour."

"Yes, Mr. Armstrong." She ached to thank him again. Ached to call him Reid, ached to step into his arms like she did at the church. But this was neither the right place nor the right time. Instead, after sharing a long look with him, they parted, he darting off to a room down the hall, she following his mother up the stairs.

The staircase was winding. At the top of the stairs, the hallway broke into thirds. To Rosalind's pleasure, she noticed each wing was painted a slightly varying shade of gray. The wing Mrs. Armstrong guided her down was faintly blue in tint. Small prints of botanicals dotted the narrow hallway. The effect was soothing.

Her room was at the end of the hall. It was small but well appointed. Though it wasn't nearly as grand as Veronica Sloane's, it was a far cry from the small room at the top of the Sloane mansion where she'd stayed with Nanci.

"I hope you will find this comfortable, dear," Mrs. Armstrong said.

"It's beautiful. Thank you." Before the lady could rush off, Rosalind said, "I don't know how I can ever thank you."

"You don't need to. We want to help you find your sister. And if that can't be done, we want to help you, dear."

"I'm grateful, but I'm afraid I don't understand why. From the very beginning, Reid, I mean, Mr. Armstrong, has been so kind to me."

"It's probably because you've been kind to him as well."

"Not all the time," she admitted.

"Well, there might be another reason. We believe in Jesus, Rosalind. Do you?"

"I . . . I think so. I mean, I have faith."

"Jesus did so much for so many, never asking them what was in it for him. He taught us all to be kind and to help those in need. We're Christians. And we have faith." She shrugged. "I'm not explaining myself very well. All I can say is that it gives me much happiness to help you. To not just say I want to make a difference in someone else's life, but to actually do so. I think Reid is much the same way."

"I'm grateful. Perhaps one day I'll be able to say I've done the same."

Mrs. Armstrong's eyes turned luminous. "Oh, you dear child, you don't see it, do you?" When Rosalind shook her head, she added, "You already have sacrificed yourself for someone you love." She waved a hand around the room. "Think of all you have already done for your sister! You've left your home, and you've worked hard to learn information. You've humbled yourself for her."

"But none of it has helped. Even though I've tried so hard, nothing has changed. I've still failed."

"You don't actually know that, do you? You don't know how the Lord has been working through you. You don't know how your efforts have rubbed off on other people and encouraged them to open their hearts to Miranda. You don't know, because you can't know. Only the Lord does."

Rosalind wanted to believe Mrs. Armstrong's words. "I hope you are right. I would like nothing better than to know that I've helped Miranda in spite of my mistakes."

"I can't promise all your efforts will have a happy outcome, Rosalind. No one can promise you that. But I can promise you that your faith will carry you through. Faith helps us all survive both the lowest points in life and some of the best."

She turned and left, leaving Rosalind to her thoughts.

She thought about what Mrs. Armstrong had said and couldn't help but be struck by how right the words sounded. After all, she knew a lot about surviving the hardest of times. But she'd certainly never thought about surviving good times too. But it did make sense. Each moment in her life made her a different person than who she was before. Both the good and the bad influenced her in ways she never could have imagined.

The fact that she was able to keep going? That was something to celebrate. To even praise God for—again and again and again.

Satisfied that Rosalind was getting settled in her guest room, Reid was doing his best to get through a large stack of his father's correspondence when his mother entered the room.

"I'm sorry to interrupt your work, but I think we need to talk."

It seemed to him that they'd been doing little but talking. "Can it wait? I want to post some of these letters before dinner this evening."

His mother sat down. "It cannot."

"All right then." He leaned back. "What is wrong?"

"It is about Rosalind."

Concerned, he got to his feet. "What is wrong?" he asked again. "She moved in on your invitation, Mother. Yours and Father's."

"Dear, I am not referring to that. Rather, I'm more concerned about your relationship with her."

"Mother, I am her friend."

"Are you sure that is all it is? Because I am fairly sure I saw something else brewing between the two of you."

He was taken aback. And more than a bit embarrassed. "I do believe I am long past the age of seeking my mother's permission for friendships."

"I agree. But, Reid, I fear you are developing a *tendre* for this girl—this maid."

She was hitting closer to the truth than he was comfortable with. He did have some feelings for Rosalind. He wanted to think they only revolved around pity and a need to improve her situation. But if he was honest, he'd have to admit that he'd found himself gazing at her with something more like desire more than once.

What he hadn't realized was that it had been noticeable to anyone else.

Feeling frustrated with himself, he lashed out. "Perhaps I am."

His mother frowned. "It is not that she isn't a lovely girl, Reid," she continued, just as if he'd not said a word. "As a matter of fact, I think she is very pretty. With the right clothes and hair? She might even be stunning."

He folded his hands across the surface of his father's oak desk. "And your point is?"

"My point is that I hope your desire to help a housemaid won't interfere with your place in society. Your father has sacrificed much to propel you into the upper echelons of Chicago. The young lady you take as your wife needs to reflect your position."

"In other words, taking an undercover maid as my wife will do me no favors."

Her eyes flashed. "I am not joking about this, Reid. Do not take my words lightly."

"I am doing no such thing. But, please, don't forget that I am no green debutante. I am a grown man who needs to follow his conscience . . . and his heart."

"I . . . I see." Standing with a flick of her skirts, she artfully arranged her gown, then left the room.

Only when he was alone again did he dare exhale and face the complete truth: no woman would ever intrigue him like Rosalind did. Actually, he was fairly sure that no woman would ever come close. He was fairly sure he was falling in love.

The only problem was that he had no idea what to do about that.

CHAPTER 28

"Well, don't just sit there, Rosie," Mr. Emerson Armstrong barked moments after his son left them alone. "Start talking."

"What would you like me to talk about, Mr. Armstrong? And I'm sorry, but my name is Rosalind."

"That's too stuffy for a girl like you. I like Rosie better."

She was momentarily taken aback. "So if you like it better, that should become my name?"

"That would be a yes." He opened one eye, the exact shade of green as his son's. "Do you have a problem with that?"

She knew she had no choice about what she should be called. The Armstrongs had taken her in and were offering her shelter while so many others had not. With that in mind, she decided she had no problem being called Rosie.

"Not at all, sir."

"Good. Now start telling me about yourself."

"You want to hear my life story?" She said the words as a bit of a joke. But by the look on his face it was apparent that that was exactly what he had in mind.

"Perhaps I should pour us some tea? This might take awhile."

"I don't want any tea. But go get yourself some. Can't have you being parched in my company."

Hiding a smile, she crossed the room to the pretty table, where a full tea service had been placed—by someone other than her. That was something to celebrate in itself.

Another thing to celebrate was Reid's father. The older man had certainly taken her by surprise. He was nothing like his son. Where Reid was polished good looks and perfect manners, his father was wrinkled, disheveled, and disarmingly blunt. Instead of speaking quietly, his words flew out of his mouth in spurts and sputters, each word hitting her with a staccato beat.

His accent wasn't nearly as formal or high-class as Reid's or even his wife's. Visiting with him made Rosalind feel completely at ease. Though she would never forget their differences in social status, the lines didn't seem as stark or strict in his presence.

Quickly, she added a bit of milk to her tea, then returned to sit next to him. "Well, I should start by saying that I grew up on a farm in Wisconsin."

"How many brothers and sisters?"

"I'm one of five."

"Five is a good round number," he said with a smile. "I'm one of five myself."

"Then we have something in common, perhaps."

One eye opened again. "We might have more in common than that, Rosie." As his eye closed, he waved his left hand impatiently. "Well, go on."

"I am the second eldest. My sister, Miranda, was the eldest. I mean, is the oldest."

His expression turned thoughtful. "What do you think, Rosalind? Do you think she's still alive?"

Reid had never asked such a direct question. She'd never dared to ask herself such a question. But to her surprise, she found she was ready to face it. Taking a breath, she gave voice to her secret fear.

"No. I don't think she was abducted. I don't think she ran off. I think she's dead."

"I see."

"You're not going to encourage me to hold out hope?"

"No." Both eyes opened this time and stared at her. His gaze was piercing. Direct. "Here's why: If she was anything like you, Miranda wouldn't simply vanish. You are too loyal. Even if she was only half as loyal as you? I doubt she would have left you all without a single word. If she were alive, she would have found some way, no matter how difficult, to contact her family."

She was stunned. This man she barely knew had been able to focus on the one trait she knew ran especially strong in her family. It was one of the reasons Miranda had left home in the first place, to help support her siblings. It was why her father had endured the ridicule of the police when he'd journeyed to the city to ask questions. It was why she'd pretended to be someone she wasn't, all in an attempt to discover the truth.

"You're right, sir."

"You needn't sound so surprised. I usually am." He chuckled softly, his laughter fading into a harsh cough that looked like it took the wind right out of him.

"Sorry."

"Would you care for some tea now?"

A look of distaste crossed his features. But he still held out his hand. "No milk. Only one sugar cube."

Rosalind hastened to her feet, then quickly poured him a cup. After stirring in the sugar cube, she carefully carried the teacup to him and helped his shaking hands maneuver it to his lips. After four sips, he leaned back with another angry cough.

Rosalind took the cup from his hands and carefully set it on his bedside table. Then she continued her story. "Anyway, after Miranda and me, there are three boys—Henry, Steven, and Ethan."

"And how old is Ethan?"

"Eight."

"And what does one do on the farm all day?"

"Any number of things. I often looked after my brothers. Gardened."

"You enjoy gardening?"

She nodded. "I do. I suppose it's because I don't mind being outside for hours at a time. I like it."

"What did you grow?"

"Everything. Beans. Corn. Potatoes." She continued, her voice warming to the memories. She told him about the cucumbers and zucchinis. About the time a squirrel or raccoon ate one bite out of every single tomato growing on the vines.

She chuckled when she relayed one of her brother's misadventures with a particularly hungry pig. Then she noticed that Mr. Armstrong's breathing had slowed and become even. Her chatter had caused him to fall asleep.

Uncertain about what to do next, she sat quietly next to him for another hour, content to listen to him breathe—and to allow herself to remember her home and the farm and the times she'd had there.

And she allowed herself to accept that she might not ever discover what happened to her sister. And that she was going to need to come to terms with the very real possibility that Miranda was dead.

Dead. It was such a stark, final word. But she needed that descriptor. She needed to accept it.

At last, she picked up the heavy tray and exited the room. Almost immediately, she saw Reid.

"Rosalind, I was just coming to check on you both. How did your visit with my father go?"

"Just fine. He fell asleep about an hour ago."

As he had just noticed the tray in her hands, he reached for it. "This is too heavy for you. Please allow me—"

"Certainly not, Mr. Armstrong." She stepped backward just enough to get it out of his reach. "I can carry this just fine."

"Are you certain?"

"I carried trays like this for the Sloane family many a time, sir."

He frowned. Stared at her a long moment, then took a step backward himself. "I see. Well, I won't keep you then. Unless you'd like my help finding the kitchens?"

"I'll find another staff member to help me." She turned and started walking down the hallway toward the stairs, then gingerly began the long journey down. Her arms were shaking from the weight of the tray. But she kept her chin up and was bound and determined not to lose her composure . . . or the tray.

Just as she got to the marble entryway, Benjamin hurried to her side. "Need a hand?"

"If you could direct me to the kitchens, I would appreciate it. And, please, may we not argue this point? It is fairly heavy."

"It's this way." With a new resolve, she followed the valet toward the kitchens, bracing herself to be unwelcomed into the private sanctuary of the servants' rooms.

She was pleased, however, to have stood her ground with Reid. The Armstrongs needed to remember who they were and where they came from as well as her own station in life. Remembering the line that neither could cross was necessary.

For all of them.

Reid watched Rosalind walk down the stairs, then accept Benjamin's guidance to the kitchens. To his chagrin, he felt a bit jealous. He, not his valet, was the one who knew her well. He should be the one helping her.

And that, he realized, was why he needed to remember his mother's warning. Maybe her words did have merit. Obviously, Rosalind still was very aware of their stations, and perhaps he should remember that too. Maybe there really couldn't be anything between him and Rosalind beyond giving her a helping hand.

Deciding that this encounter had been just the thing he needed to remember his place, he glanced at his pocket watch, saw that it wasn't too late to pay a call, and decided to go call on Eloisa Carstairs. He'd enjoyed talking with her at that dinner party, and she was the perfect candidate for a wife.

He shouldn't waste another moment in pursuing her.

As his driver drove the carriage to Eloisa's house, Reid knew he would talk to her about the Sloanes and their maids as well. Perhaps she would know something about their household staff that he wasn't aware of. After all, women were insightful like that. They were able to see many personality conflicts of which men were blissfully unaware.

He presented his calling card to Eloisa's butler. He looked at the card, gazed at Reid, and smiled politely. "Yes, sir. I'll inform Miss Eloisa that you have called."

Less than two minutes later, the butler guided him through a maze of rooms and out to a solarium. When Reid had visited before during a social call with his mother, they'd been directed to the formal receiving room. The solarium was far more private. It was also one of the prettiest rooms he'd ever been in. Bright and airy, the room boasted large picture windows and a pair of French doors that opened onto a stone patio.

And there, on the patio, stood Eloisa. Her back was to him. She was wearing a light blue frock that was undoubtedly an expensive work of art, with its many flounces, tucks, and pleats. The effect was charming. As if she sensed his presence, she turned and caught his eye. Smiled softly.

She was so beautiful that she almost literally took away his breath. Right then and there, Reid decided her gown was worth every penny.

The butler stood at attention. "Miss Eloisa is outside, sir. She asked that you join her out there?"

"Yes, that would be pleasant." With a nod, he added, "I'll let myself out. Thank you."

"Yes, sir." The butler nodded again, then left the solarium quietly, leaving Reid to stare at Eloisa a little bit longer before striding outside.

She held out both hands to him. "Reid, this is a surprise."

"But a welcome one, I hope?" he asked as he squeezed both her hands gently.

"Very much so." She smiled again, then bent down and picked up a pair of garden clippers. "I was just about to cut some flowers. My mother is hosting a dinner later this evening."

"I'll hold your basket for you."

"I was hoping you'd say that." She smiled again, then turned back to the grouping of rosebushes, their appealing fragrance warring with their red and gold beauty. Eloisa fingered a gold-tipped blossom before deftly snipping off the stem and gently placing it in the basket Reid had retrieved from a nearby table.

As she turned to clip another stem, she said, "To what do I owe this pleasure?"

"Would you believe me if I said I merely wanted to see you?"

She snipped another stem. "I would be flattered. But I wouldn't believe you." She grinned as she clipped another stem, a blood-red rose this time. "You are not the kind of man to pay calls for no reason."

He considered disputing that, but opted for telling the truth instead. "I came over for your help. And to discuss our future with you."

He saw only her profile, but he could tell that she was visibly struggling to retain her composure. "I see." With deliberate movements, she set down the clippers and reached for the basket.

When both were resting on the stone wall behind her, she stepped to the French doors. "Perhaps we should sit down."

He did the honors with the doors, then followed her back into the solarium. After she was seated, he seated himself in a sturdy-looking wicker chair at her right. Though he did his best to appear composed, inside, he was calling himself ten types of a fool. What had he been thinking? Paying a call on an elegant woman like Eloisa and being such a stumbling cad.

"Eloisa, perhaps I misspoke. What I meant to say is that I think an, uh, alliance between the two of us would be beneficial to both of us."

She neatly folded her hands. "A beneficial alliance? You intrigue me." Yet the tone of her voice indicated she was feeling anything but intrigued.

"I hold you in high esteem."

"We hardly know each other, Mr. Armstrong."

"That can be remedied."

"It could, if we both wanted that."

"I do." As soon as he heard his tone, he winced. He didn't sound as enthused as he sounded resigned. "I mean, I would like to get to know you better."

"Ah." She stared at him a good, long time. Then a new light of amusement lit her pale blue eyes. "And your other reason to see me?"

He paused, mentally debating whether to divulge Rosalind's secret or to keep it to himself a little longer. Rosalind desperately needed to know there was someone she could trust, and he was reluctant to break her faith in him.

However, he also knew time was of the essence, and that Eloisa Carstairs was the type of woman to help Rosalind's search in any way she could.

Surely Rosalind would care more about that than anything else?

Taking a deep breath, he plunged ahead. "I've stumbled upon a housemaid down on her luck and I need your help."

"Care to explain?"

"Her name is Rosalind. Rosalind Pettit, but now that I think about it, I'm not even sure if that is her real name," he admitted. "But that doesn't matter. What does matter is that she was a maid for the Sloane family, but she was only there to investigate the disappearance of her sister."

"Investigate? Is she sleuthing?"

"She is. Well, she was. Her sister, Miranda, obtained a job at the Sloane mansion for two months and was sending money home. She disappeared, though. Without a trace."

Eloisa leaned forward, her expression intent. Her attention obviously riveted. "What do you mean, without a trace?"

"One day, she simply wasn't there."

"What about her belongings?"

"Most of them were left behind."

"Still, she probably ran off. Some maids do that . . ."

"Rosalind's father came to Chicago and visited the house. The Sloanes were vague and disinterested, the police even less so."

"Yes, if they thought the sister merely left."

"However, Rosalind's father believed everyone there knew more than they were letting on. So Rosalind volunteered to come to Chicago to try to find her sister."

"Has she discovered anything?"

"No, though she did say that Douglass paid another maid to leave the house after he discovered she was with child."

"He gave her money?"

"Yes." Reid hoped she understood everything he wasn't saying.

Eloisa stared at him in shock. "That is a very serious offense, Reid."

"I agree. And I wouldn't have given much credence to it, except I was with Douglass when he was with the other maid. I've been in the house and witnessed the way he treated Rosalind. I don't know what happened to Rosalind's sister, but I do think that more has been going on than anyone wants to admit."

"I see."

It struck him, then, that Eloisa was not shocked by the allegations against Veronica or Douglass. "Have you heard rumors?"

"I've heard rumors about Douglass," she said quietly. She looked at the doorway. "I wouldn't want this bandied about, but more than one girl has alluded that he behaved less than gentlemanly with her. They were afraid to be alone with him."

"I've heard rumors as well." He stared at her, noted the concern in her eyes. "Eloisa, I must also admit something else. Though I can imagine Douglass, uh, behaving like a cad, I can't imagine him accosting a maid."

"I would have to agree." Her eyes narrowed. "So that begs the real question, Reid."

"And that is?"

"If Douglass Sloane merely pursues women and ruins their reputations, if Rosalind's sister was one of them, what happened to her? Did she run away in shame? Or did someone else have a hand in her disappearance?"

"Only the good Lord knows."

"I do believe that it's time people discovered the truth too," she said grimly.

CHAPTER 29

After leaving Eloisa's, Reid dismissed his driver and took the new elevated train to the entrance of the fair. He needed to get away, to think. Think about Eloisa, his duty toward his family, and his curious regard for Rosalind.

Something needed to change. He felt a new sense of urgency that he couldn't seem to shake. He didn't know if it was because of Rosalind, the new pressure he felt to marry well, or if it was a by-product of the disintegration of his relationship with Douglass.

After paying his entrance fee, he walked through the gates and mixed with the throng. The crowds had thinned considerably since the fair had first begun. And though there were still many fine ladies and gentlemen promenading, there seemed to be a greater number of men and women from the lower classes enjoying the sights. Their tailored suits and dresses were just a little bit shabbier, their grooming needing an extra bit of care.

As he looked at the white buildings, Reid realized the crowd had much in common with the buildings. Most of the people were looking like faint replicas of the shining statues positioned all around them.

He'd heard rumors that the buildings hadn't been built for posterity. Instead, the architects and builders had built glorious façades, covering plain buildings encompassing priceless artifacts. To his way of thinking, it felt fitting.

That was the way of it, he decided. People were born bare and helpless, relying on others for everything from comfort and love to happiness and esteem. Little by little, each person became more independent. Relationships were formed, not on kinship, but on mutual interests.

A new, hard veneer was formed, along with the proper way of speaking and clothing appropriate to their place in society. Some of the changes happened organically, without much thinking or planning. They just happened.

Some men inherited their fathers' businesses or adopted their trades. Some inherited the family's land or home. They continued on, in much the same path of their forefathers.

But not for men like him. No, for the Armstrongs, and most specifically for Reid Armstrong, little in life was left to chance. Instead, each step forward was contemplated carefully. Pros and cons and alternative paths were studied with great care and then put into action with the deliberative force of a general planning his battles.

Accents and fashion were studied. Schools and governesses and tutors were paid for. Dressers and valets, diets and polish. Acquaintances nurtured, friendships fostered.

And any failure to prosper was considered a flaw. A mistake. Something that needed to be rectified as soon as possible.

But of course, all of it could be stripped away with the loss of money or the loss of stature. Making an enemy of a former friend could do that too. And then, if a man wasn't careful, he could find the beautiful covering that he'd paid for with time and money and effort and fear slowly crumbling away. Leaving him to be the man he'd always dreaded being.

Reid sat on one of the benches, realizing that he was the White City. He had been as bright and perfect as money and careful planning had been able to buy. However, at the end of the day, his true colors were showing through the cracks in his marble façade.

Over the last few weeks, since he'd met Rosalind and had become interested in something besides his worth or acceptance in society, he'd discovered himself.

Of course, the Lord had much to do with that. He'd been the one who had encouraged Reid to continue to be involved with his church, even when it wasn't the thing to do. The Lord had kept putting him and Rosalind in each other's path. And the Lord had also given him the ability to see Rosalind for herself.

He'd begun to see beyond her stunning looks and social status. He'd begun to think of her as a whole, unique person. A child of God. And during that time Reid had realized she was important to him.

He didn't know what was going to happen next. Would he ever be able to help Rosalind enough for her to discover what had really happened to her sister? Were his puny efforts ever going to be enough?

He sincerely hoped so.

"Guvnor, you need something to eat?" A young man about twelve years of age gazed at him hopefully. Behind him was a row of thick pretzels. Suddenly nothing had ever looked so good.

Reid got to his feet. "Yes," he said. "I'll have one of those pretzels."

"Salt?"

"Of course." He got out some change from his pockets and paid generously.

The boy looked at the coins in his hand, grinned, then promptly closed his fist, just as if the metal was about to fly out of his hand. "Thanks."

Reid nodded, then bit into the pretzel, enjoying the bite of the yeasty concoction. Then he started walking. To where, he didn't know.

But for the first time, it didn't really matter.

Rosalind had just finished freshening up when there was a light knock at her bedroom door.

Curious as to who it could be, she opened the door slightly and peered out. It was Mr. Watterson.

"You have a caller, Miss Rosalind."

"I'm sorry?"

"It's a Miss Carstairs, miss."

Rosalind swallowed. "I'm afraid I have no—"

"I'll escort her downstairs, Watterson," Reid's mother interrupted smoothly as she walked down the hall.

"Rosalind, Eloisa Carstairs is one of my son's good friends. She has come to pay a call. She's hoping that she might be able to help you in your search for your sister."

Rosalind had no idea why a lady would make such an offer— or how she knew about her sister. But she was curious to find out. Quickly, she followed Mrs. Armstrong down the winding staircase, still feeling terribly conspicuous for going down the main stairs instead of the servants'.

When she entered the drawing room, she saw an exquisitely dressed young lady perched on the edge of a settee. She was fine-boned and elegant-looking. She looked up and smiled softly as Rosalind followed Mrs. Armstrong into the room. "Good afternoon," she said by way of greeting.

"This is Eloisa Carstairs," Mrs. Armstrong said with a smile. "Eloisa, may I present Rosalind Pettit, our guest."

Rosalind felt her cheeks heat. "How do you do, ma'am. I'm only here because of the generosity of the Armstrongs."

"I am pleased to make your acquaintance. Reid stopped by to see me this afternoon and told me about your situation."

"He did?"

"Yes. And don't fret. He wasn't gossiping. Rather, he thought that I might be able to help you in some way. Like Reid, I know a great many people in our circle." Looking beyond Rosalind, she added, "I've also known the Sloane family for many years. We were once friends, Veronica and I."

Rosalind felt her eyes widen. But for the life of her, she couldn't think of a thing to say.

Luckily, Mrs. Armstrong took control of the conversation. "Tell us a bit about your sister, Rosalind."

She racked her brain, but she couldn't think of anything new to say about Miranda that Reid and his mother didn't already know. "I'm sorry, I've told you all I know about her job and what I've discovered about her last days there."

"No, dear. I don't want to hear about your sleuthing," Mrs. Armstrong said. "Rather, I want to hear about her. What is she like?"

Eloisa leaned forward. "Did she do her chores without complaint? What did she like? What didn't she like? Were you close?"

"Miranda is truly beautiful. She isn't ethereal like you, Miss Carstairs, but she is striking. In many ways I'm a poor copy of her. Her hair is brighter, her eyes bluer, her figure more filled out. And she is impetuous." Her voice warmed as she thought about the person Miranda is . . . or was. "Miranda was always hatching a plan and was always a bit foolhardy. My mother depended on me to be her voice of reason."

"And were you?"

"I'm ashamed to admit that I was not. Truthfully? Her ideas always sounded like a lot more fun than mine. More often than not, I was as much her devoted follower as any of my brothers."

"So you were close?"

"We got along and were close in the way sisters always are. But in many ways we were not close. I'm a bit too much of a worrywart for her."

Suddenly, the memories poured forth. "Once she wanted to rush through our chores so we could go to the swimming hole with the family next to ours. But I was afraid we'd get in trouble." She shook her head in wonder, her eyes brimming with tears as the moment rushed forth, bringing with it both laughter and sadness.

She tried to stem the flow, but it was as if all the pressure from the past weeks was too much to contain. Or perhaps it was really the fact that she didn't need to bear the weight by herself any longer.

She could afford to feel instead of plan. She could afford to remember instead of plot.

The realization only made the tears fall harder, followed by a choking sob.

"Oh, my dear," Mrs. Armstrong murmured, moving to her side. From out of nowhere, she produced a handkerchief and folded it into Rosalind's hand. And that act of kindness only made the tears fall still harder. Before she knew it, Eloisa was sitting on her other side, her slim hand gently patting Rosalind's back.

Which, of course, only made her tears continue.

Seconds later, Reid walked in. "Mother? Eloisa? What is wrong?" he said, then added in a rush, "Rosalind? Rosalind, are you all right?"

She lifted her head just as he rushed to stand in front of her, his hands outstretched.

And she knew right then and there that if they'd been alone, he would have pulled her into his arms. And she would have gone. Gratefully.

She lifted her head and met his gaze. Forgot about his mother and Eloisa. Was only aware of Reid Armstrong. And knew that she'd fallen in love.

"Ah," Mrs. Armstrong murmured. "Now I understand."

Eloisa stood up and stepped toward the door. "I believe I do too."

Reid looked confused, but Rosalind was not. For better or worse, her heart had made a decision. And even if she spent the rest of her life on a farm in Wisconsin, she knew she would only give her heart to one man.

Reid Armstrong.

CHAPTER 30

It was probably best to be philosophical about the recent developments with Reid Armstrong, Eloisa Carstairs decided the next evening as she alighted from her carriage and walked into yet another black tie event. This one was hosted by the McCormicks, and their beautiful home was glowing from the number of gaslights and crystal chandeliers. The walls were lined with paintings, each worth thousands of dollars. They were widely known to be fans of portraits. Dozens of pairs of eyes watched the event, giving one a slightly elusive feeling of constantly being under surveillance.

All two hundred of the privileged guests.

The function was a charity gala, its purpose to raise money for Salvation Army orphans. A noble cause, indeed.

But as she studied the variety of men in black tie, escorting women wearing thousand-dollar brocaded gowns and snow-white gloves up past elbows, each dripping with enough jewels to pay for food for whole blocks of unfortunates, Eloisa couldn't help but be struck by the absurdity of it all. Surely more good would come from money donated to the cause instead of being spent to look good while supporting the less fortunate.

But perhaps that was why a man like Reid was so important to her. He was one of them, there at the gala tonight. She could see him talking intently with some friends nearby.

But he also had his toes in his parents' former pool. He understood better than most in the room the consequences of the reforms and how much good even a dollar donation could do.

It was too bad that she couldn't seem to summon more feelings for him than friendship.

After being announced, she walked down the stairs, greeted several friends, then looked up to see Douglass Sloane quietly studying her.

Douglass was everything Reid wasn't. He was vaguely dangerous and had no more concern for penniless orphans than he did for a splinter in his thumb.

Her mother thought he was eminently suitable, and resolutely had paid no mind to any of the rumors floating about him. Eloisa, however, knew better.

But because she'd promised Reid to do what she could, she smiled in Douglass's direction.

He approached, his handsome face as perfectly composed as always. "Eloisa, you look as stunning as ever."

"Thank you, Mr. Sloane."

He leaned closer. "Why will you never call me by my Christian name?"

"I'm afraid we don't know each other well enough." Then, remembering her mission, she smiled at him softly and added the one word that changed everything. "Yet."

"That can be rectified. Walk with me."

She'd arrived rather late. The ballroom was crowded. Crowded enough for her not to fear his company. In addition, she knew that she'd just been given the perfect opportunity to help Rosalind. Setting her hand in the crook of his arm, she smiled. "I would like that very much."

Something new glittered in his eyes, and she felt a flicker of unease. With a mental shake of her head, she brushed it aside. Surely her imagination was running away with her.

Douglass's smile broadened into a full grin when several men and women watched them. "Eloisa, who would have imagined the two of us could create such a stir?"

She played along, mentally calculating how long she should stay in his company for propriety's sake. And how many questions she could pepper him with without giving away her true motives.

"Not I," she replied. "Though it shouldn't be a surprise. We are much alike."

"Perhaps that is the reason, though I would put the blame solely on you."

"Me?"

"You are the most beautiful woman in the room, Eloisa."

"You flatter me."

"I speak only the truth. Your beauty is blinding."

His effusive flattery embarrassed her. They continued walking to the side of the ballroom. To her surprise, Douglass bypassed several groups of their friends. "Where are we going?"

"Somewhere private. Someplace where we can talk."

Because she did need to speak with him, she kept her silence, even when Douglass led her into a vacant hallway. As she glanced down the passageway, empty except for a few closed doors and a series of rather stuffy portraits of dead relatives, her uneasiness grew. It wasn't the norm for guests to wander uninvited into closed rooms, and it wasn't her norm to ever do so in the company of a man, with no escort or chaperone in sight.

"We will be missed. We should probably get back."

"I agree. But not yet. We still have to talk, yes?" Smiling a bit, he led her farther down the passageway, trying one door, then the next, but finding them all locked.

"Douglass, where are you taking me?" she asked, feeling more than a little vexed.

"Listen to that. You have called me by my name. At last."

His expression was so pleased, his words so boyish, she chuckled. "I guess I have."

They walked farther down the hall, away from everyone else. "Here we are." He paused at a door that had swung open. "Will you come inside with me?"

"Of course not, Douglass. I wanted to talk to you about something important."

"I won't have a conversation out in the hall. Anyone could overhear us."

His statement was ridiculous. No one was around. No servants. Certainly no other guests. She pulled away from his grasp. "I am going back."

"No," he said in all seriousness. "No, Eloisa, I don't believe that will be happening. Not yet."

To her shock and dismay, he pulled her into the room and closed the door firmly behind them.

"Douglass!" she cried out.

But there was no way she could continue, because then his mouth was on hers, and his arms held her firmly against him.

And just as she was about to struggle, he pressed one of his hands against her neck, preventing her from breaking away.

Then, as he grasped her dress, all thoughts of orphans and Reid Armstrong and maids named Rosalind evaporated. All she felt was humiliation and pain.

Reid had just called for his carriage when he saw Eloisa standing all alone, just beyond a copse of trees. He wouldn't have recognized her, wouldn't have even noticed her, if not for the broad beam of light that a carriage made as it exited the home's driveway.

Alarmed, he murmured to his driver that he would be a few minutes and strode toward her. When he got close enough, he realized she was shuddering and sobbing into her hands — and it looked like she could be injured.

A sixth sense warned him to approach her with great care, as if he was approaching a scared child. "Eloisa? Eloisa, yes, I thought that was you. Are you all right?"

She didn't answer, only pressed her hands more completely against her eyes. Her shoulders curved, hiding her face from view.

His concern grew. He reached out to touch her, gently placing a hand on her arm.

With a cry, she flinched from his touch. Then, at last, lifted her face to his.

Her eyes were swollen from her tears. But even in the dark evening he could see that her golden hair was mussed, her lips looked swollen, and her skin was deathly pale. "Eloisa?" he whispered. "Eloisa, it's Reid. My dear, what has happened to you?"

Her eyes widened, her lips formed a small o, and then she closed her eyes. "Reid?" Slowly, recognition and relief filtered through her gaze, followed closely by worry. And something that looked very much like pain.

"Oh, Reid," she said at last. "What am I going to do?"

Conscious of where they were standing, as well as his carriage waiting for him, he made a decision. "Eloisa, I'm going to escort you home in my carriage. I'll tell the doorman to tell your driver to go ahead on his way."

She began to tremble. "I can't go home. Not yet."

"All right then. I'll take you to my home. I live with my parents, you know," he said conversationally, as he slowly reached for her elbow and guided her to his side. "We'll go there for a bit."

"I don't know if I can face your mother."

"Then we'll sit in the kitchen," he soothed. "It's late. No one will bother us there."

"No . . . no one will mind?"

"Not at all. And if you do choose to speak to my mother, I promise, she'll be honored by your visit." He smiled lightly. "You know what she's like," he teased, hoping she would take his over-the-top remarks for what they were—a light attempt at humor in a distressful situation.

However, she gave no response other than a weepy sigh. Glancing at her once more, he pulled off his overcoat and draped it around her as they walked to his carriage. The fact that he was leaving with a woman who was wrapped in his coat would cause some talk, but hopefully he would bear the brunt of it. He was hoping that no one would be able to identify the lady he was with.

Billy, his driver, looked at him in surprise when Reid helped Eloisa into the carriage. But like the well-trained servant he was, he wisely kept to business. "Where to, sir?"

"Billy, we'll be going home. But first, please inform the doorman that Miss Carstairs has left with one of her lady friends and that he needs to tell her driver."

"Right you are, Mr. Armstrong," he said without missing a beat. "I'll go deliver that message right away."

Reid smiled his thanks, then entered the carriage and sat across from Eloisa. "Billy's going to send word that you left with a lady friend," he explained.

"Do you think anyone will believe that? I didn't even retrieve my cloak."

"All that really matters is that no one will actually be able to disprove it."

In reply, she huddled a little farther into his coat. Moments later, Billy got into the driver's seat, snapped the reins, and guided the horse for the short drive home.

Reid debated whether to ask any questions, but decided against it. Eloisa needed a fortifying cup of tea and, hopefully, would allow his mother's soft, steady presence. Already, he suspected that Eloisa was the victim of something terrible. His concern for her, along with his fierce disdain for anyone who preyed on women, was threatening his composure. Though he would do everything he could to not frighten her in any way, he feared his best might not be enough.

When they arrived at his house less than a half hour later, he carefully helped her out of the carriage, then escorted her into the house.

Watterson eyed them with surprise. "Sir?" he asked diffidently.

"Good evening." Reid turned to Eloisa, who was standing by his side. She looked pale and fragile, her bearing as stiff as a rail. It was obvious that she was doing everything she could to keep in control. "Where would you like to sit down, my dear?" he asked gently. "In the drawing room? The library? The kitchens? I promise, the choice is yours."

Wide eyes stared at him in confusion, then slowly focused. "Your library."

"Very well, dear." He turned to Watterson. The man was almost his parents' age and was a trusted member of their house. Reid had always believed he could accomplish almost anything; he'd certainly done his best to make Reid into a gentleman.

"I need you to summon someone in the kitchen to fetch us a pot of tea and bring it to the library."

"Yes, sir. Will your mother be joining you as well?"

"Would you like my mother's company, Eloisa?"

She winced at the use of her name, then, after a long pause, nodded.

"Please summon Hannah to wake my mother and ask her to join us. Perhaps in ten minutes or so."

Watterson bowed slightly. "Yes, sir. A fire has already been laid in the library."

And with that, Reid guided Eloisa with the lightest of touches at the small of her back into his father's library, just off the foyer. Watterson knew Reid often spent time there after an evening out before going to bed.

Reid took care to seat her by the crackling fire, then lit a lamp. Then another.

At last, Eloisa faced him. The dim glow highlighted her golden hair, her striking blue eyes. And the bruise on her cheek. Then the marks on her neck.

And the tear in the lace of her gown.

Every muscle in his body tensed as his worst fears were confirmed. "Eloisa, you've been attacked."

She bit her lip, then nodded. "Yes."

"Do you need a physician?"

She winced. "No."

"Do you have other wounds?" He didn't know how else to ascertain how serious her injuries were. Though he felt a little foolish, he held out a hand. "Perhaps you'd feel better with your gloves off?"

To his relief, she placed a hand in his, letting it limply rest in his right palm as he unfastened the buttons, then smoothed down the kid glove. He did the same for her other hand. Then, before she could pull her hands away, he held them both in his and looked for any bruises on her wrists.

He found several.

His mood darkened. "Eloisa, we need to talk about what happened. Would you like to discuss this with me privately or when my mother joins us?" Thinking about his sister and how shy she was, he swallowed. "Or perhaps you'd rather I leave the room when my mother arrives?"

She shook her head. "No."

He wasn't sure what she was referring to. "No, you don't wish me to leave?"

"No, I don't want to talk about it ever."

"I'm sorry, I can't allow that. Something must be done. Someone hurt you."

"Reid, you offered me shelter and some tea. That is what I accepted."

He nodded. Unable to take his eyes from the dark marks on her neck, he said, "Perhaps I should summon the police."

She sighed. Looked at him as if he were a green boy instead of a grown man. "We both know I cannot allow you to do that. No one can ever know what happened."

As her words registered, a curious sense of peace rolled over him. He knew. He now knew what had happened to her. She had been raped. He was as sure of it as he was of anything.

After the briefest of knocks, the library door opened. His mother walked in first, wearing her favorite embroidered violet dressing gown. She was followed by Cook, who was looking a bit disheveled in a rumpled plain black dress. In her hands was a tea tray, complete with three china cups and saucers, a large pot of tea, cream, lemon and sugar, and a small platter of sandwiches and cookies.

With barely the briefest of glances at Eloisa, she set down the tray and placed three starched napkins next to it. "Would you like me to pour, sir?"

"I'll do it, Anne," his mother said as she took a seat next to Eloisa.

"It weren't nothing."

When they were alone, his mother took a long look at Eloisa, then picked up the teapot. "How do you take your tea, Eloisa? Cream? Lemon? Sugar?"

"Lemon. If you please."

His mother prepared three cups, handing one to Eloisa, then the next to him, with efficient movements born of many years hosting guests under varying conditions.

Then she spoke. "What can we do to help you?"

Eloisa clasped her hands together on her lap. "There is nothing you can do."

Reid shared a look with his mother, then said what had to be asked, no matter how uncomfortable it made their guest. "Who did this, Eloisa?"

She averted her eyes but said nothing.

Hating to cause her further discomfort but feeling duty bound, he prodded a bit more. "I'm guessing that you were violated?"

Her face paled. For a moment, he feared she would faint. Then she nodded. Twin tears traipsed down her cheeks. After a ragged sigh, she lifted the cup, but her hands were shaking so badly, his mother had to help her guide the china to her lips. For a moment, he considered sending a servant to the kitchens to ask for a drop of brandy. They kept it for medicinal reasons, and he believed this was definitely a time of need.

But he was also afraid to spook her, and the offer of spirits might do that.

Therefore, he did the only thing he could, which was to promise her that he would take care of things. "Eloisa, who harmed you?"

She pursed her lips, then set down the cup. "I don't want to press charges. It would only be my word against his. And I don't want my parents to know."

"Your mother would want to help you, dear."

"No. My mother would say I was ruined. That all those years of grooming and schooling and French and deportment classes were all for naught."

Reid wanted to say he was surprised, but he wasn't. Any woman who was ruined held the blame. And it wasn't just in the upper classes that this was true. It was in the middle and lower classes as well.

"If you tell me, I won't reveal your name. But you need to be avenged."

"I don't need to be avenged, Reid. But . . . I do believe that what happened to me tonight is the missing link to your mystery."

He blinked, trying to follow her train of thought.

"With Rosalind and her sister?" Then, "Was it Douglass, Eloisa?"

"I would never say his name aloud."

But her eyes said differently. Her whole body's stance and posture said differently. And his heart and soul did too. "I understand."

Reid stood up. He thought of trying to reassure her, let her know that justice would be served, but he wasn't so naive as to spew false promises.

"My mother and I will pay a call on Sloane House tomorrow."

Eloisa shook her head. "He will deny everything."

"I imagine he will. But his parents and his sister might tell a different story."

"I don't want my name bandied about. I couldn't bear it."

"I'm not asking for that. All I am going to say is my experience, when I saw him with Nanci at the fair, then saw her after being with him. I am sorry to say that she looked much the same as you do now."

"He's done this before."

"I had heard rumors."

His mother said, "Eloisa, do you believe that he has preyed on other young ladies of your social stature?"

"There is reason to believe so." She, too, stood up, wrapped her arms around her slim waist, hugging herself so tightly he felt his heart ache. "D–Douglass forced me into an empty room. And he kept whispering that I would be fine if I didn't fight him. That no one would know." She shivered again. "I believed him after he hit me."

A dozen choice words filled Reid's head, none of which were suitable for mixed company. "I will do my best to see that your suffering is not in vain."

Eloisa looked at his mother. "I believe I need to go home now. I hate to impose, but could you, perhaps, summon a maid to help me repair myself? I can't go home like this."

His mother smiled. "I know just the person to help you, dear. Rosalind. She is staying up in one of the guest bedrooms. Of course, she knows how to dress hair and mend torn hems and seams. We'll have you looking as fresh as can be in no time."

"Thank you, Mrs. Armstrong."

Every trace of humor left his mother's expression. "Please don't thank me. It is the very least we can do. And I promise, it is not all we will do, either. Now, Reid, please go knock on Rosalind's door and tell her that I'll be walking Eloisa to her room in five minutes' time. And then you may go to bed."

"Mother—"

"Your day will be tomorrow, son. For now, I think it might be best if Eloisa and I have a few moments to speak privately. And the only way that will happen is if you remove yourself from the situation."

He knew she was right. With a new resolve, he strode to Eloisa and bowed in front of her formally. "Miss Carstairs, I bid you good evening."

"I can never thank you enough."

"I assure you, it was an honor and a privilege to assist you."

After kissing his mother lightly on the cheek, he left them and strode up the stairs to quietly make his way to Rosalind's room, hoping all the while that they were all doing the right thing.

Only God knew. Perhaps only the good Lord would ever know for sure.

CHAPTER 31

How far she'd come. As Rosalind methodically pinned up Eloisa Carstairs' hair and applied cold compresses to her bruised cheek, she realized that in many ways she'd grown into herself while in Chicago.

Just a few weeks previously, she'd been a timid, rather self-centered girl. Not spoiled, but rather unaware of the world around her, her family, her small farm in Wisconsin. The problems one faced while living in a big city like Chicago had been as foreign to her as the United States must be to the natives from West Africa at the fair.

Rosalind remembered her first glimpse of the foreigners. She'd stared at them curiously, quite unable to fathom that they were all the same human race. The men had seemed too different from the men she'd known. Their dress—or lack of it—such a distraction that she'd forgotten that such things didn't really matter at the end of the day.

As she calmly completed dressing Miss Carstairs' hair and then painstakingly repaired the torn hem of her dress, the tear in its lace, and the rip in its sleeve, Rosalind felt less dismay and shock and more concern and sympathy.

That was the difference. She was less inclined to do nothing, more determined to make a difference as best she could.

Forty minutes after Reid had awoken her with two firm raps of his knuckles on the face of her door, Rosalind was saying good-bye to Miss Carstairs.

"Are you certain there isn't anything else I may do for you, miss?"

"You are too kind." Eloisa gave her a shaky smile. "Thank you, but I think I am sufficiently presentable to make it past our butler without him alarming the household."

"I know this is none of my business, but wouldn't it be good if your family knew what happened?" Reid had prepared her with the truth, knowing that she would never betray Miss Carstairs.

"It wouldn't be good at all. All a woman has is her reputation, you know."

Rosalind did know that. She also knew that no good would come of her interfering in things that were not her business. "Good evening, miss. I will hope and pray that one day this evening will be just a faint memory."

"I doubt that will ever happen. But perhaps it doesn't need to be," she said before walking out of Rosalind's room with the elegance of a young lady who had nothing more on her mind than satin slippers and brand-new hair ribbons.

▬

Five hours later, Rosalind was facing Reid across the breakfast table, where he had insisted she dine rather than in the kitchens. He was as immaculately dressed as always, but there were new lines of stress around his lips and shadows under his eyes.

He was sipping coffee but not eating. She was doing the same thing.

"I hope Miss Carstairs arrived at her house safely last night?"

"She did. Our driver took her home. She also sent a missive this morning that everything was fine. No one suspected a thing, not even her lady's maid."

"I am glad of that."

"She asked me to convey her thanks to you, by the way. If not for your willingness to rouse out of a deep sleep to repair her hair and gown, she wouldn't have been able to go home with no one the wiser."

"It was nothing. I was glad to help."

"Everything happens for a reason, isn't that so? I guess it was fortuitous that you were staying here."

"I can't help but wish that she hadn't been . . . attacked."

"That goes without saying."

"Children, go to the sideboard and fix yourselves a plate of breakfast," Mrs. Armstrong said as she entered the room.

"Mother, I'm not hungry."

"I imagine you are not, but that hardly matters. Eat. We have a long day ahead of us, Reid."

He stared at his mother for the span of two beats, then nodded and stood up. "You're right, of course."

Mrs. Armstrong pointedly looked at Rosalind. "You too, Rosalind. You won't make Eloisa's day brighter by refusing to eat. I can promise you that."

The commonsense advice sounded so like something her own mother would say that Rosalind got to her feet and dutifully followed the instruction. As she took a generous spoonful of eggs and a rasher of bacon, Reid winked.

"My mother is a force to be reckoned with," he teased.

"So I am learning." After adding two pieces of toast to her plate, she returned to her place, content to eat quietly while Reid and his mother discussed plans they had previously made.

She concentrated on pushing her troubles to one side and consuming her small breakfast, paying little attention to talk about Mrs. Armstrong's dress fitting and Reid's intention to visit the bank at the end of the week. But then their conversation turned to Douglass and Veronica. Almost immediately, it became apparent that they were planning to go to Sloane House—without her.

All traces of her appetite vanished.

Reid apparently noticed that she pushed the last triangle of her toast to one side and guessed what she was thinking. "I hope you are not disappointed that you will not be joining us?" he asked.

She couldn't imagine why they wouldn't want her to be there. "Forgive me, but I think I need to go as well."

Reid looked a bit taken aback by her firm manner. "That is not a good idea."

"I don't understand why that is a concern," she said pertly.

"I beg your pardon?"

"None of what has happened has been a good idea," she explained. "That is what I meant."

Reid and his mother exchanged a long look.

As if taking up the gauntlet that had just been passed, Mrs. Armstrong spoke. "Rosalind, I can understand your need to keep involved. But your appearance would only cause concern."

Rosalind thought quickly. "You don't need to make me out to be your equal, ma'am. I could go as your companion."

"But I will be there. She won't need a companion if she isn't alone," Reid pointed out.

Rosalind waved her hands. "Then be unusual. I just feel like I need to be there." Looking beseechingly at Mrs. Armstrong, she pressed her case. "Please."

The older woman stared at her a long moment, her mouth set in a grim line. "Rosalind, other factors need to be taken in consideration as well. I fear our visit is going to be difficult."

"Which would be putting it mildly," Reid interjected.

Mrs. Armstrong continued. "All things considered, I would rather you not be there to get mixed up in it. They could say some harsh things that I'd rather you not hear."

Rosalind wondered if Mrs. Armstrong had any idea about things that happened and were said outside the stately walls of her beautiful home. "I appreciate your concern, ma'am, but I think it's only fair that you allow me to make this decision. After all, I am already involved. And my journey here began because my sister went missing. It's possible that we'll learn something about Miranda."

"I'm afraid this has every indication of being a volatile conversation," Reid warned.

"I promise I will sit quietly."

"I don't feel good about this, but I suppose we have no choice."

Reid looked resigned. "But, Rosalind," he continued, "if I allow you to accompany us, you must remain in the background. Let me drive the conversation. Any interference on your part will only make things worse."

"I promise. I'll be quiet and unobtrusive."

Gazing at her, he shook his head. "If only that was something you could do."

When she met his eyes, her heart flipped a bit. Suddenly, she understood that he wasn't only speaking of the visit to Sloane House. He was talking about them.

Caught off guard, she sipped her coffee and then bit into the remains of her toast. The funny thing was that she did understand. Whereas before she might have been tempted to rush headlong into each conversation, certain that only she could make a difference to Miranda, she was now learning the benefits of biding her tongue and time—and remembering that she wasn't alone.

And that sometimes it was even better to rely on others, because they could do things much better than she could herself. It was both humbling and exhilarating to realize that the simple act of trusting another could reap great rewards.

"Thank you for allowing me to go and for everything you have done. Already, you have done so much for me. I am grateful to you both."

Mrs. Armstrong took a bracing sip of tea, then said darkly, "Let's just hope our efforts aren't in vain."

And on that note, Mrs. Armstrong stood up and walked out of the room.

Only later did Rosalind realize that Reid's mother had never followed her own advice. Her only breakfast had been a pot of strong tea.

CHAPTER 32

The three of them set out for Sloane House on foot a few minutes after ten. It was, of course, far too early to respectfully pay a social call. But they weren't calling on the family for social reasons.

For most of the five-block journey, Rosalind had walked behind Reid and his mother. Though he'd attempted to coerce her to walk by their side, she'd murmured something about being more comfortable trailing them. Only when they'd stopped in front of Sloane House did she join them, her eyes wide and her mouth set in a tight line.

His mother looked no less apprehensive. "Do you truly think this is the right thing to do, Reid?" she asked, for at least the fifth time since they'd begun their walk.

Remembering the shadows under Eloisa's eyes, he said the same thing he'd uttered the other four times. "Of course it's the right thing. We cannot simply stand back and do nothing." Looking at Rosalind, he asked, "Will you be all right? I have a feeling this will be difficult for you."

Rosalind lifted her chin. "I will be fine."

Reid almost smiled. He did admire her spunk.

Looking up at the broad façade of Sloane House, with its lime-stone bricks and many gables, Reid vividly recalled his first visit there. He'd been in awe not only of the house but of the family and every-thing the Sloane name represented. He'd been proud to make such an acquaintance. Now he knew better. Now he knew what the name really signified and what the grand home hid inside.

Beside him, his mother gazed at the house as well. She wore a frown, and a small wrinkle marred her forehead. "I sometimes wish the right thing wasn't always so hard."

"I've wished that a time or two as well. But as you once told me years ago, the Lord doesn't promise us an easy life. Only a fulfill-ing one."

His mother wrinkled her nose. "I fear I said that before I had ever been tested."

He chuckled. "Ladies, shall we soldier on?"

Rosalind nodded while his mother shook out her skirts and then led the way up the steps. "Of course. I may be nervous, but even I know nothing gets done by putting it off."

Hodgeson answered their bell within seconds. His normally impassive face softened in recognition. "Mrs. Armstrong, Master Armstrong, good morning." When he looked at Rosalind, he inhaled sharply. "I hope all is well with your family, sir?"

Reid nodded. "Good morning, Hodgeson. My mother and I are here to pay a call on the Sloane family."

The butler's expression became more guarded. "Whom did you wish to see?"

"All of them," his mother said crisply. "We need to see as many Sloanes as are home."

The man had just stepped backward so they could enter the grand foyer. "Beg your pardon?"

"We'd like to see Douglass, Veronica, and Mr. and Mrs. Sloane, if they are available," Reid murmured. "And please convey that it would be in their best interests if they were."

"I will see who is receiving at this early hour."

"It's a matter of some importance," Reid said. "Otherwise we would not have dreamed of infringing upon their privacy at this time of day."

"Please, let me escort you to the drawing room."

As they followed him across the black-and-white-checkered marble floor and into the almost stark drawing room, its elegance and spaciousness something of a surprise in the current Victorian fashion of excess, Reid thought again about his first visit.

He'd been struck dumb by the grandeur and the pure beauty and quirkiness of the home. Only then did he truly appreciate the place the Sloanes occupied in Chicago's social circles. Here was a family that didn't rush to adopt every new fad or trend. Instead, they set them—or ignored them, thumbing their noses at the rest of the world. As a product of two people's extreme efforts to make him into the mold of a gentleman, the pure disdain for the accepted decorating styles felt both freeing and vaguely scary.

Now Reid realized that he hadn't had the confidence in himself to trust his own judgment. He'd also been forgetting some very important tenets about who—and what—truly mattered in life.

Hodgeson led them into the formal drawing room. Then, with another curious look at Rosalind, abruptly turned and left. Reid could only imagine how he would approach each family member. After a few minutes, he said, "Rosalind, who do you think will join us first?"

"Mr. Sloane. He is always up first."

"Do you think Douglass and Veronica will grace us with their presence?"

After a moment's thought, Rosalind nodded. "They will be too curious not to. Your appearance is rather unusual. I have a feeling by now—even after only a few minutes—every person in the house is wondering why the Armstrongs have paid a visit so early. With a former maid in tow," she added with a grimace.

After looking at a collection of silver kaleidoscopes, his mother perched on the edge of a dark eggplant-colored velvet settee. "Come sit down, Rosalind."

"I'd rather stand."

She clucked her tongue. "I think not. Now's not the time to waver, dear. You wished to join us? Then join us you will. Please sit."

With obvious reluctance, Rosalind sat next to his mother.

Reid took one of the chairs on their right. They sat in silence. He supposed each was lost in their thoughts. He, for one, couldn't help but keep returning to his finding Eloisa in the shadows the night before. He doubted he would ever forget the look of pain and humiliation on her features.

Hodgeson returned. "The family will receive you within the half hour." His disapproving tone conveyed the disdain both he and the family felt for the timing of their visit. "I was told to ask if you would care for refreshments while you wait?"

"I think not," Mrs. Armstrong replied.

"Very well." The butler bowed slightly before retreating.

When they were alone, Rosalind leaned back against the cushions with a sigh. "Oh, he is not happy."

"Good," Reid snapped.

"I hope this is the last time I'm ever in this home. Something feels off, don't you think?" his mother mused. "I don't want to come back."

Twenty-eight minutes later by Reid's count, they heard footsteps and the low murmuring of voices in the foyer. "Here we go," Reid said as the double doors to the room opened and all four Sloanes entered the room.

He rose to his feet.

His mother straightened but remained sitting. She pressed a hand on Rosalind's thigh when she made a move to stand up as well.

"Armstrong," Mr. Sloane boomed. "Carlotta."

"Hello, Clayton," she replied graciously. "I apologize for the timing of this visit, but I'm afraid it couldn't be helped."

"Hmm." Mr. Sloane, his wife, and Douglass all took chairs facing Reid. Each wore varying expressions of curiosity and boredom. Veronica sat down on the settee opposite his mother and Rosalind, looking vaguely amused.

None of them acknowledged Rosalind.

"Reid, Carlotta," Mrs. Sloane said with a patently fake smile. "Now that we are all settled, perhaps you would care to share to what we owe this honor?"

"At this ungodly hour," Veronica said under a yawn.

"And why do you need to see all four of us?" Mr. Sloane groused.

Douglass looked at Rosalind. "And why is she here?"

"Is someone in trouble?" Olympia Sloane asked.

Douglass eyed Reid curiously. "I must admit that you have us all intrigued."

An expectant pause descended over their group. Reid knew it would be up to him to begin and to put out the story about Eloisa as circumspectly as possible.

He'd gone over several ways of breaking the news in his head, each one sounding more jumbled and convoluted than the next.

Finally, he let his heart and instincts guide him. "Over the last several months, rumors have been circulating about you, Douglass."

"Me?" His dark eyes narrowed.

Reid folded his hands together. "I'm sure you've heard them. Your behavior has become more volatile. Your activities and proclivities more dark. More shocking."

To Reid's surprise, it was Veronica who came to her brother's rescue. "And?" she asked in her trademark bored way. "I fail to see how Douglass's affairs affect you at all." She raised a brow. "Unless the two of you now make it a habit of calling on homes for the sole reason of spreading malicious gossip?"

"It is not mere gossip," Reid retorted.

Douglass glared at Rosalind. "If you are referring to a little harmless flirting with housemaids . . ."

"It was more than flirting," Rosalind said, already breaking her promise to leave the talking to Reid.

"Can you prove it?"

"We came over because the rumors have spread from Douglass forcing his attentions on housemaids to something far different," his mother interjected. "As much as it pains me to admit, it seems his behavior has finally crossed the line."

"Which line is that?" Mr. Sloane asked.

Reid sat down and looked directly at the man he'd once called his best friend. "A young lady of good quality informed me last night that you, Douglass, violated her."

Before his parents could shrug off Reid's statement as outlandish, Douglass leaned forward. "And when did this violation happen?"

"At the gala held last night in the McCormick mansion." He paused, then added succinctly, "In one of the empty rooms."

"I have no idea why this 'woman' would say such a thing," Douglass scoffed. "Anyway, it's only my word against hers."

Reid held his temper in check . . . barely. "I saw the bruises around her neck, Douglass. I also believe her."

"If you believe her, then you're a fool."

"What does she want?" Veronica interjected, her voice sounding like it was on the verge of breaking. "I still don't see why her misfortune concerns you. I know of no lady who would dare make such accusations aloud, even if they were true."

Reid's mother leaned forward. "It has been my experience, Miss Sloane, that most women are afraid to admit such things occur because they fear they will be blamed."

"Perhaps that is because they should be blamed," Mrs. Sloane said with a sniff. "I don't mean to disparage this, uh, lady, but if what she says is true, then she must have put herself in a bad situation." Brushing a nonexistent crumb off her skirts, she added, "Not all women take as much care with their reputation as they should."

"This lady is of the highest tier in our social circle. Furthermore, she did nothing wrong. Nothing."

Yawning rudely, Douglass leaned back, folding one leg over the other. "Again, I am mystified as to why you are here. If she is so perturbed about my supposed vicious attack, then I would have thought she would want to be here," he drawled.

Mr. Sloane was looking slightly pale. "Carlotta, did you speak to this woman?"

"I did, Clayton. I also have seen her bruises. She was badly injured."

"Why are you here, Reid?" Douglass demanded, his face ruddy with anger. "No matter what happened, it doesn't concern you."

"I am here because I can't let this incident be overlooked," Reid said quietly. "She is a lady of quality, a lady of much esteem. And you,

Douglass, have ruined her. That is unforgivable. It is unforgivable for any woman to be violated."

A muscle twitched in Douglass's jaw, but that was the only indication that he took any of Reid's accusations seriously. "I'd like to see her try to blacken my name." He looked around at his family. Glanced at his mother. Stared hard at Reid. "I'm a Sloane. That name carries a significant amount of weight in some circles. In most circles." He raised a brow and stared meaningfully at Reid. "Or have you forgotten?"

"I haven't forgotten anything," Reid retorted. But this time, he didn't back down. He stared hard at Douglass. "If you are referring to the way you lied for me back in boarding school, I believe I can safely assure you that that debt has been repaid. Tenfold."

For the first time, Douglass looked a bit nervous. He pulled out an immaculate handkerchief and wiped his brow.

Veronica paled. "This woman, will she be all right? And does anyone else know about what happened to her?"

"I don't believe anyone else knows. As for her future? I'm afraid I do not know that answer."

She leaned forward. "Mr. Armstrong, who was it?"

"You know I cannot divulge that information, Veronica," he said gently. "Once more, I think you know why."

Veronica's eyes widened. "Why would you say that?"

Reid looked around the room, feeling as if he had the weight of the world on his shoulders. As each face stared back at him, in various stages of anger, disbelief, and pain, he knew he had made the right decision.

This was one of the hardest things he'd ever done, but it was a choice he would never regret.

"You and I both know that this has happened before to other

ladies of quality, and the reputation of any woman he violated would be ruined as well if what happened became known."

He went on. "But we also both know that this is not as big of a shock to you as you are pretending it to be. Douglass's behavior has ruined your chances for a successful match as well. No man of good standing wants to be tainted by such an association."

Mrs. Sloane clenched her hands together. Mr. Sloane looked stunned. Veronica paled further, and his own mother looked shaken. Rosalind looked dazed.

Only Douglass sat complacently.

And that, Reid believed, was the most telling reaction of all.

CHAPTER 33

But Douglass's apparent complacency was soon replaced by a dark look.

"I had no idea your gifts included such oratories, Armstrong," Douglass murmured with a tightness in his voice. With wooden movements, he stood up, crossed the room, opened a cabinet, pulled out a bottle and snifter, and poured himself a shot. When he sat down again, Reid noticed that the muscles around his lips had loosened, but there was an increased amount of stress looming at the corners of his eyes.

For the first time since they'd arrived, Reid felt a small amount of relief. At last, Douglass was rattled. Maybe far more shaken than any of them realized.

Mr. Sloane coughed. "Forgive me if I am mistaken, Douglass, but you have not once denied either Reid's or Carlotta's claims. Why not?"

"I don't believe this is the time or the place, Father."

"Forgive me, but I disagree," Mr. Sloane said. "You are here with your family."

"And with the Armstrong family. And with a . . . a maid." Douglass rolled his eyes. "Forgive me if I don't harbor the same allegiance to them that you feel toward yours."

His father closed his eyes with a sigh. When he opened them again, anger lit his features. "Douglass, did you violate this lady?" he barked. "Do you know what Reid is alluding to?"

"He knows," Veronica said, her eyes flashing. "Everything Reid said is true. Douglass is the reason I've become the laughingstock of our social circle." Bitterness poured through her voice. "And because no one in polite company will dare mention what Douglass has done, they only point out that the wealthiest woman in their midst is slowly becoming an old maid."

After shooting a spiteful glare her way, Douglass shrugged. "I might have been a touch too eager with my attentions. But it is certainly nothing to be concerned about. It's not like I have really harmed anyone."

His father slumped. "So the allegations are true." Turning to Reid, he said softly, "How much does this woman want?"

Reid exhaled. The family's response wasn't too much of a surprise, but it was still disappointing. Here Douglass wasn't even bothering to refute Eloisa's claims, and yet all his parents were worried about was saving his reputation.

"She is not asking for anything," he said at last. "I, however, would like Douglass to tell us about the other women he's ruined."

"The other women were of no account."

"I believe one of the others was a maid in your household."

Douglass lurched to his feet, frustration evident in the lines of his face. "That blasted girl! I gave Nanci more than enough to keep her silence. She took every penny and promised not to tell. So what did she say, Armstrong? Or was it Rosalind who talked?" he sneered. Turning to her, he glared.

"What did you learn? Did she tell you all about Wooded Island? Did she tell you how she went with me easily enough? Did she lie and tell you she was with child?"

Reid stared at Douglass, stunned as his worst fears came to light. "I wasn't speaking of Nanci."

"You hurt Nanci too?" Veronica was on her feet now. "She'd been with me for years!"

"She was nothing. Just an uppity lady's maid." His voice lowered, took on a far more bitter tone. "And she knew she was in good looks too. Every day, she taunted me. Teased. It wasn't my fault that I could no longer ignore her."

Warily, Reid glanced at Rosalind. Her face was ashen but she remained composed. His mother was holding her hand. She looked shocked. Mr. Sloane sat motionless while the lines around his wife's lips increased.

As Douglass and Veronica continued to argue.

"Douglass, you should have left her alone," Veronica said with a fierce glare. "After all, she was a servant in our home."

"But that was all she was. She was only a servant."

Veronica folded her arms over her chest. "You must have hurt her feelings if she left so abruptly. Where did she go?"

"I don't know and I don't care. I gave her enough money to go anywhere she wanted." Brushing a piece of lint from the arm of his suit jacket, he eyed the rest of the room. "Wasn't that enough?"

Reid had thought he was far beyond being shocked. Obviously he was wrong. He stared at Douglass while his insides twisted. How had he ever become this man's friend?

At last, Mr. Sloane stood up. His face was a mask of disdain, but whether it was for Reid bringing the tragedies out in the open or for his son's admittance without remorse that he'd violated at least two women, Reid wasn't sure.

"Mrs. Armstrong, Reid," he intoned. "Rest assured this, uh, situation will soon be resolved. However, it would be best done in the privacy of our home, at the discretion of this family."

They'd been dismissed.

Reid wanted to leave. He ached to leave. But he had promised Rosalind that he'd see her quest through. And that meant he could never leave the house without bringing up her sister.

"What about Miranda Perry?" he asked baldly.

"Miranda?" Douglass raised his brows. "What concern is she of yours?"

"Miranda was my sister," Rosalind blurted. "I mean, she is my sister."

"Your sister?" Olympia Sloane said. She looked genuinely confused, reminding Reid once again that many of the employees of the great house weren't really seen as people by the Sloane family. Instead, they were warm bodies assigned to do a job to make the family's lives easier. "I'm sorry, did we know you were related?"

"Not at all. I came to Sloane House to search for her. Secretly."

"I don't understand. Are you really stating that you only entered our employ to discover information about your sister?"

"Yes, ma'am."

"That was a bit extreme, don't you agree?" Douglass sat back down, resting one foot atop his knee. "Any number of things could have happened to the girl." He waved a hand. "Most likely, she fell in love with a peddler or something."

"No," Rosalind retorted. "That is not what happened."

"What do you think did?" Veronica eyed her with a wary expression.

"I'm not sure. I . . . I'm still trying to figure that out." Unable to merely sit and answer questions, Rosalind stood up. "But . . . I think someone in this house had something to do with her disappearance."

"Such as?" Veronica asked.

Oh, but this was hard! Facing the whole family together was far more difficult than she ever would have imagined it to be. But she had Reid and his mother there. And she was stronger too. Far stronger than she'd been just a few weeks ago.

She also felt the reassurance of the Lord deep inside her. He had sent her on this mission, and he was pushing her forward. She knew it with every fiber of her being. That gave her all the strength she needed.

"I've heard from several people that Douglass paid a lot of attention to her. Some of the staff said Miranda had been warned to keep quiet, but I think Douglass and Veronica were angry with her because she was going to talk. She was going to go to the police or even go to some of the other servants in other homes."

Looking around the room, she added, "There was talk, you see. I think she was in danger."

"Are you trying to say I did away with her?" Douglass looked completely incredulous. "I certainly did not do any such thing."

"What kind of talk?" Mr. Sloane blustered.

Veronica slumped against the cushion of the sofa like a petulant child. "Oh, Father. Have you really been so oblivious to anything but work? Douglass's reputation for violence and poor treatment of women stopped being whispered speculation over a year ago. Now it is regarded as common knowledge. No one decent calls on either of us anymore."

Her father shook his head. "What your brother did shouldn't have mattered. You have the Sloane name."

"A name means whatever people want it to mean," Veronica pointed out. "At the moment? It means many bad things." She glared at Reid. "But you were my hope. I thought you, at least, would see me for who I am. Not that I was tainted by my brother's reputation."

"I wasn't in love with you. I had already given my heart to someone else."

Rosalind saw the softening in Reid's gaze. Knowing that he was most likely speaking of Eloisa hurt. She'd seen how concerned he'd been about her, how much he wanted to help her. A combination of jealousy and despair spiraled inside of her as she realized that Reid Armstrong could never be hers.

She pushed aside the pain as Mr. Sloane's booming voice broke the sudden silence. "Did you violate Miranda, Douglass?"

He squirmed. "I didn't violate her . . ."

"But you did compromise her," Reid pointed out.

Douglass raised a brow. "Can a maid be compromised? I'm not sure." He cleared his throat. "Regardless, she was an uppity thing too. Threatened to tell all sorts of people." He laughed. "She actually said she had proof that I'd molested other women as well."

"What kind of proof?"

Douglass's expression tightened, but it was obvious that he was determined to act blasé. "She said she'd talked to other women . . . and even a lady. That they were willing to damage their reputations to bring out the truth. They were even going to tell the police, if you can believe that."

Rosalind stepped forward. "What happened next to her?"

"Nothing," Douglass blurted. "She made all these threats . . . then one day she was gone."

Looking at Veronica, Rosalind said quietly, "Do you know what happened?"

"I know nothing."

"But Nanci said her belongings were left here. She wouldn't have left on her own without her clothes."

Veronica shrugged. "I truly have no idea what happened to her, Rosalind. I knew Douglass had made her his latest conquest, but that is all." She looked at her mother after a split second. "Do you know, Mother? I now remember Nanci telling me that you went to their room and boxed up Miranda's clothes for the workhouse."

Mrs. Sloane's expression tightened, but she said nothing.

"I remember you threatening her," Douglass said to his sister. "I remember you continually asking her to deliver your breakfast tray and that she was often white as a sheet whenever she left your room."

"If I challenged her, I was justified," Veronica said. "If I reminded her once or twice about our family's power? Well, it was nothing more than the truth."

Reid sighed. "I've heard enough. Rosalind, let's go to the police. If we talk to them, maybe now they will, at the very least, consider investigating Miranda's disappearance."

Mrs. Sloane stood up. "Reid, you cannot involve the police."

"We have no choice," Mr. Sloane murmured. "As much as it pains me to admit it, there is a good chance that something untoward happened to the girl. It is in everyone's best interests if we all cooperate."

Mrs. Sloane looked from her husband to her daughter in obvious panic. "I think not."

"We have no choice."

"Of course we do. If we continue on as if nothing happened, no one will ever suspect anything."

Mr. Sloane paused. "What do you mean, as if nothing happened?"

As Rosalind stared at Mrs. Sloane and saw a flash of guilt cross her features, she realized that she'd underestimated the formidable lady. "You've known what happened to Miranda all along, haven't you?" she whispered.

"I've known what I needed to do to protect this family," she replied.

Reid leaned forward. "What are you saying?"

She sighed. "I'm saying . . . I'm saying that our family's reputation means more than each of us." Turning, she glared at her children. "We've given you everything, but you didn't understand the depth of your good fortune. Douglass, you let your spoiled, selfish nature threaten to ruin everything generations of Sloanes accomplished. And you, Veronica? You haven't even been able to make a match. I had to do something."

Silence filled the room as each person stared at her in shock.

Finally, Mr. Sloane asked the one question Rosalind assumed they were all thinking. "What did you do?"

"I got rid of her," Mrs. Sloane bit out. "I took her down to the pier. By the lake. I pretended to fall. And then, when she bent down to assist me? I picked up a rock and hit her on the back of the head."

Douglass jumped to his feet. "Mother!"

"I had to do something. Miranda was going to ruin you and Veronica. She was going to taint our name. Our reputation! And the fair had just opened. Anyone who is anyone was here in Chicago and would have heard about it. We could have been ruined."

It took everything Reid had inside him to force out the next words. "What did you do after you hit her?"

"I dumped her into the lake."

Her husband's color turned ashen. "What?"

"I had no choice, Clayton. We had to protect our name."

As the rest of the group stared at Mrs. Sloane in dumbfounded silence, Rosalind felt her heart break. She was almost too proud to show her tears, almost too proud to let them know just how overcome she was. But she couldn't help but let out a sob. And then Mr. Sloane, of all people, reached over and handed her one of his monogrammed white handkerchiefs.

She knew those small pieces of cloth well. Had ironed dozens of them during her time working at the home. When she'd first arrived at the mansion, the linen had intimidated her. She'd never imagined something so fine could be used for wiping tears and noses. But as she crushed the fine linen in her palm and brought it up to her eyes, she realized it meant nothing to her anymore.

Now all it did was allow her tears to fall.

At last, she'd gotten an answer. She swiped her eyes again, tried to tell herself that the news was what she had expected. Truly, it had been the only thing that had made sense. She had never really thought headstrong Miranda could have been snatched from the streets of Chicago. It wouldn't have been like her.

Besides, the secrets of Sloane House had been powerful, calling all the time from beneath a veneer of privilege and wealth.

And then the reality of it all sank in. And it became too much. Her sister had been molested. Murdered. Her body had been dumped. With a lurch of her stomach, she stood up. Tried to run from the room. But all she really was aware of was the floor spinning and her head pounding.

At last, she'd discovered the truth. But instead of giving her freedom, it only served to make things worse.

Her sister was gone, and she was never coming back.

CHAPTER 34

Reid barely had time to reach for Rosalind before she fell to the floor in a faint. With her body limp in his arms, he gently eased her to the carpet, situating himself so that he could cradle her head. Worry for her, mixed in with the blow of what Douglass and his mother had just admitted, made him feel almost as weak as Rosalind. Their admissions rang through his head as he smoothed her hair from her brow.

"Oh, Rosalind," he murmured. "I am so sorry."

He was barely aware of someone in the room calling for smelling salts until his mother was kneeling by his side. After sharing a worried glance with him, she opened a vial and waved it underneath Rosalind's nose. "Don't worry, Reid," she murmured. "It's just a faint. She'll come around in a moment."

To his surprise, Veronica appeared at his side with a glass of water. "This will help when she wakes," she said simply.

Seconds later, Rosalind's eyes fluttered open. She coughed a bit, then studied her surroundings. She looked at him, at his mother, at the floor on which she was reclining, in confusion. And then it was obvious that reality consumed her again. A weary look transformed her expression.

And broke his heart. "I'm so sorry," he said again. It was inadequate, but at least it encompassed everything he was feeling.

She blinked and lifted one shoulder, conveying so much.

"I'll tend to her, dear," his mother said.

Reid rose to his feet and walked to Mr. Sloane.

The man looked like he'd aged ten years, and as if he, too, were in danger of passing out. Reid wouldn't have blamed him in the slightest. The latest revelations had gone far beyond his wildest imaginations.

Reid cleared his throat and did what he needed to do. What he hoped his father would have done if he could have been there himself.

"Sir, we need to contact the police," he said baldly.

Mr. Sloane nodded. "Yes. I'll send a footman to the nearest precinct." Looking beyond Reid, the man motioned toward Hodgeson, who looked as if he, too, was trying to stay steady on his feet. "Send Jerome to the police."

Hodgeson nodded. "What would you like him to say?"

Mr. Sloane's expression was so dark, Reid almost smiled. But of course, he understood the butler's question. Nothing—especially not information like this—left the house without the Sloanes' approval.

Mr. Sloane glanced at Veronica and Douglass, who were sitting separately, each some distance away from the other and from their parents. They looked as shaken as the rest of them.

"Ask Jerome to say that we are experiencing a matter of some urgency. If someone asks for more details, Jerome should admit that he is not at liberty to say." His lips pressed together. "That should get them here in a hurry."

The butler bowed slightly. "Very well, sir." When he reached the doorway, he paused. "Would . . . would you like a tea tray to be delivered, perhaps?"

"The last thing we need is tea, Hodgeson."

"Yes, sir. But . . . perhaps for the ladies?"

"Bring it. Or don't. I don't care." He stood up, glanced at his children, glanced at his wife, who was as white as a sheet, and then turned to Rosalind, who was now standing next to one of the windows with Reid's mother.

Minutes passed like hours. A maid brought in the tea tray. She set it on a side table and walked out without a single person in the room acknowledging her service.

Then the most curious expression fell over Mr. Sloane's features. "How did this happen, Reid?" he asked quietly.

Reid wasn't sure if the man expected an answer or not. But he felt foolish not answering him. "I don't know, sir. Perhaps one thing leads to another?"

"But how did this happen to my family?" He shook his head. "Douglass was always so willful. Impetuous. But I never imagined he was preying on innocent women. But my wife? I fear she must have gone mad."

Still looking weary, he sat down next to Mrs. Sloane.

She raised her chin. "What should we tell them?" she asked, breaking the silence.

"To whom are you referring?"

"The police, of course. We must have a story to tell them about what happened to that maid." She paused and looked curiously at

Rosalind before sitting up a bit straighter. "Would it help if we said she was a thief? I'm sure they would believe that."

Behind him, Reid heard Rosalind cry out, and his mother comforting her.

Everything inside of him ached to yell at the woman, to shake her by the shoulders. To do everything in his power to convince her that no longer could the Sloanes simply hide behind a name. But he held his silence, hoping, praying that Mr. Sloane, at least, understood that the time to worry about appearances was long gone.

"We are going to tell them the truth," Mr. Sloane said finally. "That is all that can be said. That is all that can be done."

Veronica gasped. "But, Father, they could put Mother in jail."

Douglass laughed low. "They could do worse than that, Veronica. And most likely they will."

"We'll cross that bridge when we come to it," their father said.

Fear and panic had mottled Veronica's face. Reid feared she was about to slip into a rage, but then the door opened. "The police have arrived, sir," Hodgeson announced. Just as if he was announcing a visit from Mayor Carter Harrison himself.

Two policemen walked through the door, one in street clothes, the other in a blue uniform. "Hello, sir. My name is Detective Lt. Sean Ryan. This here is Officer Carter."

Mr. Sloane nodded. "Thank you for coming so quickly."

The detective eyed all of them in the room with a sharp eye. "We heard there was an emergency here? What seems to be the problem?"

The other policeman looked a little dumbstruck by the grandeur of his surroundings.

With a weary hand, Mr. Sloane gestured to two empty chairs. "Detective Ryan, Officer Carter, you two might as well take a seat."

He gestured to Rosalind and to Reid's mother, to Veronica and to Reid. "You all had better take a seat as well. I have a feeling this is going to take awhile."

When Officer Carter pulled out a pencil and pad of paper and Detective Ryan leaned forward, Clayton Sloane began.

Beside them, the overflowing tea service lay gleaming on the sideboard, stacks of Haviland china beside it. All of it unnoticed or ignored.

CHAPTER 35

The police had questioned all of them. Then, once they were clear about the severity of the situation, more officers were called upon to take statements.

Only after Rosalind had given her statement to both the officer and a detective dressed in a brown tweed suit was she allowed to leave Sloane House. However, she'd been given a stern warning not to leave Chicago anytime soon.

At least three hours after they had arrived, the three of them left. Reid walked in between Rosalind and his mother, offering an arm to each.

Rosalind accepted his help, though she felt conspicuous walking by his side.

For once, not even his mother could think of anything to say. Each of them seemed lost in their thoughts as they slowly walked the five blocks back to the Armstrong residence.

Just as they arrived, Mr. Watterson greeted them at the door with an anguished expression.

"It's Mr. Armstrong, ma'am," he said to Reid's mother, apology in his tone. "I'm afraid he's taken a turn for the worse."

Rosalind watched Mrs. Sloan's eyes widen with a strike of pure shock, then she slowly composed herself. "How bad is he?"

"We've sent for the doctor."

Reid turned to her. "Rosalind, I am sorry to leave you—"

"Please. Go." She waved her hands and put on a brave smile. Seconds later, both Reid and his mother were up the stairs and out of sight.

She sighed. Could this day be any worse?

"Are you all right, miss?" Erin, the maid who had been attending her, asked.

Rosalind shook her head. She didn't really know Erin. She didn't know any of the servants here at the Armstrong house. But they knew the truth about her, that she'd been dismissed from the Sloane mansion and was only living here out of the Armstrongs' charity.

But she saw no reason to lie or prevaricate. "We discovered this morning that my sister, Miranda, was murdered. All this time I've been hoping and praying that I would find her, you see. That I would be able to take her home. Back to Wisconsin. But . . . that is not going to be possible. She's dead."

Erin's eyes flashed. "I'm very sorry. May I bring you something?"

"Thank you, but no." If she knew anything now, it was just how busy the staff was in a big house like this. She certainly didn't want to create more work or cause confusion. So even though she didn't want to be alone, she also knew that her room was the best place for her to be. It was out of sight and out of everyone's way.

"I'll be in my room if the family needs me."

"W–would you care to come sit in the kitchen? Most everyone's having some tea in the servants' hall. Not much to do while we're waiting."

Being in their company sounded much better than waiting for news in the silence of her guest room. "You wouldn't mind? You don't think Cook would mind?"

Her face warmed a bit. "I have a feeling you might be pleasantly surprised about the many differences between here and the Sloane mansion." She turned and started walking. "Follow me."

Rosalind did as she was bid.

⸻

The room was dark with the thick velvet curtains tightly shut. The air was still and thick with emotion as Reid, his mother, and the doctor all watched his father continue to labor through each breath.

His father seemed to have drifted from their presence for the most part. Only his mother's clinging seemed to prevent him from ascending into heaven. It was a painful thing to see. And, Reid realized, brought back painful memories of sitting by his brother's side.

After taking his father's pulse, Dr. Nolan readjusted his glasses on his nose as he straightened. "I'm sorry, ma'am," he said, "but there is really nothing more we can do."

Tears glistened in her eyes as she nodded. "I understand." Turning from them both, she leaned close to her husband, took hold of his hand, and brought his knuckles to her lips.

Reid felt like his heart was in a vise, the pain was that overwhelming. And he wished Beth were here. She'd be so devastated that she wasn't. With effort, he pushed it away and headed to the door. "I'll walk you out, Doctor," Reid murmured. When they were at the stairs, Reid asked the question he was most dreading. "How long, do you think?"

The doctor pursed his lips. "A day? Perhaps two? I'll stop by tomorrow morning. If something happens this evening, don't hesitate to send for me."

"Thank you, Doctor."

After he left, Reid walked back to his father's room, prepared to stand vigil with his mother for as long as was needed. But when he peeked in, he changed his mind. His mother was sitting on the bed next to his father and talking softly.

Reid doubted his dad could hear or understand what she was saying. But whatever his mother was saying, it was obviously important to her. And private.

He backed away, deciding to check on Rosalind instead. When he didn't find her in her room, he strode downstairs and peeked in the parlor and the drawing room.

Unfortunately, he saw only Erin. "Have you seen Rosalind, by chance?"

"Yes, sir. She's having tea in the servants' hall."

He was surprised, but not shocked. "I'm glad she's not sitting by herself." Suddenly, he was wishing he wasn't either. But a man certainly couldn't beg for company. It was his duty to stand firm and strong.

"Mr. Armstrong, do I understand that your father has taken a turn?" Erin asked hesitantly.

Reid didn't fault her asking. He knew how much the servants cared about his father, and how worried and concerned they must be feeling too. "He has." Swallowing hard, he added, "The doctor says he won't have much longer. Maybe a day or two at the most."

"Do you need anything? Maybe some lunch?"

He was a little hungry. But just as importantly, he hoped the meal might help steady his nerves. "Bless you, Erin. Thank you."

"Yes, sir. I'll let the staff know." After a beat, she said, "I'll ask Miss Rosalind to let you know when the dining room is ready."

He couldn't bear to sit in that room by himself. "Not there. Just a tray in my office. I mean, my father's office."

Her bottom lip trembled. "Yes, sir."

He wandered into his father's office in a daze, reflecting as he did that the day couldn't have been a more difficult one. Ignoring the desk, he sat in his father's favorite chair in front of the fireplace, perching his feet on a stool.

And realized that there was very little chance of his father ever taking his place here again. More to the point, there hadn't been a chance for some time. He'd only been holding out hope. Praying for a miracle.

"But you don't grant dreams and wishes, do you, Lord?" he asked the empty room. And for the first time in a very long time, he didn't expect an answer.

That made him feel even less whole. All his life, he'd hugged his faith close to his heart, clung to it with the zest of a temperance worker. Oh, he'd made sure to give thanks to God every night. And he did have many, many reasons to feel blessed and grateful. But now, he wondered, what had he been praising the Lord for? Things that didn't matter?

When had he really given thanks for having parents like his own? For the simple fact that they loved each other? That they had never acted like he and Beth weren't poor substitutes for Calvin?

Now he and Beth and his mother would become an awkward trio.

For a moment, he realized that he still had not done the one thing his dad had wanted him to do so badly—marry well.

Of course, he wasn't married at all. And the woman he was currently thinking about was far from a lady of means. He paused, waiting to feel guilt. Instead, all he felt was a curious sense of righteousness.

Thinking about Douglass and Olympia Sloane's staggering revelations, he realized that he was still in a state of shock. He'd never truly realized that Douglass felt no shame or remorse for his actions.

And Reid had never guessed that a woman as regal as Mrs. Sloane could murder—and then expect everyone to lie to protect her. She was such an elegant lady, and she hailed from one of the finest families in the nation.

But did it really matter? And what was "fine," anyway? Surely not men and women like that.

"Knock, knock," Rosalind said as she entered with a tray laden with a sandwich, cookies, and what looked to be a bowl of soup. "I hope you're hungry, Reid. Your cook outdid herself."

"I am hungry. Starved." He jumped to his feet. "But I didn't imagine the staff would ask you to bring me my tray."

"I asked to. Erin was going to bring it, but she needed a little break. Besides, I told you, I've gotten pretty good at carrying trays by now."

Only she could make his mood lift at a time like this. "So I see."

After she set down the tray on a table near the fire, she glanced at him with a bit of trepidation in her eyes. "Do you mind if I sit in here with you while you eat? Your staff is very kind, but they have things to do and I was only getting in their way."

"I don't mind at all." Today she was wearing a plain brown dress. It should have washed out her color, made her look mousy. But instead, the plain clothes only accentuated her natural beauty.

And reminded him of how he was tempted to simply stare at her. Gesturing at one of the empty chairs opposite where he was sitting, he added, "Actually, I can't think of anything better than having you keep me company."

After she sat, he took the chair next to hers. With a tug and a pull, he shifted it so they almost faced each other, next to the table with the tray. Now little separated them except for his flaws and her hesitancy.

Next, he closed his eyes, gave a quick blessing, then at last dug into his meal. "So how was sitting with the staff in the kitchen?" he asked after he'd consumed a few spoonfuls of his cream of broccoli soup.

"I liked it very much. Your maid, Erin, promised me the staff here was different, and she was right."

That interested him. "Different how?"

"Different, happy. Less stressed."

He had to smile at that. "It's probably because we don't know how to act properly for the servants."

"No, it's probably because you all are nicer to them. I also heard that your mother doesn't like to entertain all that much."

"No. Well, not grand parties."

"That's something your staff is grateful for. Preparing for a grand dinner can be an exhausting business."

"So I've been told." He tucked into his sandwich, thinking about the differences in staff. Thinking about how comfortable he felt just being around Rosalind.

She seemed to be feeling contented too.

He hated to ruin their few moments of peace, but he knew something had to be said. "Rosalind, I truly am sorry about your sister. But perhaps one day you might find comfort by knowing that justice will be served."

"Perhaps." Her bottom lip trembled, but she held her composure. "I am upset, but not shocked. I think I knew in my heart that she wasn't alive and she was probably a victim of foul play. I told your father as much."

Unable to stop himself, he reached out and rested his palm on her

299

back. When he felt her muscles loosen, he gently rubbed the line of tension between her shoulder blades. "If it's any consolation, one day you will know that the truth was only discovered because of you," he murmured.

"Perhaps one day I will be glad I discovered what really happened to her." She rested against his hand for a moment before straightening abruptly. "I'm wondering if my parents are ever going to be pleased about my discovering the truth, having to accept that Miranda is dead."

"But that's why they sent you here," he pointed out. "You cannot help that the truth wasn't what they hoped to hear."

"They sent me here with grand dreams. For some reason, my parents imagined that I would be able to single-handedly find Miranda, wrestle her from whatever situation she was in, and bring her straight home." Clenching her hands into fists, she whispered, "For a time, I actually thought that was possible. Now I realize it was all a pipe dream." She stood up, turned away to gaze out the window.

It would be so easy to stay where he was. To remind himself that nothing was between them. Not really. Instead, he crossed the room and curved his hands around her slim shoulders. Hoping to remind her that she wasn't alone. "You tried your best. And what you did accomplish was noteworthy. Your family will be proud of you."

She didn't turn. Didn't acknowledge his touch. "I doubt that. When I return and tell them everything, all we'll have left is our reality. All their hopes will be shattered."

"But you will have the truth. That is something."

"Yes, though it's sometimes easier to live with denial."

Thinking about his dreams of making his parents proud by marrying a woman of elevated circumstances, about his decision to continually ignore his qualms about Douglass's behavior out of a misguided feeling of obligation, made him nod. "I suppose that is true."

He'd put up so many boundaries where the two of them were concerned. He'd pretended her social station mattered, though his wasn't all that exceptional.

He'd pretended they were too different, because he'd had so many opportunities in his life while she'd had far too few.

And he'd tried to refute his attraction to her by imagining that her looks weren't as polished as any young debutante's. Or that he shouldn't be noticing that a young maid in a misshapen uniform could stir him as much as an expensively clothed girl in silk.

Hmm. It turned out that he, too, hadn't been all that ready to accept the truth.

He knew he had two choices now. He could concentrate on the truth and a future he wanted, or he could continue to pretend to want things that would never be.

Put that way? He had only one choice.

"I don't want you to leave," he whispered into the nape of her neck.

She swayed a bit, leaning into his touch. Or maybe it was his words? "I can't leave, remember? I promised the police I wouldn't leave the city until they said I could."

Had she misunderstood him? Or was she merely choosing to pretend she did?

He parted his lips, ready to explain himself, ready to at last kiss her neck, to pull her closer . . . when a burst of insight helped him see things more clearly.

He needed to go slowly.

She'd just been told her sister had been murdered. His own father was upstairs dying. Perhaps now was not the best time to declare his feelings.

But—just perhaps—he could hint at things a bit?

He ran his fingertips down her arms.

"Rosalind, if you weren't here, I would miss you."

She trembled under his touch, but she did not turn to face him. "I can't imagine why. I've brought you nothing but trouble."

"That isn't true. You've brought me something very special."

"And what was that?"

"A new belief in myself. Hope for the future. If you go, I don't know what I'll do. I don't want you to go." He swallowed, then made himself think of her needs. "Unless . . . unless you want to leave me."

After the span of a heartbeat, she sighed. "I would miss you too. I hate to admit it out loud, Reid. But I would miss you too."

He could no longer resist the temptation. He brushed his lips against the nape of her neck. Leaned closer, kissed her jawline. She sighed.

"You know what?" she said. "God is so very good, don't you think? Here, even in the darkest hours, he gives us light. Here, my sister was murdered and your father is dying. I'm out of a job, and you have lost someone you once thought to be a good friend. Even in times like this, we've found each other. He reminds us that we cannot completely give in to despair."

He wrapped his arms around her waist, liking the way she felt against him. Liking the feel of her in his arms. "You are right, Rosalind," he murmured. "God is, indeed, so very good."

She was right. For a few scant moments this day, he'd been doubtful and depressed. Sad and despondent. He'd let himself forget so many things.

But then God had brought Rosalind into his life, into this room. And in doing so, the Lord had reminded Reid just how much he had to be grateful for.

And he was, indeed, so grateful.

CHAPTER 36

By noon the following day, the Armstrong household had already welcomed four callers. Dr. Nolan arrived to sit vigil, saying that it was only hours—or even minutes—now until his father passed into heaven.

Next, Eloisa came and refused to leave, admitting that she'd rather help in any way she could instead of sit alone with her thoughts at her own house. When Reid said that her presence eased them all, she picked up his mother's embroidery basket, scooped out a rat's nest of jumbled floss, and asked if she could sit with Rosalind while she untangled the strands.

Reid summoned Rosalind right away.

After a few minutes of shyness, Rosalind accepted Eloisa's offer of friendship with alacrity. She knew the young lady had been through a lot. She also knew she was a lady through and through and was so happy that a woman like Eloisa wanted to get to know her better.

A little over an hour later, Detective Ryan and Officer Carter called. After handing Watterson a card, they requested a private audience with Rosalind Pettit, who was now going by her real name, Rosalind Perry. Reid attempted to intervene and join her, but the police were firm, Detective Ryan even going so far as to say that they were already doing Rosalind a favor by conducting the interview at the Armstrongs' home instead of at the police station.

Though Reid had looked like he had quite a bit to say about that comment, he held his tongue and only indicated that he would be waiting in the drawing room at the end of the interview.

After sharing a look with Eloisa, Rosalind followed the policemen into Mrs. Armstrong's private sitting room, where she answered many of the same questions once again.

The detective looked perturbed when she told them how her father's visit to their headquarters had been handled. But still the questions and statements continued.

Though their questioning was difficult, Rosalind actually didn't mind it all that much. She'd felt as if she had been on a wild-goose chase by herself—at least until Reid stepped in. She'd had no resources, little knowledge of the city, and no true knowledge of Miranda's life in Chicago. All she'd really had was a strong sense that something had happened to her sister and enough stubbornness to attempt to see her search to the end.

They eventually confided that Mrs. Sloane had been sent to a private mental hospital. No charges had been made against Douglass, on the other hand, because no woman had ever come forward. For a split second, Rosalind wondered if Eloisa would be willing to stand up against him, but she quickly pushed that idea to one side. She was worldly enough now to realize that Eloisa's testifying would do little good. Douglass would dispute her and she would lose a little bit more of herself.

It was obvious that the Sloane family was extremely influential, perhaps even with members of the police. They also had an army of lawyers at their disposal.

Detective Ryan did promise that a number of officers would once again look for Miranda's body, which Rosalind supposed would be a blessing. She knew she and her family would like to give Miranda a Christian burial.

However, she didn't hold out much hope. Months had now passed. The police detective had described a variety of things that could have happened to her sister's body, each one more upsetting than the last. Rosalind began to think that perhaps it would be best—for her parents at least—to always remember Miranda as she had been when she left their farm. Determined and beautiful. Headstrong and optimistic. Full of life.

Two hours later, the interview was over. After giving them her address in Wisconsin, she was told she could leave Chicago.

"We are sorry about your sister, miss," the detective said as he shook her hand good-bye.

When she was alone, she sat back down on the settee. Her mind felt numb. At last, her adventure was over. The tears started to fall. Whether from grief for her sister or relief that she'd at last discovered the truth, she wasn't sure.

Maybe she was even sad to be leaving Chicago and all the people she'd met and gotten to know. As frightening and emotional as her time here had been, she knew she was going to miss her new friends. She was going to miss her life here.

Two hours after that, Mr. Armstrong went to heaven.

As black bunting was draped over the windows and the house settled into mourning, Rosalind made a decision. She was going to stay a little bit longer. After visiting with the housekeeper and the cook, she slipped on a clean white apron and began to help out as much as she could. It was the least she could do for the Armstrong family, the very least she could do for Reid.

And, she realized, exactly what she did need at the moment. She needed to do something for someone else. There would be plenty of time to go home and return to her old way of life. Just not yet.

She simply wasn't ready.

———

Two weeks later

Her old carpetbag and a new one were packed. She was ready to go.

Sitting on the steps in the foyer, Rosalind waited for Reid and his mother to come downstairs. Mrs. Armstrong wanted to give her a final good-bye, then Reid was going to take her to the train station in his carriage.

He'd insisted on paying for her train ticket home.

"Oh, good, miss. You're still here," Cook proclaimed as she trundled forward, carrying a metal pail covered in floral linens in her hands. "All of us downstairs have been wantin' to give you this."

Rosalind took it and peeked inside. In the pail was an assortment of sandwiches and cookies, an apple, and a little note too. "This all looks wonderful. Thank you so much."

"It was the least we could do for you." Cook shook her head. "I've never met a girl like you. You stepped right in and helped everyone in the house. We'll be sad to see you go."

Only by sheer force of will could she keep her bottom lip from trembling. "Thank you." Fingering the note, she said, "Shall I read it now?"

"Definitely not! You'll make us all blush. Read it when the train leaves the station. It will give you something to do."

"I'll do that, then. Thank you again."

Cook leaned forward. "Just between you and me? We were all hoping that you would be able to stay. You've been a real ray of sunshine, you have."

"You all were so welcoming that you made my time here quite pleasant. But this household is so well run, there's no opening for me, I'm afraid."

Cook looked at her in surprise. "None of the staff was thinking about you working here. We were hoping that something would have happened between you and young Mr. Armstrong."

"Of course nothing could have happened," she said, a bit shocked. "I'm only a maid."

"Miss Rosalind, let me tell you a secret. You're a right help, you are. But you aren't all that good of a maid or kitchen helper. You'd probably make a better wife for him."

Rosalind was so shocked, she laughed. "Don't tell Mr. Armstrong that!"

"Too late, I'm afraid. I overheard," he said from the doorway of his office off the foyer.

This time, both she and Cook turned beet red.

"I didn't know you were standing there, sir," Cook retorted.

"I hope not. I'd hate to think my staff had decided to start telling me what to do with my life to my face."

Cook pulled back her shoulders. "Never that, sir."

With a wink, he held out his arm. "Rosalind, are you ready to go? My mother said to tell you that she'll write to you. She's something of a watering pot right now. She didn't want to cry all over your new dress."

This time, Rosalind wasn't sure if Reid was joking. At his urging, his mother had sent her shopping with Eloisa two days ago. Though Rosalind protested, Mrs. Armstrong paid for two ready-made dresses, a lovely felt bonnet, a new pair of kid gloves, and a beautiful pair of black boots. She'd enjoyed spending time with Eloisa, and now she was dressed in a fashionable blue gown that fit her almost perfectly. On her head was her new bonnet. Its brim framed her eyes just right, and the ribbons that decorated the brim made her feel feminine and pretty.

"Every woman needs a new dress now and then, dear," Mrs. Armstrong had remarked when Rosalind tried to protest that it was too much.

Just as importantly, she couldn't deny that she felt pretty and, for once, attractive. She looked like a young lady, not someone's servant. And after a lifetime of living in Miranda's hand-me-downs, followed by these months of working as a housemaid, Rosalind felt a real need to be seen as herself.

Now, looking at Reid, seeing his appreciative gaze, she felt herself blush. "I wouldn't have minded if your mother dampened my dress. I will miss her."

"I'll let her know you said that." Escorting her out the door, he lifted her into the carriage and away from the best home she'd ever had.

CHAPTER 37

To her surprise, they took his family's big carriage, not the smaller one he usually used. He sat in the seat next to her while Charley drove them.

Never before had they been alone in the enclosed space. She was aware of everything, the way the ends of his brown hair curled at the edges, the way her sapphire-blue dress brushed against his suit.

Even his scent drew her notice. He smelled of soap and pine and horses, as if he'd gone to their carriage house for a bit before greeting her.

Closing her eyes briefly, she hoped and prayed that she wouldn't forget a second of their last few minutes together. She knew she'd hold these memories tight to her heart for the rest of her life.

He seemed to notice her expression. "Everything all right?"

"Oh. Yes." There was no reason to lie. "I was simply trying to make this moment last. It's a good memory."

His gaze drifted over her face, as if he, too, was hoping to imprint each last second they had together in his brain. "Because you're finally returning to your family?"

Did she dare tell him that it was much more than that? "Partly," she allowed.

There was traffic on the street. Through the windows, which were cracked open, they heard Charley yell at a pair of boys running through the street and greet the driver of a lumbering milk wagon. The carriage lurched, then darted forward in a rush.

Rosalind gripped the seat and laughed. What used to feel so foreign and scary now felt almost exciting.

Reid winked. "Before you know it, all the sights and sounds of Chicago will be a distant memory."

That was what she was afraid of. "I hope not a memory for too long. I want to come back here one day."

"I hope that happens."

"I do too." She took a chance and met his gaze, thought about being completely honest with him, then remembered her place. Forcing her voice to brighten a bit, she added, "I'm going to miss many things here."

A new, bright interest filled his gaze. "What are you going to miss?"

You.

"The farmer's market. The grip cars."

You.

"Is that all?"

"Oh no." She tried to giggle, though the noise came off sounding a bit like a braying mule. "Believe it or not, I'm going to miss the noise of the trains. The flower sellers, the newsboys."

"Anything else?"

You.

"All the people." And because his gaze was so intent, she added quickly, "And the fair, of course."

"Of course." Leaning a bit closer, he picked up her hand. Rubbed a thumb along her knuckles. "Will you miss anything else? Anyone else?"

"Yes." She swallowed. "I'm going to miss Eloisa. And your mother. And even most of the servants at Sloane House."

"You'll even miss them? In spite of everything that's happened?"

"In spite of everything, I've learned that most people will go out of their way to help others. Even a coarse country girl like myself."

He shook his head. "That's never been you. You've been a pleasure to get to know."

"Thank you, Mr. Armstrong."

"You call me Reid now, remember?"

"I haven't forgotten." No, she hadn't forgotten a thing.

The carriage was moving steadily down the street now. In no time, Rosalind realized, they would be at the train station. And their relationship would be at an end.

She changed her mind. It was time to thank him properly. There was no way she was going to leave him without being honest. She owed it to him.

But even more importantly, she owed it to herself.

"Reid, before I leave, I wanted to be sure I said something."

"What is that?"

"I—I wanted to let you know that while I will miss so many things about Chicago, and I will always remember the many friendships I've made, I will miss you most of all." She felt her face flame, but she held his gaze steadily.

His body stilled. "Why is that?"

Her words were forward. Not at all in keeping with their relationship. Not at all in keeping with the things her mother had taught her, for that matter. But perhaps her mother and society had never imagined the things she and Reid would go through together.

Taking a deep breath, she began. "From the first time I met you, you've always made it seem like I was more to you than a mere maid at Sloane House. You made me feel like I was a real person. Like I was Rosalind."

"You were real to me." He rubbed her knuckle again. "Rosalind, from the first moment I saw you standing in the hallway of Sloane House, I knew I'd never forget you."

Her heart started beating faster. Her pulse raced. Here, at last, was everything she was dreaming of . . . but of course, he was merely being kind.

She swallowed. "Also, uh, Reid, you've helped me in so many ways. You've given me your time. You've listened to my troubles. And no matter how outlandish everything sounded, you believed me." She looked down, then peeked at him from under her lashes. "At least, it felt that way to me."

"I did believe you. Your story was fantastical. But it was also something that could happen."

"In addition, you helped me with Douglass, and you even gave me shelter when I had nowhere to go. I owe you so much, Reid. I doubt I'll ever be able to repay you."

Now that her little speech was over, she smiled. If nothing else, she'd be able to leave knowing that she'd done her best to be honest with him. Almost.

Still looking at their joined hands, Reid slid his palm so their fingers linked. "Is that what you thought I wanted? You thought I wanted to be repaid?"

His tone sounded faintly accusing. It stung, though she wasn't sure why. "I didn't know what you wanted."

"It wasn't repayment. I never thought of you as a job or an assignment, Rosalind." Releasing her hand, he leaned his head back against the velvet cushion, then chuckled softly. "You know, if you are going to be completely honest, then I suppose I had better be too."

She couldn't reply. All she seemed capable of doing was sitting next to him and breathing.

Yes, that was good. Inhale. Exhale.

"Rosalind, haven't you figured it out yet? I did feel sorry for you, and I did want to help you. I did. But that was never why I wanted to spend so much time with you. I never stayed away, because I liked you, Rosalind." At her wide-eyed stare, he laughed. "Come now. You had to know."

"I knew that I cared for you. I know that I do care for you."

"So we care about each other. And you know that I like you." He smiled softly. "I feel as awkward as a foolish teen. But perhaps that's not a bad thing. I need some brashness, all the sudden."

But the tables had turned. Now he was leading the conversation and she was the listener. "What are we going to do, Rosalind?"

"I think that is something for you to decide."

He grinned. "What if I told you that I want you to stay here? In Chicago. What if I told you that I want to have you here with me always?"

"I . . . I . . ."

He cut her off. "What if I told you that I don't just 'care' for you, Rosalind? That I don't just 'like' you? What if I told you that my feelings are deeper, more intense?"

"Um . . . intense?"

"I love you, Rosalind. It was all I could do not to tell you that a couple of weeks ago, to take you in my arms and kiss you. I love you and I want to marry you."

"Love? Marry?" She felt like a puppet on a string, echoing his words in wonder.

He grinned. "I am speaking of love and marriage, Rosalind. And of you and me. What do you say about that?"

If she wasn't surrounded by horns and animals and skyscrapers and dust, she would have been sure she was dreaming. "Reid, your mother—"

"My mother loves you. It's been killing her these past two weeks that I haven't made my intentions known."

"Why haven't you? Why did you wait until now?" she blurted, then ached to take it back. "Sorry, I didn't mean to say that out loud."

"I didn't want to overstep myself. I didn't want to rush you, not after you just found out the awful truth about your sister. And truthfully? I was afraid you wouldn't want to take the chance."

"Chance?"

"Take a chance on love, Rosalind. Take a chance on doing something new. On being something new."

She shook her head. "Is that even possible?"

"Of course it is. Haven't you learned by now that only good things come from taking chances?"

He did have a point about that. Only by stepping out of her comfort zone, only by reaching for something better than she imagined, had she been able to turn her dreams into realities.

Reaching out, he clasped her hand in between the two of his. "Say you'll think about this. Say you'll consider everything I'm saying."

She certainly didn't need him to explain. Almost everything of worth had happened ever since she'd started taking chances. She'd discovered what had happened to her sister and had even helped some other women by stopping Douglass's scheming and dangerous ways.

But something unexpected had also happened when she'd started taking chances. She'd also discovered that she was more than she'd ever imagined.

She was stronger, smarter, and braver than she'd realized.

Which was why, before, she probably would have tried to tell Reid that she didn't deserve a man like him.

Now she knew that she did.

"I love you," she said. "I just want you to know that."

"Because?" For the first time, he looked unsure.

"Because I'm going to say yes," she said with a soft smile.

"Yes to staying? Yes to Chicago?" His brows lowered. "Or yes to me?"

"Yes to everything, but most especially yes to you."

Just then, the carriage stopped. It shook a bit as Charley hopped off the driver's seat, then threw open the door. "Here we are, Miss Rosalind. Union Station."

Reid grinned as he leaned toward the door. "There's been a change of plans, Charley."

"Sir? Where do you want to go now?"

"Rosalind, you want to tell him?"

She took a breath, then changed her life. "Charley, Mr. Armstrong and I would like to go back."

His eyebrows rose. "Back to Sloane House?"

"Oh no. To Armstrong House," she said with a smile.

Reid grinned. "We've a wedding to plan, Charley. Miss Rosalind Perry has just consented to become my wife."

Charley looked at Reid, at their clasped hands. And finally, at Rosalind's smiling face. "Congratulations! It's back home now, then. For all of us."

"Take your time, would you?" Reid murmured as Charley started closing the door.

"I'll do my best, sir."

When the carriage started rolling again, Reid pulled her into his arms and kissed her tenderly. "I'm so happy, Rosalind. I'm so happy and grateful and blessed. And loved."

"Me too," she murmured as he pulled her close and kissed her again.

Then she followed her heart, wrapped her arms around his neck, and kissed him right back.

It turned out that some things didn't need to be explained at all. Only repeated. Again and again and again.

DISCUSSION QUESTIONS

1. I used the following scripture verse as a guide while writing this book. How does it resonate with you? "Though your sins are like scarlet, I will make them as white as snow. Though they are red like crimson, I will make them as white as wool" (Isaiah 1:18).

2. Setting the novel against the backdrop of the 1893 Chicago World's Fair was fascinating for me. Through my research, which included a lengthy visit to the Chicago History Museum, I learned a lot of new things about Chicago and life in the 1890s. Is there something about this time period which you found interesting?

3. One thing I enjoyed about Rosalind's character is she never shied away from what she knew about her sister. She accepted both Miranda's good qualities and flaws, which in turn enabled her to uncover everything she could about her sister. What were some of Rosalind's best qualities? What were some of her flaws?

4. What did you think about the staff at Sloane House? Who did you find sympathetic? Was there a staff member you didn't trust?

5. Reflect on Victoria Sloane's character. Did she have any redeeming qualities? What do you think will happen to her in the future?

6. I felt like Reid Armstrong was walking a tightrope through much of the book, balancing his past with his future. Was he successful in this balancing act? Was there something he could have done in order to make his life different?

7. Was Reid right to feel so indebted to Douglass Sloane? What do you think Reid's life might have been like if Douglass had never stood up for him back in boarding school?

8. How do you envision Rosalind and Reid's future? What hurdles do you think they might face in the future?

9. Reid's faith throughout the book is unwavering. How do you feel this impacted his character? Did it affect Rosalind's faith?

10. Eloisa Carstairs is the heroine of the next novel in this series. What do you imagine will be some of the obstacles she might face?

11. Much of the mystique about the fair's White City is that the buildings were ornate and beautiful, yet not made to last. Can you think of anything in today's world that feels much the same?

12. Which characters would you enjoy reading an epilogue about?

One woman's search for the truth leads her
to deceit and danger in 1893 Chicago.

Deception at

SABLE
HILL

The Chicago World's Fair Mystery Series

Available Spring 2015

AN EXCERPT FROM

DECEPTION AT SABLE HILL

by SHELLEY GRAY

CHAPTER 1

Chicago
September, 1893

"Don't keep me in the dark for another second, Eloisa," Quentin Gardner teased as they waltzed across the gleaming parquet floor of his family's crowded ballroom. "Where have you been for the last three months? No one has seen you in ages."

"I've been the same places you have," she replied, taking care to keep her voice light and steady. "Though to be honest, it would be a wonder if you were able to spy me among this year's debutants clamoring for your attention."

He chuckled. "I've hardly been that in demand."

"The *Tribune* did just list you as one of society's most eligible bachelors." She raised a brow, half expecting him to act surprised. Quentin enjoyed pretending that he was above such things as the society pages.

However, instead of denying the article, his cheeks flushed. "The only reason I was on that list was because of my family's money."

"And perhaps your good looks, too." Tapping his shoulder lightly with her gloved hand, she murmured, "I've been told that blue eyes and coal black hair are an irresistible combination."

"You and I both know that article was mere gossip."

"One that has a shred of truth, though."

"Even if I was surrounded by a bevy of young ladies—which I was most definitely not—I would have noticed if you were in our midst. You have not been out, Miss Carstairs."

With effort, she kept her expression impassive. "You sound so sure about that."

"That's because I am."

Just as she was developing a reply, Quentin twirled her around. Then, as she chuckled at his exuberance, he eased her a bit closer. "I've missed your company, Eloisa. What made you decide to suddenly be so elusive?"

She had a very good reason. A very good reason that only a handful of people knew about. It was also imperative that she keep it that way, too.

As she felt his warm breath on her neck, her unease returned. Pressing on his shoulder, she attempted to gain back her space. "Quentin, there's no need to hold me so close."

Something flashed in his eyes before they filled with hurt. "I'm not doing anything inappropriate. I simply want to talk to you without having to raise my voice."

She tried to pull away again but his arm holding her waist was very strong. "The way you are holding me is rather improper . . ."

"Hardly that. Besides, I can promise that no one is paying the slightest attention to us. It's a veritable crush here. I think my mother's guest list included every dignitary associated with the Fair."

He was talking about the fair to commemorate the four hundredth anniversary of Columbus' discovery of America, the World's Columbian Exposition, of course. Though some were still scratching their heads, wondering about the need to celebrate such a thing in such a grand fashion, no one could deny that the World's Fair of 1893 had certainly made Chicago feel as if it was the center of the universe.

The excitement surrounding the fair had been exhilarating and wondrous. And exhausting. Every dignitary and society matron had used the event as a reason to hold a soiree, dinner party, gala, or ball. And because her mother was intent on Eloisa marrying well, she'd encouraged her daughter to attend as many events as she could.

The only excuse she would hear of for Eloisa to decline was of a migraine headache. Therefore Eloisa had made sure she'd had as many such "headaches" as possible.

When Quentin twirled her again, Eloisa tried to relax. Tried to remind herself that he was doing nothing but dancing with her—in plain sight of everyone, too. "Soon everyone will go back to their homes and Chicago will seem almost empty."

"Yes, the fairgrounds will close on All Hallow's Eve, you know."

"I'll be glad when it's over."

Quentin nodded. "As will I. Our city feels filled to the brim with miscreants and vagabonds." Tilting his head back so their eyes met, he added, "I know how independent you are. I hope you are taking care when you go out. It's no longer safe for young ladies to go anywhere unescorted."

"It hasn't been for some time."

Regret filled his clear blue eyes. "Forgive me for frightening you.

I imagine you're still reeling over the news about Douglass Sloane's death. It has only been two weeks."

She stumbled. "Yes. His death has been something of a shock. I can still hardly believe the news is true."

"I'm still trying to figure out why he'd decided to go boating in September. It isn't quite the thing, you know. He was never one I would call a friend, but still...drowning in Lake Michigan? That's a terrible way to go."

Hardly able to even think about Douglass, she nodded and prayed for the dance to be over soon. Or, at the very least, for Quentin to change the subject.

And as if on cue, he did just that. "Now, of course we have even more to worry about, what with the recent string of attacks on women of substance."

"Indeed. It, ah, is a wonder any of us ever leave the house."

"How many women have been attacked with a stiletto?"

"I'm afraid I don't recall," she lied. Three. Three acquaintances of hers had found themselves at the mercy of a crazed madman intent on ruining their looks.

"You're looking pale, dear. Forgive me. I'm not usually such a clumsy conversationalist."

"I am perfectly fine." She attempted to smile while peeking over Quentin's shoulder at the orchestra. Hopefully the waltz would be over soon. Then she could quietly make her escape and return to the sanctity of her room. Leaving it had been a mistake.

The faint wrinkle that had been marring Quentin's perfect features smoothed. "Please don't be concerned about your safety here, dear Eloisa. I'll look after you."

"That is very kind, but people will talk if I monopolize all of your attention."

He laughed. "I don't care. Actually, my mother would practically start crowing if everyone believed that you and I had formed an alliance. I might be this week's most eligible bachelor, but you, Eloisa, have been the focus of every man's attention between the age of eighteen and eighty since you made your debut."

"You flatter me."

"It's the truth. You are the object of many a man's attentions. Believe me, I've heard."

She shuddered. "Your observation doesn't make me feel any safer."

"How about this, then? My father hired two off-duty policemen to keep watch over the event this evening. I promise, all evening you've been closely guarded."

"Truly?" She looked around the room. "I saw a couple of officers near the front door, but I thought they left."

"No, dear. They're right here with us. In the ballroom."

"I haven't seen any men in uniforms."

"They're here undercover. One is Detective Owen Howard. Have you made his acquaintance?"

She relaxed. "Of course. We've known each other for ages." Just like the rest of them had. Everyone in their circle stayed the same, only got older. Owen was the exception, which made her admire him all the more.

"He is a good man, to be sure, though I have to admit to still being somewhat shocked about his chosen profession. He could have done much better."

"Perhaps he enjoys the work?"

"That would be doubtful. His father is a banker."

"Perhaps banking isn't for everyone."

"Well, he is a fourth son. With no chance of inheriting much, he elected to go into the police business." After a pause, his voice turned haughty. "It's his partner who looks a bit more swarthy. His name is Sean Ryan."

"Sounds Irish."

"Trust me, he's as Irish as a clover. He had also been lurking about in an ill-fitting tuxedo. I don't know if the poor fit is from an inferior tailor, his bulky weapon, or the fact that he likely borrowed it from some unfortunate soul."

As Quentin guided her across the marble floor, she scanned the crowd. "I don't see him."

"You will. I promise, once you start looking, you won't miss him. He sticks out like a sore thumb! However, Owen has vouched for his character, which is the only reason my parents allowed him to be in our midst." He leaned closer to drawl into her ear. "So don't worry about a thing, Eloisa. As long as they're here, everything is going to be just fine. As far as I'm concerned, they're worth every penny of their exorbitant fee. If they keep you safe, it will be money well spent."

It took a lot of effort to pretend she believed him. But what Quentin didn't realize was that it wasn't only the threat of being accosted by scoundrels that frightened her.

It was the knowledge that much worse things could happen by someone she knew.

━━

"You're staring again," Owen Howard blurted as he reached Sean's side. "If you're not careful, someone besides me is going to notice."

"I'm merely scanning the area," Sean lied. Only through careful effort was he able to refrain from flushing. "There are a lot of people here, you know. Hundreds."

"Yes, but only one Eloisa Carstairs."

"I'm sure I don't know whom you are referring to."

"Of course you do," Owen countered with a wink. "But don't be embarrassed, chap. You aren't doing anything the rest of us haven't done a time or two. Or ten. Eloisa is perfection. Angelic even."

Sean raised his brows at the descriptor. It was at times like these that he truly wondered why Owen had elected to join the police force. Though he wasn't quite as high in the instep as the majority of the gentlemen and ladies in attendance, he was certainly far and above Sean's social standing.

In addition, Sean was fairly certain that if he had made such a social stumble like joining the police force, he certainly wouldn't be showing up at society functions like this. It seemed an odd choice.

He, however, was making a small fortune for Hope House this evening. That was what he needed to focus on. His fee alone would cover the expenses of the women and children who lived there for almost a month. That was reason alone to be standing around in an ill-fitting borrowed tuxedo attempting to look vigilant.

"Ready to split up again?" Sean asked. "I'll check the balconies and alcoves while you check the perimeter's grounds."

Owen pulled out his timepiece. "That suits me fine. Meet back here in an hour?"

As the set ended and the men escorted their partners off the dance floor, Sean watched Owen walk in the direction of the outdoor patio, decorated in a flurry of white candles.

Then, unable to help himself, he looked for her pale lace gown the color of spring grass. He exhaled as he saw Eloisa being escorted off the floor and toward one of the private rooms off to the side. She was in Quentin Gardner's company, which was reason enough for Sean to pretend he didn't see her. Quentin's father was not only paying his fee, the family was also believed to be above reproach. In short, Quentin was everything Sean was not. He was exactly the type of gentleman Eloisa should be near.

But then Sean noticed that her expression had become strained and she was trying to pull her arm from Quentin's grip. Her eyes were darting around the room, as if she was looking for anyone to give her assistance.

He stilled. Stared at her hard, not caring if his attention was garnering notice.

He knew the exact moment she recognized him. Her lips parted. Her pleading look told him everything he needed to know.

It didn't matter who she was or who she was with. Eloisa Carstairs was looking to him for help.

And he would do almost anything to go to her assistance.

AUTHOR BIO

Photo by The New Studio

Shelley Gray is a *New York Times* and *USA Today* best-selling author, a finalist for the American Christian Fiction Writers' prestigious Carol Award, and a two-time HOLT Medallion winner. She lives in southern Ohio, where she writes full-time, bakes too much, and can often be found walking her dachshunds on her town's bike trail.

She also spends a lot of time online. Please visit her website, www.shelleyshepardgray.com to find out her latest news, or find her on Facebook at Facebook.com/ShelleyShepardGray